D1103825

Guide to the
Battle of
Chickamauga

Edited by Matt Spruill
University Press of Kansas

© 1993 by the University Press of Kansas
All rights reserved

Published by the University Press of Kansas (Lawrence, Kansas 66049), which was organized by
the Kansas Board of Regents and is operated and funded by Emporia State University, Fort Hays
State University, Kansas State University, Pittsburg State University, the University of Kansas,
and Wichita State University.

Library of Congress Cataloging-in-Publication Data

Guide to the Battle of Chickamauga / edited by Matt Spruill.
    p.   cm. — (The U.S. Army War College guides to Civil War
battles)
   Includes bibliographical references and index.
   ISBN 0-7006-0595-9 (hardcover) — ISBN 0-7006-0596-7
(paper)
    1. Chickamauga (Ga.), Battle of, 1863. 2. Chickamauga-Chattanooga
National Military Park (Ga. and Tenn.) — Guidebooks. I. Spruill,
Matt. II. Series.
E475.81.G85   1993
973.7'35 — dc20   92-46288

British Library Cataloguing in Publication Data is available.

Printed in the United States of America

10 9 8 7 6 5 4 3 2 1

The paper used in this publication meets the minimum requirements of the American National
Standard for Permanence of Paper for Printed Library Materials Z39.48-1984.

Guide to the
Battle of Chickamauga

The U.S. Army War College
Guides to Civil War Battles

CONTENTS

MAPS AND ILLUSTRATIONS

Maps

Illustrations

ACKNOWLEDGMENTS

A book is not the work of a single individual, but is rather the product of work and support from a team of friends and colleagues. Foremost in this instance are Professor Jay Luvaas and Colonel Harold Nelson of the U.S. Army War College, who started me on the trail that led to this book and provided invaluable aid and editorial work. Jim Cissell, Chief Ranger at Chickamauga National Battlefield Park earned my thanks by reviewing the manuscript and giving many helpful suggestions. I owe hearty thanks to Rangers Connie Vogel-Brown and Rex Williams for their cheerful assistance and ready supply of answers to my endless stream of questions. I owe an unpayable debt to my friends Colonel Robert Lee "Cold Steel" Powell and Colonel Jim Sheppard for walking the battlefield with me and helping to fit Reports to terrain. I am indebted to Mrs. Corless Doughman Ferris and Mr. Thomas J. Doughman for providing me the transcript of the diary of Private T.J. Doughman, Company G, Eighty-ninth Ohio Infantry, which is included at the end of Appendix II.

A special thanks goes to Colonel Roy Strong (Ret.), Executive Director of the U.S. Army War College Foundation, for having the vision to see the need for the entire battlefield series and for encouraging the project. John Kallmann has been especially patient with the difficulties imposed by a distant battlefield and an even more distant editor for this volume.

My deepest gratitude and love go to my wife Kathy, my mom Helen, and my sons Matt and Lee, all of whom walked parts of the field and read parts of the manuscript with me, acted as photographers, and constantly provided that special support that only a family can. My part in this book was done for those of our family who will follow us.

Matt Spruill

INTRODUCTION

This new volume in the U.S. Army War College *Guide* series is similar to its predecessors. Built upon the after-action reports of officers who fought the battle, it uses maps, detailed directions and short editorial comments to put the reader on the critical terrain so that those soldiers' words, and the impressions and actions they recall, will be clear in the reader's mind. A detailed order of battle for each army is included in the appendix, and a second appendix addresses an important dimension of the military art as it was applied during the Civil War. Only this latter appendix is offered as traditional *history*.

Throughout the text the editors have resisted the temptation to adjudicate contradictions and explain details. We believe that the inquiring reader, confronted with problems in the original sources, asks valuable questions that are rarely apt to arise when reading traditional narrative histories. The success of the earlier volumes in this series, together with the continued enthusiasm that this method engenders during our own staff rides over the old battlefields, confirms this belief. Readers encountering this method for the first time may be skeptical, but they will soon find themselves reconstructing the battle in ways they otherwise might not have thought possible.

* * *

By the 1880s—when the Civil War veteran was about as remote in time from his battlefields as Viet Nam veterans today are from theirs—old soldiers from the North and South returned to their battlegrounds in increasing numbers. To judge from the programs of their reunions it was an occasion for oratory, dedicating monuments to the past and expressing faith in the future, and the National Military Parks created over the next decade were established in large measure as shrines "for patriotic devotion for the future generations of American youth."[1] At the dedication of the Chickamauga and Chattanooga National Military Park in 1895, two former Confederate Generals spoke of the positive results of the war. "It was a remarkable war in all its aspects," John B. Gordon proclaimed, most remarkable of all because "it bequeathed a legacy of broader fraternity and more complete unity to America." James Longstreet, forever the "old war horse," invoked Lincoln's Gettysburg Address and then appealed to his old comrades, former enemies, and all of their sons "to lock shields . . . to prevent any future occupation by Great Britain in Venezuela and resist any further amercement by England in Nicaragua."[2]

In contrast to the battlefield park at Gettysburg, which had been established in 1864 by a private corporation chartered by the Pennsylvania legislature to preserve portions of the battlefield, mark *Union* battle positions, and supervise the location of monuments and markers, the Chickamauga Memorial Association, organized twenty-five years later, included veterans from every state, North and South, that had sent troops into the battle. This was to be a *national* military park.

But even before the establishment of the Chickamauga and Chattanooga National Military Park by act of Congress in 1890, there was a secondary and less publicized mission: to preserve and mark the battlefield "for historical *and military study*."[3] This probably started with former Brigadier General John B. Turchin's study of the battle published in 1887. Basing his history upon the newly published *Official Records*, correspondence with "veracious" participants and his own personal experiences, Turchin produced an analysis of the battle with the hope that it "may prove instructive to the students of the military art." The book is filled with what modern soldiers would call "lessons learned." Among the particular lessons of this campaign, General Turchin, a well-educated professional soldier who had previously served on the General Staff in the Imperial Russian Army and had participated in the campaigns in Hungary in 1848–49 and in the Crimea in 1854–55, identified the following:

First. A topographical map is the headlight of an army operating in enemy's country. With a topographical map, all the movements and concentration of troops can be perfectly planned. . . . Without such maps, an army gropes in the dark. . . .

Second. The scattering of various columns of troops at a distance from the enemy is necessary and useful, but to do it in proximity to the enemy is dangerous.

Third. For a daring expedition choose rather a reckless and rash commander than one who is methodical and scientific. Hindman was not the man to attack Negley and Baird at Dug Gap . . . still less was Polk a fit man to quickly and impetuously attack Crittenden.

Fourth. When an important movement is projected, on which the success of the campaign depends, the commander-in-chief who planned it must assume the command and carry it out, instead of giving written orders to his subalterns, as Bragg so often did during this campaign.

Sixth. Night movements are sometimes indispensable; such was our passing the army to the left in the night from September 18 to 19. But night attacks, such as Cleburne's on our left in the evening of the 19th, are to be avoided; they hardly ever attain the desired object, and result in a great deal of noise and very little execution.

Seventh. No army can be complete without the staff-officers being thoroughly educated and specially prepared for this important duty. . . . Our staff officers were selected at random, and being utterly unprepared for their duties, encumbered rather than facilitated our operations. . . . Almost all our assistant-adjutant-generals were mere clerks, instead of real military helpers to their generals.

Eighth. A continuous formation of a deployed front in an uninterrupted line that crosses hill and dale, often disregarding the topographical . . . changes of the ground, belongs to the time of Frederick the Great. . . . We often too strictly adhered to it. . . . If you adopt your formation for defensive purposes to . . . varying ground, you never will have the line of your formation straight, but broken, consisting in salients, points, and recesses which . . . if properly occupied, will make your position strong. Salients give a cross-fire in front of the intermediate spaces. . . . That salient of our breastworks on the left, where Gen. Baird had a few guns planted so that they could enfilade the line, did a great deal of damage to the enemy.

Ninth. We had no general reserve. . . . A strong reserve is indispensable. It is the means of repulsing the enemy in case he penetrates the line. . . . If we had had two divisions by Dyer's farm standing in reserve, we could have met Hood's column after it broke our line and have forced it back.

Tenth. The shifting of troops from one point of the line to another during the action is always dangerous. And here is another proof of the importance of having a reserve.

Eleventh. It is infinitely better to spend the whole night in toilsome marching in order to get into a good position, than to risk meeting the enemy in a faulty position. We did not have a proper position where we fought on the 19th. . . .

Twelfth. It is always better to use troops in the battle in their proper organization if possible. . . . Mixing of parts of commands interferes with the highest usefulness of the troops. . . . In the battle of Chickamauga too much of that sort of breaking and mixing up of commands occurred. . . . and it was a great disadvantage.

Thirteenth. It is pernicious usage to appoint separate commanders of wings. What was good in the last century is out of date now. . . . Our army consisted of three army corps; to make two wings it was necessary to break one of the corps, and . . . the commander of the broken corps. . . . did not know where to stay.

Fourteenth. The battle . . . proved to the full satisfaction of our own and the enemy's soldiers that barricades—even of old rails and rotten logs—make a good protection against the rifle. (4)

In November 1888 Turchin revisited the battlefield with other former Union officers to locate positions of Union units for the purpose of correcting the official War Department map of the battle. The following year a group of former Union and Confederate officers organized the Chickamauga Memorial Association and then petitioned Congress for aid in acquiring land at Lookout Mountain, Missionary Ridge, and "the entire field of Chickamauga." In its *Report* the House Committee on Military Affairs National Military Park urged the establishment of a National Military Park for reasons that Turchin would have approved.

The preservation for national study of the lines of decisive battles, especially when the tactical movements were unusual both in numbers and military ability, and where the fields embraced great natural difficulties, may properly be regarded as a matter of national importance. . . . The preservation of these fields will preserve to the nation for historical *and military study* the best efforts which . . . noted officers, commanding American veterans, were able to put forth. The two together form one of the most valuable object lessons in the art of war. . . . The national value of the preservation of such lines for historical and professional study must be apparent to all reflecting minds. (5).

Congress passed the legislation without a dissenting vote.

From the first the army was actively involved with the effort. The Secretary of War, who was officially responsible for developing and administering the park, appointed three Commissioners—each a veteran of one of armies that had fought here—to locate and mark the battle lines.

The army delivered condemned artillery and other ordnance to help mark appropriate sites and built a 70 foot high steel tower on the highest hill along Horseshoe Ridge so that officers could have an overview of the terrain. Finally, in 1896 a bill was passed specifying that all national military parks—which by this time included Gettysburg and Shiloh (but not yet Antietam, still officially designated a battlefield *site*)—were to be utilized as "national fields for military maneuvers for the Regular Army . . . and the National Guard." In urging this legislation Representative John P. Tracy of Missouri claimed that Chickamauga-Chattanooga could not be excelled

> as a theatre for military instruction. . . . A month's campaigning for practical study on such a field of maneuvers by the corps of West Point cadets, where the lines of battles and the movements . . . of nearly every organization of each side have been ascertained and . . . marked . . . would be worth an entire course in textbooks on the strategy of a campaign and battle tactics.[6]

As hoped, soon after the park was established the land was used for encampments by the Georgia State Militia, and early in 1898 Regular Army troops arrived to train on the ground. During the Spanish-American War it served as a mobilization camp, with some 72,000 troops—more than had been present in either army during the battle—having camped and trained at Fort Thomas in the vicinity of the Wilder Tower. Indeed, more soldiers died of disease at Chickamauga in 1898–99 than were killed in battle during the war with Spain.[7]

In 1902 Congress authorized the army to purchase acreage adjacent to the park for a regiment-sized cavalry post, and with the completion of Fort Oglethorpe both the army and militia from neighboring southern states "made frequent and increasing use of park lands," sometimes in ways that had not been anticipated—training camps and cantonments in 1918, with trenches along the slopes of Snodgrass Hill that resembled the Western Front; biplanes tethered on Wilder Field in the 1930s; and a Woman's Army Corps (WAC) training center during World War II. Only in the 1950s could it be asserted that "the military use of the park had entered a new day."[8]

Turchin and the House Military Affairs Committee of 1890 would have been pleased to see the group of honor graduates from the advanced Leavenworth Staff College course and their instructor, Major Eben Swift, visit the area in 1906. Swift was especially interested in Sherman's campaign from Ringgold to Atlanta, but the following year the Leavenworth Staff Ride also included Chickamauga and Chattanooga.[9] The student officers and their instructor rode over the battlefield, stopping at various points to discuss the application of some principle to the battle and the terrain. The "applicatory method" of instruction then in vogue at Leavenworth was based upon the assumption that principles were best learned by their application rather than through abstract study, and for these students, who had applied the accepted principles in Map Problems, the *Kriegspiel*, Tactical Rides, and Maneuvers, this Historical Staff Ride served as the capstone course. Each officer previously had been assigned to research some phase of a particular battle for analytical study, and after his presentation on the field the class would consider the action and how it might relate to modern conditions.

For the next four years the Staff Ride was an integral part of the Leavenworth curriculum, and in 1983 Leavenworth returned to the tradition by reinstituting the Chickamauga Staff Ride as an elective. Thanks to the popularity of this course, a number of Leavenworth Staff Rides to Chickamauga are now conducted each year, while various of the Army Branch Schools and groups from nearby military installations organize their own staff rides over the battlefield. Most participants probably would agree that the value of "professional study" of these staff rides "must be apparent to all reflecting minds."

* * *

The principal editor of this volume, Colonel Matt Spruill, is a 1986 graduate of the U.S. Army War College. Matt was an enthusiastic participant in our monthly staff rides during his student year. A number of other students have developed studies of minor battlefields or details of a major battle, and we have acknowledged help from a few in earlier volumes. Some of these have gone on to lead staff rides for their units on subsequent assignments. But Matt is unique in having sustained his interest by devoting nearly every free moment in off-duty hours during the ensuing two years he was stationed at U.S. Army Forces Command in Atlanta to write a complete manuscript. His dedication, hard work, and experience as a staff ride leader enabled him to produce this manuscript, and the Army's continued interest in historical staff rides gave him early opportunities to test it in the field.

A graduate of the Citadel who later earned his Master's degree in history, Matt has been a successful troop commander in armor, cavalry, and special forces assignments. He has led soldiers in Vietnam, Germany, and the United States, and he has been a key staff officer in Japan, the U.S. Forces Command, and now in NATO. He has taught in ROTC, at his branch school, and at the Command and General Staff College, Fort Leavenworth. We were fortunate when he turned his talents to the battle of Chickamauga.

As we read this manuscript, several things that differed somewhat from what we had been studying in the Eastern Theater caught our attention. We were impressed by the remarkable professionalism of many brigade commanders, Union and Confederate, who bore the brunt of the fighting. These men fought their brigades magnificently and wrote their reports well. While debates may continue between the parochial advocates of one theater or another, we are convinced that strong leadership at the principal tactical level can be found in ample measure in every army by this stage of the war.

This professionalism is not limited to fighting. The ability to resupply units with ammunition while in contact seems superior to anything we have seen in Eastern battles to this point in the war, and the quick improvisation of offensive and defensive fortifications, while less extensive than at Chancellorsville, seems to have made a greater impression upon participants.

We were struck, too, by the many high-quality memoirs written by senior officers engaged in this battle. They had a sense of the importance of their actions and tried to extract lessons that would improve performance or explain battle outcomes. This volume does not rely on those memoirs, since we try always to deal with the impressions of the moment rather than subsequent reflections or explanations, but many of the excellent after-action reports foreshadow the later writings of Generals William B. Hazen, John B. Turchin, and others.

We noted the ways in which compartmentalization of the Union army slowed the application of improved methods. This is most striking in the organization of the infantry-artillery team. The Army of the Potomac, learning many of these lessons from the Army of Northern Virginia and from its own experiences at Antietam, Fredericksburg and Chancellorsville, already had a chief of artillery who commanded a reserve artillery and directed the efforts of fairly senior artillery officers commanding artillery brigades. This structure was responsive to the needs of senior infantry commanders while exhibiting tremendous flexibility on the march, in the attack, or when defending. These ideas had not yet penetrated the Army of the Cumberland, and Union artillery actions at Chickamauga were often clumsy, late, or ineffectual because of this difference.

We were also reminded that "high tech" units, well-led and equipped with proper doctrine as well as the newest equipment, can be genuinely decisive. In this battle, Colonel John T. Wilder's brigade of mounted infantry is a case in point. Armed with Spencer repeating carbines and detached from their parent division, these soldiers combined tremendous firepower with an improved edge in tactical mobility. Freed from organizational constraints, they were inserted at the critical point again and again by senior commanders. Their combat power was decisive at the minor tactical level, but the Union Army had not yet developed the ability to transform this tactical advantage into operational achievements. This seems to be a recurring dilemma for armies seeking "high tech" solutions to tactical problems.

And finally, we are impressed by the insistence of survivors that this battlefield be preserved so that army officers might use it for professional study. The School of Application for Cavalry and Infantry at Fort Leavenworth – established by another product of the western armies, General W. T. Sherman – had been in existence for less than a decade, and already the notion was accepted by veterans and the House Military Affairs Committee that such a battlefield offered unique opportunities for junior officers to study leadership and tactics.

*   *   *

We are pleased to add this volume to the U.S. Army War College Guide series. As teachers we take pardonable pride in Matt's achievement, and while Chickamauga lies well beyond the range of our own regular staff rides, the book should be of value to anyone visiting the battlefield. The work and the basic text was done by Matt; our role was essentially to assure that the volume conforms to others in the Series in style, historical content and technique. It is appropriate here to acknowledge our appreciation to Col. D. G. Hansen, chairman, Department of National Security and Strategy, U.S. Army War College, for providing support and making the necessary time available to devote to the manuscript; Col. Roy Strong, of the War College Foundation, who made it possible for us to go over the battlefield – manuscript in hand – one last time; and to Ms. Traci Durff for her cheerful and capable assistance in preparing the final manuscript for the publisher.

Jay Luvaas
Harold W. Nelson

1. John C. Paige and Jerome A. Greene, *Administrative History of Chickamauga and Chattanooga National Military Park* (Denver, 1983), pp. 18–19.
2. H. V. Boynton, *Dedication of the Chickamauga and Chattanooga National Military Park* (Washington: Government Printing Office, 1896), pp. 39, 41; "The National Military Park," *Century Magazine* (vol. L, Sept. 1895), p. 705.
3. Ronald F. Lee, *The Origin and Evolution of the National Military Park Idea* (Washington: National Park Service, Office of Park Historic Preservation, 1973), p. 31. Emphasis added.
4. John B. Turchin, *Chickamauga* (second edition, Chicago: Fergus Printing Company, 1889), pp. 167–74 *passim*. There are additional "lessons" expounded by Turchin, but these apply directly to the experience at Chickamauga.
5. H. V. Boynton, *The National Military Park Chickamauga-Chattanooga: An Historical Guide* (Cincinnati: The Robert Clarke Company, 1895), pp. 252, 257–58. Emphasis added.
6. *Ibid.*, pp. 259–60; Lee, *Origin of the National Military Park Idea*, p. 35.
7. Paige and Greene, *Administrative History of Chickamauga*, p. 176.
8. *Ibid.*, pp. 171–99 *passim*.
9. Carol Ann Reardon, "The Study of Military History and the Growth of Professionalism in the U.S. Army before World War I," Unpublished Ph.D. Dissertation, University of Kentucky, 1987, pp. 104–7.

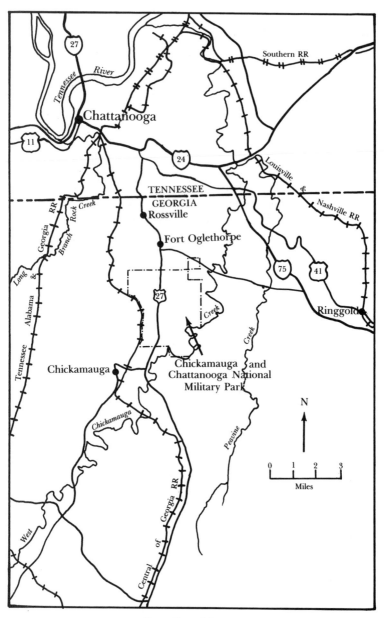

Location Map

TO REACH THE BATTLEFIELD

Traveling north from Atlanta, Georgia or south from Chattanooga, Tennessee on Interstate I-75, leave the Interstate at Exit 141 and travel west on Battlefield Parkway (Georgia Route 2) for 6.2 miles. Turn left on the La Fayette Road (U.S. Highway 27) and drive 0.9 mile. The stone building on your right as you enter the battlefield area is the Park Headquarters and Visitor Center. Turn right and park in the parking lot.

You will start your tour here, but you may wish to spend a few minutes in the Visitor Center before you begin. It houses an excellent small arms collection as well as the usual sources of information and comfort.

As you proceed around the battlefield you will see signs indicating "Tour" or "STOP 1," etc. These signs are for the Park Service tour and have no relation to the directions and stops in this book. Please disregard them.

STOP 1 – OPENING MOVES

Lee and Gordon's Mill on the Chickamauga River (U.S. Army Military History Institute).

THE MOVEMENT TO CONTACT
September 8 to September 18, 1863

The Battle of Chickamauga, fought September 19 and 20, 1863, was the culmination of a series of maneuvers and counter-maneuvers by Major General William Rosecrans' Union Army of the Cumberland and *General Braxton Bragg's* Confederate Army of Tennessee. The series of events that led to the bloodiest battle in the western theater began in early September 1863, when Rosecrans outflanked *Bragg's* defensive position at Chattanooga.

Report of General Braxton Bragg, CSA, Commanding Army of Tennessee

Closely watched by our cavalry, which had been brought forward, it was soon ascertained that the enemy's general movement was toward our left and rear in the direction of Dalton [Ga.] and Rome [Ga.], keeping Lookout Mountain between us. . . . It was therefore determined to meet him in front whenever he should emerge from the mountain gorges. To do this and hold Chattanooga was impossible without such a division of our small force as to endanger both parts.

I marched from Chattanooga on the 8th instant [September 1863] with the whole force, and took position opposite the enemy's center, extending from the crossing of the Chickamauga to La Fayette, Ga. This movement checked the enemy's advance, and, as I expected, he took possession of Chattanooga, and looking upon our movement as a retreat, commenced a concentration and pursuit. As soon as his movements were sufficiently developed I marched on the 17th instant from La Fayette to meet him, throwing my forces along the Chickamauga between him and my supplies at Ringgold. [*The War of the Rebellion: A Compilation of the Official Records of the Union and Confederate Armies* (Washington 1880–1901) Series I, Volume XXX, Part II, pp. 23–24 & 27. Hereafter cited as *O.R.*, XXX, Part I or II.]

After occupying Chattanooga with the extreme left of his army, Rosecrans continued to maneuver in an attempt to maintain pressure on *Bragg's* army from the north while at the same time outflanking him on the west by moving through the passes of the mountains running in a southerly direction from Chattanooga.

Report of Major General William Rosecrans, USA, Commanding the Army of the Cumberland

The weight of evidence, gathered from all sources, was that *Bragg* was moving on Rome, and that his movement began on the 6th of September. General Crittenden [XXI Corps] was therefore directed to hold Chattanooga, with one brigade, calling all the forces on the north side of the Tennessee across, and to follow the enemy's retreat vigorously, anticipating that the main body had retired by Ringgold and Dalton.

Additional information, obtained during the afternoon and the evening of the 10th of September, rendered it certain that his main body had retired by the La Fayette road, but uncertain whether he had gone far. General Crittenden was ordered, at 1 a.m. on the 11th, to proceed to the front and report, directing his command to advance only as far as Ringgold, and order a reconnaissance to [Lee and] Gordon's Mills. His report, and further evidence, satisfied me that the main body of the rebel army was in the vicinity of La Fayette.

General Crittenden was therefore ordered to move his corps, with all possible dispatch, from Ringgold to [Lee and] Gordon's Mills, and communicate with General Thomas [XIV Corps], who had by that time [crossed over and] reached the eastern foot of Lookout Mountain. General Crittenden occupied Ringgold during the 11th, pushing Wilder's mounted infantry [First Brigade, Fourth Division, XIV Corps] as far as Tunnel Hill, skirmishing heavily with the enemy's cavalry. . . . The whole [XXI] corps moved rapidly and successfully across to [Lee and] Gordon's Mills on the 12th. [*O.R.*, XXX, Part I, pp. 53–54.]

On September 14, Rosecrans realized that his army, which was deployed into three major and separated groups, was in danger of being attacked and defeated piecemeal.

Report of Major General William Rosecrans, USA, Commanding Army of the Cumberland (Continued)

It was ascertained that the enemy was concentrating all his forces, both infantry and cavalry, behind the Pigeon Mountain, in the vicinity of La Fayette, while the corps of this army were at [Lee and] Gordon's Mills, Bailey's Cross-Roads, at the foot of Steven's Gap, and at Alpine. . . . It had already been ascertained that the main body of *Johnston's* army [the Department of the West] had joined *Bragg*, and an accumulation of evidence showed that the troops from Virginia [the lead elements of *Longstreet's* I Corps, Army of Northern Virginia] had reached Atlanta on the 1st of the month. . . . It was therefore a matter of life and death to effect the concentration of the army.

General McCook [XX Corps] had already been directed to support General Thomas, but was now ordered to send two brigades to hold Dougherty's Gap, and to join General Thomas with the remainder of his command. . . . As soon as General McCook's corps arrived General Thomas moved down the Chickamauga towards [Lee and] Gordon's Mills. Meanwhile, to bring General Crittenden within reach of General Thomas and beyond the danger of separation . . . [General Crittenden] was withdrawn from [Lee and] Gordon's Mills, on the 14th, and ordered to take post on the southern spur of Missionary Ridge, his right communicating with General Thomas. . . .

Minty, with his cavalry [First Brigade, Second Division, Cavalry Corps], reconnoitered the enemy on the 15th and reported him in force at Dalton, Ringgold, and Leet's [Tan-Yard], and Rock Springs Church. . . . The same day General Crittenden was ordered to return to his old position at [Lee and] Gordon's Mills, his line resting along the Chickamauga via Crawfish Spring [today the town of Chickamauga].

Thus, on the evening of the 17th, the troops were substantially within supporting distance. Orders were given at once to move the whole line northeastwardly down the Chickamauga, with a view to covering the La Fayette road towards Chattanooga. . . . [*O.R.*, XXX, Part I, pp. 54–55.]

As can be seen from *Bragg's* report, Rosecrans' understanding of the immediate danger to his army was correct.

*Report of General Braxton Bragg, CSA, Commanding
Army of Tennessee (Continued)*

Immediate measures were taken to place our trains and limited supplies in safe positions, when all our forces were concentrated along the Chickamauga, threatening the enemy in front. *Major-General Wheeler*, with two divisions of cavalry, occupied the positions on the extreme left, vacated by *Hill's* corps, and was directed to press the enemy in McLemore's Cove, to divert his attention from our real movement. *Brigadier-General Forrest*, with his own and *Pegram's* divisions of cavalry, covered the movement on our front and right. *Brig. Gen. B.R. Johnson*, whose brigade had been at Ringgold, holding the railroad, was moved towards Reed's Bridge, which brought him on the extreme right of the line. *Walker's* corps formed on his left opposite Alexander's Bridge, *Buckner's* next near Thedford's Ford, *Polk's* opposite Lee and Gordon's Mills, and *Hill's* on the extreme left. . . .

The following orders were issued on the night of the 17th, for the forces to cross the Chickamauga, commencing the movement at 6 a.m. on the 18th by the extreme right, at Reed's Bridge. . . .

1. *Johnson's* column (*Hood's*), on crossing at or near Reed's Bridge, will turn to the left by the most practicable route and sweep up the Chickamauga, toward Lee and Gordon's Mills.

2. *Walker*, crossing at Alexander's Bridge, will unite in this move and push vigorously on the enemy's flank and rear in the same direction.

3. *Buckner*, crossing at Thedford's Ford, will join in the movement to the left, and press the enemy up the stream from *Polk's* front at Lee and Gordon's Mills.

4. *Polk* will press his forces to the front of Lee and Gordon's Mills, and if met by too much resistance to cross will bear to the right and cross at Dalton's Ford, or at Thedford's, as may be necessary, and join in the attack wherever the enemy may be.

5. *Hill* will cover our left flank from an advance of the enemy from the cove, and by pressing the cavalry in his front ascertain if the enemy is re-enforcing at Lee and Gordon's Mills, in which event he will attack them in flank.

6. *Wheeler's* cavalry will hold the gaps in Pigeon Mountain and cover our rear and left and bring up stragglers. . . .

The resistance offered by the enemy's cavalry and the difficulties arising from the bad and narrow country roads caused unexpected delays in the execution of these movements. Though the commander of the right column was several times urged to press forward, his crossing [at Reed's Bridge] was not effected until late in the afternoon. At this time *Major-General Hood*, of *Longstreet's* corps, arrived and assumed command of the column. . . . Alexander's Bridge was hotly contested and finally broken up by the enemy just as *General Walker* secured possession. He moved down stream, however, a short distance, and crossed, as directed, at Byram's Ford. . . . [*O.R.*, XXX, Part II, pp. 31–32.]

Report of Major General William Rosecrans, USA, Commanding Army of the Cumberland (Continued)

The position of our troops and the narrowness of the roads retarded our movements. During the day [September 18] while they were in progress, our cavalry, under Col. Minty, was attacked on the left in the vicinity of Reed's Bridge, and Wilder's mounted infantry were attacked by infantry and driven into the La Fayette road. It became apparent that the enemy was massing heavily on our left, crossing Reed's and Alexander's Bridges in force while he had threatened [Lee and] Gordon's Mills.

Elements of Minty's Cavalry Brigade delaying the Confederate advance at Reed's Bridge on September 18, 1863 (U.S. Army Military History Institute).

Orders were therefore promptly given to General Thomas to relieve General Crittenden's Corps, posting one division [Negley's Second Division, XIV Corps] near Crawfish Spring, and to move with the remainder of his corps [behind Crittenden's corps] by the Widow Glenn's house to the Rossville and La Fayette road, his left extending obliquely across it near Kelly's house.

General Crittenden was ordered to proceed with Van Cleve's and Palmer's divisions, to drive the enemy from the [La Fayette and] Rossville road and form on the left of General Wood, then at [Lee and] Gordon's Mills.

General McCook's corps was to close up on General Thomas, occupy the position at Crawfish Spring, and protect General Crittenden's right, while holding his corps mainly in reserve.

The main cavalry force was ordered to close in on General McCook's right, watch the crossing of the Chickamauga, and act under his orders.

The movement for the concentration of the corps . . . was begun on the morning of the 18th, under orders to conduct it very secretly, and was executed so slowly that McCook's corps only reached Pond Spring at dark, and bivouacked, resting on their arms during the night. Crittenden's corps reached its position on the Rossville road near midnight.

Evidence accumulated during the . . . 18th that the enemy was moving to our left. Minty's cavalry and Wilder's mounted brigade encountered the enemy cavalry at Reed's and Alexander's Bridges, and toward evening were driven into the Rossville road. At the same time the enemy had been demonstrating for 3 miles up the Chickamauga. Heavy clouds of dust had been observed 3 or 4 miles beyond the Chickamauga, sweeping to the northeast.

In view of all these facts, the necessity became apparent that General Thomas must use all possible dispatch in moving his corps to the position assigned it. He was therefore directed to proceed with all dispatch, and General McCook to close up to Crawfish Spring as soon as Thomas' column was out of the way. Thomas pushed forward uninterruptedly during the night, and at daylight the head of his column had reached Kelly's house on the La Fayette road, where Baird's division was posted. Brannan followed, and was posted on Baird's left, covering the roads leading to Reed's and Alexander's Bridges. [O.R., XXX, Part I, pp. 55–56.]

THE INITIAL CONTACT
Morning September 19, 1863

Report of Maj. Gen. George H. Thomas, USA,
Commanding XIV Corps, Army of the Cumberland

At 4 p.m. [on September 18th] the whole corps moved to the left along Chickamauga Creek to Crawfish Spring. On arriving at that place [I] received orders to march on the cross-road leading by Widow Glenn's house to the Chattanooga and La Fayette road, and take up a position near Kelly's farm, on the La Fayette road, connecting with Crittenden [XXI Corps] on my right at [Lee and] Gordon's Mills. The head of the column reached Kelly's farm about daylight on the 19th, Baird's division in front, and took up a position at the forks of the road, facing toward Reed's and Alexander's Bridges over the Chickamauga. . . .

Kelly's house is situated in an opening about three-fourths of a mile long and one-fourth of a mile wide, on the east side of the State [La Fayette] Road, and stretches along that road in a northerly direction, with a small field of perhaps 20 acres on the west side of the road, directly opposite to the house. From thence to the Chickamauga the surface of the country is undulating and covered with original forest timber, interspersed with undergrowth, in many places so dense that it is difficult to see 50 paces ahead. There is a cleared field near Jay's Mill, and cleared land in the vicinity of Reed's and Alexander's Bridges. A narrow field commences at a point about a fourth of a mile south of Kelly's house, on the east side of the State road, and extends, perhaps, for half a mile along the road toward [Lee and] Gordon's Mills. Between the State road and the foot of Missionary Ridge there is a skirt of timber stretching from the vicinity of Widow Glenn's house, south of the forks of the [Glenn-Kelly] road to McDonald's house, three-fourths of a mile north of Kelly's. The eastern slope of the Missionary Ridge, between Glenn's and McDonald's, is cleared and mostly under cultivation. This position of Baird's threw my right in close proximity to Wilder's brigade; the interval I intended to fill up with the two remaining brigades of

Reynolds' division on their arrival. General Brannan, closely follow-ing Baird's division, was placed in position on his left, on the two roads leading from the State road to Reed's and Alexander's Bridges. [*O.R.*, XXX, Part I, pp. 248–249.]

Before beginning the battlefield tour it would be informative to visit the bridge sites where the delaying actions were fought on the 18th.

Depart the park headquarters and visitor center. As you leave the parking lot turn left onto the La Fayette Road and drive 0.1 mile to the stop light at the intersection of the Reed's Bridge Road.

Turn right onto Reed's Bridge Road and drive east for 2.6 miles to Reed's Bridge. Pull off to the side of the road just before the bridge.

You are now at the location where Colonel Robert Minty's cavalry brigade fought the final part of its delaying action against the northern-most advancing Confederate column. Minty's delay actually began on the east side of the range of hills you see a mile to the east of your location. Minty's final act before being pushed from this position was to severely damage the bridge and again cause the Confederates further delay. A look at the Chickamauga Creek at this point gives some appreciation of the obstacle it imposed to the rapid movement of a large force.

Report of Col. Robert Minty, USA, Commanding
First Brigade, Second Cavalry Division,
Army of the Cumberland

The Rebel line advanced and I was steadily driven back across the ridge.

My only means of crossing the creek was Reed's Bridge, a nar-row, frail structure, which was planked with loose boards and fence-rails, and a bad ford about 300 yards higher up. I masked my artillery behind some shrubs near the ford, leaving one battalion of the Fourth Regulars to support it, and ordered the remainder of that regiment to cross the bridge, holding the Seventh Pennsylvania and Fourth Michi-gan in line to cover the movement. Before the first squadron had time to cross, the head of the rebel column . . . moving at the double-quick as steadily as if at drill, came through the gap not 500 yards from the bridge. The artillery opening on them from an unexpected quarter evidently took them by surprise and immediately checked their ad-vance, causing them to again deploy. [*O.R.*, XXX, Part I, p. 923.]

Depart from Reed's Bridge and continue to drive east for 0.4 mile to the intersection with the Burning Bush Road. Turn right (south) on the Burning Bush Road and drive for 2.1 miles to the Alexander Bridge Road intersection.

Turn right onto the Alexander Bridge Road. (If you come up to a red brick church on your left, you have gone too far and need to go back 0.1 mile and find the Alexander Bridge Road.)

Drive west on the Alexander Bridge Road for 1.2 miles. After you cross Alexander Bridge there is a place to stop on your left. Park your car and walk back to the bridge.

This is the location where the second critical delaying action was fought on the 18th. The Union unit in this area was the mounted infantry brigade of Colonel John T. Wilder, whose soldiers, armed with Spencer repeating rifles, were deployed north and south of the road on the west side of the creek. This position was supported by the Eighteenth Indiana battery deployed on higher ground to your right rear. There were no trees in that area in 1863 and a clear field of fire was presented to the artillery. The Confederate force approaching this position was *Liddell's* division.

Report of Col. John T. Wilder, USA, Commanding First Brigade (Mounted Infantry), Fourth Division, XIV Corps, Army of the Cumberland

On the 18th, at 10 a.m., we were attacked by a brigade of rebel infantry, but our position being a strong one we repulsed them easily. . . . Soon after three brigades of rebel infantry again attempted to carry my position. We repulsed them, however, with severe loss to them. At 5 p.m. a picket stationed in my rear reported a strong force of rebel infantry in my rear. Having driven the cavalry away from the ford below me, I immediately commenced withdrawing my forces in the direction of [Lee and] Gordon's Mills, and intercepted the force that was trying to surround me, when, being re-enforced by two regiments of infantry from General Wood's division . . . we held the rebels from farther advance until morning, although they made a desperate attempt to drive us at 9 o'clock at night. [*O.R.*, XXX, Part I, p. 447.]

Return to your car. Resume driving in the same direction on the **ALEXANDER BRIDGE ROAD** for slightly more than 0.6 mile. **TURN RIGHT onto JAY'S MILL ROAD and drive 0.9 mile. TURN**

LEFT onto BROTHERTON ROAD (Jay's Mill was near this intersection). Drive about 0.3 mile and PARK in the turnout on the left near the sign pointing toward BRAGG'S HEADQUARTERS. DISMOUNT and walk about 35 yards farther on the left side of the road. TURN RIGHT to face across the road toward the trail junction in that vicinity.

STOP 1, POSITION A – BRANNAN'S ATTACK

The right flank of the position occupied by Brigadier General John M. Brannan's Third Division, XIV Corps, was 150 yards down this trail. Brannan's division was the lead unit arriving near the Kelly house, where he was met by Thomas and directed to move east. This movement brought Brannan's troops onto the low ridge traversed by the trail. Here the Union infantry made contact with *Brigadier General Nathan B. Forrest's* cavalry, protecting the north flank of the Army of Tennessee as it moved to a position thought to oppose the Union north flank.

Report of Brig. Gen. John M. Brannan, USA, Commanding Third Division, XIV Corps, Army of the Cumberland

On arriving at a point on the La Fayette road known as Kelly's house, I received orders from Major-General Thomas to capture, if possible, a rebel force represented by Col. Dan McCook to be a brigade cut off on the west side of the Chickamauga Creek; failing in this, to drive it across the creek. . . . I advanced the Second Brigade of my division, by the Reed's Bridge road toward the rebel left, while the remaining brigades of my command advanced by the Daffron's Ford [Reed's Bridge] road to strike the supposed right of the enemy's position.

Shortly after 7 a.m. on the 19th instant the Second Brigade, having advanced about three-quarters of a mile toward the Chickamauga, came upon a strong force of the enemy, consisting of two divisions instead of the supposed brigade. . . . [O.R., XXX, Part I, p. 400.]

Col. John T. Croxton, who commanded the Second Brigade in this action, was wounded the next day. His senior regimental commander wrote the after action report for the brigade.

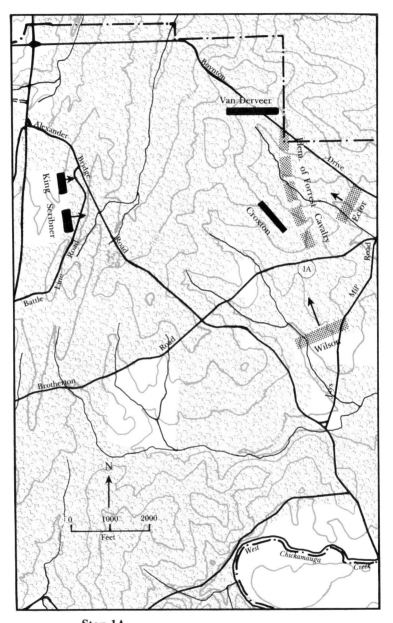

Stop 1A
Situation Early Morning
September 19, 1863

Report of Col. Charles W. Chapman, USA, Commanding Second Brigade, Third Division, XIV Corps, Army of the Cumberland

The brigade was on the march all night of the 18th instant; arrived in the vicinity of the enemy about 6 o'clock in the morning of the 19th. After halting and taking a hasty cup of coffee, firing was heard in front; the column was immediately on the march forward, on the Ringgold road. The colonel commanding was here informed that a brigade of the enemy had been cut off, and was immediately in our front . . . in the vicinity of the Chickamauga Creek.

We advanced about 1 mile on this road and formed line of battle in the woods, facing nearly east, the Seventy-fourth Indiana on the right . . . the Fourth Kentucky . . . on the left, the Tenth Indiana . . . in the center, these three regiments forming the front line; Fourteenth Ohio . . . [and] Tenth Kentucky . . . forming the reserve. Skirmishers were thrown out in front, under command of Major Van Natta. . . . They advanced but a short distance when they were charged upon by the rebel cavalry, supposed to be those under the command of *Forrest*. The skirmishers immediately returned to the line. The advance line gave them one volley, fixed bayonets, and charged, which caused them to "skedaddle" in haste, with considerable loss.

The line of battle was immediately reformed, and skirmishers advanced . . . about 500 yards, when they came in contact with the enemy's skirmishers. After considerable firing on both sides, a flank movement was discovered. The reserve regiments were at once brought forward, the Fourteenth Ohio on the right and the Tenth Kentucky on the left. . . .

An advance being ordered, the troops moved forward steadily, and with a determination to drive the enemy from the field, but, instead of finding one brigade to contend with, we had the combined forces of *Longstreet* and *Breckinridge*. [Actually *Forrest's* four brigades of cavalry and *Ector's* and *Wilson's* infantry brigades.] [*O.R.*, XXX, Part I, pp. 415–416.]

Report of Brig. Gen. Nathan B. Forrest, CSA, Commanding Cavalry Corps, Army of Tennessee

On the morning of the 19th, I was ordered to move with my command down the road toward Reed's Bridge and develop the enemy, which was promptly done, and their advance was soon engaged at the steam saw-mill near that point. Finding the enemy too strong for *General Pegram's* force, I dispatched a staff officer to *Lieutenant-General Polk's* quarters for *General Armstrong's* division. He could only spare *Colonel Dibrell's* brigade, which arrived shortly after we engaged the enemy; was speedily dismounted and formed, and, with *General Pegram's* division, were able to hold position until infantry re-enforcements arrived, the first brigade of which, under *Colonel Wilson*, formed on my left, advanced in gallant style, driving the enemy back and capturing a battery of artillery, my dismounted cavalry advancing with them. The superior force of the enemy compelled us to give back until re-enforced by *General Ector's* brigade, when the enemy was again driven back. [*O.R.*, XXX, Part II, p. 524.]

Ector's brigade was deployed northeast of this location and moved westerly against the Union force. *Wilson's* brigade attacked northwest from the location where you are now. This was the first of many flank attacks and counter attacks that would be made by both sides on this part of the battlefield. If you face north and look over your left and right shoulders you will see the regimental monuments that outline the battle line of *Wilson's* brigade as he moved forward and attacked Croxton's brigade.

Report of Col. Claudius C. Wilson, CSA, Commanding Brigade, Walker's Division, Army of Tennessee

General Forrest . . . informed me that the enemy in considerable force were engaging his cavalry to the right and front of my position, and he directed me to select a position and form line of battle on the left of the road. I formed my line on the ridge of the long hill, which from the northeast overlooks and commands the plain where our first encounter with the enemy took place, posting the artillery by sections on the most elevated positions and opposite to the intervals between regiments. We had not remained in this position long when an order from *General Forrest* informed me that the enemy were pressing him sorely in front and directed me to move up on his left. This order was promptly executed, the brigade moving off by the right flank, and, filing up the Alexander's Bridge road about three-eighths of a mile, was formed forward into line.

The line was scarcely formed when firing commenced on the left. The order was given to move forward at once, and the line stepped off with the enthusiasm of high hope and patriotic determination, and the precision and accuracy which only disciplined and instructed troops can attain. The enemy's skirmishers were encountered at once and driven in on their first line, which opened upon us a terrific fire. Steadily the line moved forward and poured into the enemy's ranks a well-directed fire, which very soon caused his line to break and flee from the field in confusion. . . . The command still pressed forward on the retreating foe and soon encountered a second line of battle, which seemed to have been drawn up 300 or 400 yards in rear of the first. Then again the contest was renewed with great energy and the position disputed with stubborn resolve. [*O.R.*, XXX, Part II, p. 248.]

If you want to walk the ground described in these accounts, follow the directions to Positions B and C. Disregard the monuments used as landmarks for this walk since they refer to a later phase of the battle.

To walk to **POSITION B**, take the left of the two trails that enter **BROTHERTON ROAD** across from **POSITION A**. Walk about 150 yards to the large stone monument to the Seventy-fourth Indiana (about ten yards off the trail on your right) to follow the center of Wilson's attack.

POSITION B – WILSON'S FLANK ATTACK

This is the right flank of the initial battle position occupied by Croxton's brigade after he had attacked *Forrest's* cavalry and was counterattacked by *Wilson's* brigade. Croxton's line generally faced to the east and southeast.

Report of Col. Charles W. Chapman, USA, Commanding Second Brigade, Third Division, XIV Corps, Army of the Cumberland (Continued)

We succeeded in checking them, but they soon recovered, and being in force they soon commenced flanking us on the right. We were compelled to fall back, which was done in good order.

A new line of battle was now formed on the right, and nearly at right angles with the first, for the purpose of meeting the flank movement being made by the enemy, and again advanced this line, driving the enemy before us a short distance. At this time, our ammunition being nearly exhausted, we fell back to a ridge and there

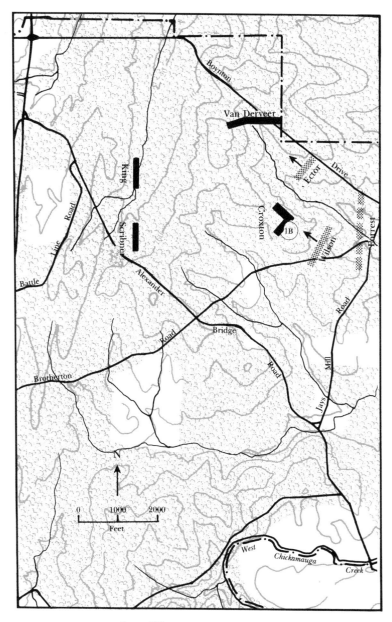

Stop 1B
Situation Mid Morning
September 19, 1863

held our position until we were relieved by King's brigade of General Baird's division. The brigade then returned to the rear of the battery [Battery B, First Ohio Artillery] (which had been ordered back about 300 yards, to take position on a ridge commanding an open field in our rear, so that if the enemy forced us back beyond it the battery could rake them with grape and canister), forming line of battle on the right and left of it, and replenished the men with 60 rounds of ammunition. [*O.R.*, XXX, Part I, p. 416.]

Report of Lieut. Col. Myron Baker, USA, Seventy-fourth Indiana Infantry, Second Brigade, Third Division, XIV Corps, Army of the Cumberland

The Seventy-fourth Indiana held the right of the front line, the Tenth Indiana being on its immediate left. At about 10 a.m. the line was advanced, changing direction slightly toward the right. When the line had advanced about one-half a mile . . . the skirmishers thrown forward in our front became engaged and in a short time were driven in by the rebel cavalry, which in turn was repulsed by a volley from the Fourth Kentucky, Tenth Indiana, and Seventy-fourth Indiana. The skirmishers again being thrown forward the men were ordered to lie down to screen themselves from shells which were being thrown into the line by a rebel battery. In a few minutes after the attack by the rebel cavalry in front, it was discovered that the enemy was attempting to turn our right, and the line was immediately changed fronting in that direction at almost right angles with the original line of battle. The Seventy-fourth Indiana executed the movement under a sharp fire from the rebels. The skirmishers in front having changed direction parallel with the line were soon driven back and the whole line became engaged with the line of the enemy. In a short time it became apparent that the right wing of the Seventy-fourth Indiana was thrown too far forward, being exposed in its new position to a terrible fire on the right flank, in consequence of which Col. Chapman ordered that flank to be thrown farther back.

Up to this time, although exposed to a severe fire under which the loss in killed and wounded had been considerable, the regiment held its position unwaveringly and returned the enemy's fire with commendable coolness and alacrity. When the order to retire the right flank was given it was misunderstood for a command to retire the whole line, and the regiment was momentarily thrown into confusion, but immediately rallied and took position on the right of the

Tenth Kentucky, where it fought unflinchingly until its 60 rounds of cartridges had been expended, when it was relieved and went to the rear for ammunition. [*O.R.*, XXX, Part I, pp. 418–419.]

Shortly after Brannan's division became engaged, Thomas ordered Baird's First Division, XIV Corps, forward to reenforce along the line of contact. This division moved forward from the area south of Kelly's farm and, upon making contact, attacked the flank of *Wilson's* brigade. In time the right portion of Baird's line would be attacked in the flank by additional Confederate reenforcements.

Report of Brig. Gen. Absalom Baird, USA, Commanding First Division, XIV Corps, Army of the Cumberland

I formed General King's brigade upon the left, with orders to dress and close upon General Brannan, and a portion of Colonel Scribner's force upon the same line to be guarded by King's right, and the rest of his force I had bent to the rear so as to march by flank in rear of his right, and be ready to front in that direction or toward the south should it be required. To General Starkweather I gave orders to move in column in rear, holding his brigade as a reserve. I had particularly in view the support of our right flank. The artillery could not advance in line with the infantry, nor, indeed, could it have been used except at rare intervals. It could not, at the same time, be left behind for want of protection, and it was directed to follow closely the brigades, making its way through the trees.

I had scarcely got my line formed when General Brannan's men, a little in advance, began to skirmish hotly. My men were soon after engaged. We drove the enemy before us, and covered the ground quite thickly with his dead and wounded, besides sending 200 prisoners to the rear, some just from the Army of [Northern] Virginia. During this forward movement, I received orders from the general commanding to push rapidly toward the left to support Colonel Croxton's brigade of Brannan's division, then hard pressed by the enemy and almost out of ammunition.

About the same time, General Starkweather . . . received an order of similar effect, and at once acted upon it. I was not . . . aware of this, and thus lost my knowledge of his position. Before I had closed up with General Brannan's left, word was brought me that General Palmer had arrived upon my right, and that his skirmishers were then passing across my front. I sent a caution . . . to my men not to fire into them. . . . Men of our forces were in the position indicated; but to whom they could have belonged, or how they came there, I cannot now conjecture.

[Having] arrived close up to General Brannan, and the enemy having disappeared from our front, I halted to readjust my line. We had now advanced about three-fourths of a mile from where we first became engaged, and the troops had behaved admirably. While arranging my line, I learned from prisoners that there had been but one division in our front, while the main body of the rebel force, which they exaggerated at 90,000, had crossed the river at Alexander's Bridge . . . and was then upon my right flank. I immediately ordered General King to change his front so as to face the south; his left being supported by General Brannan's troops, in order to face the new danger. I also dispatched staff officers to General Starkweather to bring him to the same point, but having moved toward the left . . . they failed for some time to find him. I went myself toward Colonel Scribner to see his command properly posted, but before I could reach him, the attack had been made in such force that he was unable to withstand it, and I met his men coming back in disorder, driven by the enemy across the rear of what had been our previous position. . . . Complete destruction seemed inevitable. Four pieces of Colonel Scribner's battery were captured after firing sixty-four rounds, and the enemy, sweeping like a torrent, fell upon the regular brigade before it had got into position, took its battery, and after a struggle in which whole battalions were wiped out of existence, drove it back upon the line of General Brannan. [*O.R.*, XXX, Part I, pp. 275–276.]

To reach POSITION C, where an attack from *Liddell's* Division hit the right flank of King's Brigade, continue along the trail about 400 yards to the monument and guns on the right marking the position of Battery H, Fifth U.S. Artillery.

POSITION C – DEFEAT OF KING'S BRIGADE

This position marks the general location of the left flank of King's brigade, when he moved forward with the rest of Baird's division to re-enforce Brannan. After assisting in the counterattack against *Wilson's* flank, King's brigade halted. Here, along with Scribner's brigade to his right rear, King in turn was counterattacked by *Liddell's* division, composed of *Walthall's* and *Govan's* brigades. King's line was initially oriented to the east.

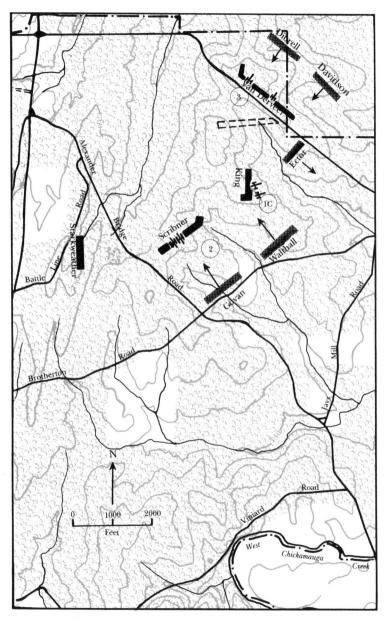

Stops 1C, 2, & 3
Situation Late Morning
September 19, 1863

*Report of Brig. Gen. John H. King, USA, Commanding
Third Brigade, First Division, XIV Corps, Army of the
Cumberland*

I pushed everything to the front, my first line driving the enemy before them for a mile, and meeting General A. Baird, . . . at about 10 a.m., was ordered to make a new front at right angles with the other. I had only time, however, to get the [First Battalion] Sixteenth Infantry and battery in position before being assailed by an overwhelming force; at this time the troops on my right were giving ground to the enemy in confusion. I immediately gave orders for the battery to limber up, but it could not be done as the horses as they were brought up to the guns were shot down.

The officers and men, finding it impossible to retire, remained with their pieces (firing) until they were forcibly taken from them by the enemy. It was at this time that I lost the First Battalion Sixteenth Infantry (made prisoners), with the exception of 5 commissioned officers and 62 men. . . . I reformed my command some 400 yards in the rear of the battery. . . . [*O.R.*, XXX, Part I, p. 309.]

*Report of Capt. Robert E. Crofton, USA, Commanding
Sixteenth U.S. Infantry, Third Brigade, First Division
XIV Corps, Army of the Cumberland*

We moved into line of battle, the First Battalion, Eighteenth, being on our right, and the First Battalion, Nineteenth, being on our left; our front was covered by a strong line of skirmishers. Very soon the skirmishers on our left opened fire, and almost immediately it extended along the entire line. After a pretty sharp skirmish fire the enemy broke, and we drove him about three-quarters of a mile, taking several prisoners and killing and wounding several. From this point we moved changing our front to the right, and were ordered to support Battery H, Fifth [U.S.] Artillery, on a ridge about a quarter of a mile from our last position. We were formed directly in front of the guns, and the men ordered to lie down. Here, without any warning whatever, the rebels came up on our right flank and got right on us before any disposition could be made to meet them. Consequently nearly the entire battalion was killed, wounded, or captured, and at the same time the battery was also taken. Of the men engaged in this action, about 62 escaped, some of them slightly wounded. This remnant was, by order of General King, attached to the Nineteenth Infantry. . . . [*O.R.*, XXX, Part I, p. 318.]

Return to your car. Resume driving in the same direction on BROTHERTON ROAD. After driving about 0.3 mile, pause and look to your right front as you enter WINFREY FIELD. *Liddell's* division crossed the ground between this position and the tall monument. Continue driving, and when you have gone a total of 0.5 mile, just before reaching the STOP sign at ALEXANDER BRIDGE ROAD, TURN LEFT and use the picnic area turnout to REVERSE DIRECTION on BROTHERTON ROAD. Drive slightly more than 0.1 mile and park in the turnout on the right with the sign pointing toward the BALDWIN MONUMENT. Dismount and walk to the tall monument pointed out earlier in the drive that is now to your left front. This monument memorializes a unit that was here in the afternoon and was not a part of this action. It is used here solely as a landmark.

STOP 2 – LIDDELL'S ATTACK AND SCRIBNER'S RESPONSE

When you paused to look at this position from the edge of the field you were in the center of *Liddell's* attack. Leaving its position near Alexander's Bridge. *Liddell's* division moved north through that location to attack the right flank units of Baird's division. Part of this attacking force caused the damage to King's brigade.

Report of Brig. Gen. St. John R. Liddell, CSA, Commanding Division, Walker's Corps, Army of Tennessee

About 8 o'clock the firing of *General Forrest's* cavalry and *Ector's* and *Wilson's* brigades became very heavy in the rear of the direction we were taking and on the right of our intended line of battle. The country around was mostly oak woodland, and in places thick underbrush. About 11 o'clock *Major-General Walker* asked me to go with him on a reconnaissance to know what the demonstration meant then being made on our right. . . .

We found the enemy pressing back *General Ector's* and *Colonel Wilson's* brigades, the latter more or less in confusion, and other evidences of attack, making it apparent that a heavy force was bearing down upon us. I replied to *General Walker's* inquiry as to what I thought of it, "that I was satisfied a corps of the enemy was about being thrown forward to turn our right wing, which it was absolutely necessary for us to meet promptly with heavy re-enforcements."

He agreed with me . . . and immediately wrote the same to *General Bragg*. At the same time orders were received . . . from *General Bragg* to attack the enemy immediately with all his force, upon which . . . *[Major General Walker]* instructed me to bring up my force to the relief of the two brigades already mentioned, and to retard, if possible, the farther progress of the enemy.

As soon as my command could reach the place I formed the line facing northward, *General Walthall* on the right, *Colonel Govan* on the left, and at once moved forward to the attack . . . , cautioning *Colonel Govan* to look well to his left, as I apprehended that wing would strike the enemy first, although he was not then visible on account of the thick undergrowth. In a few minutes we became hotly engaged with the enemy's infantry and artillery, and pressing forward with a shout we captured all the artillery in our immediate front, with many prisoners of the Fifth, Fourteenth, Fifteenth, Sixteenth, Eighteenth, Nineteenth, and Twenty-first U.S. Regulars and Fourth Kentucky. . . .

We had now broken through two lines of the enemy immediately in our front, and were just engaging the third when it was discovered that their extended lines were overlapping and flanking us right and left, upon which it became necessary to retire rapidly by a flank movement to the right, to avoid destruction or capture. After reaching the next hill in rear of us, we found *General Cheatham's* division taking position, having just come up a little too late to our support in action. [*O.R.*, XXX, Part II, pp. 251–252.]

On *Walthall's* left was *Govan's* brigade. The Fifth and Thirteenth (Combined) Arkansas, on the right of *Govan's* attacking line, was one of the regiments that struck Scribner's brigade in the wood line to the northeast.

Report of Lieut. Col. John E. Murray, CSA, Commanding Fifth and Thirteenth Arkansas Infantry, Govan's Brigade, Liddell's Division, Army of Tennessee

After moving about half a mile over a flat, rocky, and wooded country we suddenly came in contact with the enemy. The country being covered with a thick undergrowth of wood was such that it was impossible to see the enemy until we were very close upon him. He was posted in strong force in a slight depression in the ground, with his artillery on a slight ridge or elevation immediately in his rear. This position was immediately charged by this command, and after a short but sanguinary struggle the enemy was driven back in great confusion, leaving his artillery in our possession.

In this charge *Col. L. Featherston* was killed while gallantly leading his men. . . .

I at once assumed command of the regiment and ordered it to press forward on the enemy's second line, which was done in gallant style, and this line of the enemy's was soon broken and scattered as the first had been, and more artillery was captured, as well as a good many prisoners, who were at once ordered to the rear. My command continued to press forward and soon engaged the third line of the enemy. While fighting this line the troops upon my left began to give way in some confusion. Not understanding the reason for this, I made strenuous exertions to keep my men from falling back, but while I was thus engaged I was notified by *Major Green*, who had been nearer the left, and could consequently see better what was going on there, that the enemy had succeeded in turning the left of the brigade and were then in my rear. I was convinced that his report was correct by being fired on at this time from the rear. The command was immediately moved by the right flank. After moving in this manner for about three-quarters of a mile, the command was halted and reformed in rear of *Major-General Cheatham's* line. [*O.R.*, XXX, Part II, p. 263.]

SCRIBNER IS PUSHED BACK

You are now in the area of Scribner's second position as he attempted to face the attack falling on his flank. A line of monuments to the units of Scribner's brigade runs in a westerly direction just inside the wood line.

Report of Col. Benjamin F. Scribner, USA, Commanding First Brigade, First Division, XIV Corps, Army of the Cumberland

The advance on my left having ceased, I halted in front of the field and placed the battery in position, bearing to my left and the point where the enemy attempted to place a battery. About this time I was informed by my skirmishers that the enemy was passing to our right. I immediately sent a staff officer to notify General Palmer, who, after proceeding a short distance in the supposed direction of General Palmer's line, found himself within 20 paces and confronting a strong skirmish line of the enemy. After adroitly making his escape, and being unable to find my intermediate commander, [he] reported in person the presence of the enemy on the right to Major-General Thomas, who immediately directed him to order any forces that could be found in the woods to meet the enemy in his new position. Three separate commands were thus notified. I was immediately after informed that my right was being turned. Dr. Miller, my brigade surgeon, coming up, reported the enemy in my rear; that he had been in their hands. As information like this came in I dispatched the same to the general commanding division, and threw a company of skirmishers to my right and rear.

Scarcely had their deployment been completed when the enemy opened upon them a destructive fire. To form a front to the right by causing the Thirty-eighth Indiana to change their front to the rear and to change the Tenth Wisconsin to the right of the Thirty-eighth Indiana and limber the battery to the rear, between the two regiments, employed but a few moments; this, too, under a heavy fire.

The enemy charged down upon me along my whole line, pouring in canister and shell. I now dispatched every staff officer and orderly with information of my position, asking for support, expressing my intention to hold my place with desperation until assistance arrived. . . . Thus, contending with an overwhelming force in my front and on my flank, was [fought] one of the most stubborn and heroic fights that ever fell to my lot to witness. The gallant Lieutenant Van Pelt was shot down at this guns, having fired 64 rounds into the midst of the enemy as they came charging down the hill, the two regiments on the right and left of the battery at the same time pouring in a well-directed fire. The enemy would hesitate but a moment, when they continued to press on. Their augmenting forces at length broke my lines, and forced me to fall back. The nature of my line, being in a right angle, the intricacies of the woods, overwhelming numbers, and the impetuosity of the charge rendered it impossible to withdraw in order, and not until they had reached a point near the road could order be restored. [*O.R.*, XXX, Part I, pp. 286–287.]

As you face the road the left flank regiment was the Second Ohio, in position to your left rear.

Report of Capt. James Warnock, USA, Commanding Second Ohio Infantry, First Brigade, First Division, XIV Corps, Army of the Cumberland

The Second Ohio Regiment, under the command of Lieut. Col. O.C. Maxwell . . . . formed into line of battle. About 8 a.m. two brigades passed our regiment toward the left of the field, and soon afterward heavy firing of musketry was heard in that direction. The First Brigade was put in motion, the Second Ohio being in the front line of battle, and marched in the direction of the firing. . . . In half an hour the regiment came within sight of the enemy and opened a rapid and steady fire, advancing all the time, firing, loading, and cheering loudly. The enemy in a few minutes gave way and fled, leaving about a dozen killed and wounded in our immediate front, also about 15 or 20 prisoners, who were sent to the rear. A section of *Martin's* (Georgia) battery was in our front. The regiment killed all the horses belonging to one of the guns, and it was left on the field . . . because we had no means to bring it off.

Idealized version of the fight around Van Pelt's battery (Battery A, First Michigan Artillery) in the northwest edge of Winfrey Field on the morning of September 19, 1863 (U.S. Army Military History Institute).

The firing here ceased in front, and our line was halted about an hour. Skirmishing was then heard on our right flank; the regiment changed front forward, facing a corn-field through which the enemy was coming massed in heavy force. Immediately the engagement was renewed with great fury, the enemy pressing forward heavily on the right. So overwhelming was his force that the right of the brigade gave way by regiments, successively, until the Second Ohio, being on the left, retired, after all the regiments on the right had been driven from their position. In falling back from this position we expected to find a line of our troops supporting us, behind which the regiment would halt. In this we were disappointed, and the result was that the line retired thereafter in considerable confusion, but the regiment was rallied about half a mile to the rear. . . . Here also the regiment lost heavily, particularly in missing, most of whom fell into the hands of the enemy. [*O.R.*, XXX, Part I, pp. 292–293.]

Report of Lieut. Col. Daniel F. Griffin, USA,
Commanding Thirty-eighth Indiana Infantry, First Brigade,
First Division, XIV Corps, Army of the Cumberland

Company F, Captain Jenkins commanding, my line of skirmishers, . . . reported the enemy advancing and moving to our right, as though intending to flank the position and gain our rear. . . . I was ordered to change my line perpendicular to the rear, forming almost a right angle with line of the Thirty-third Ohio, next on my left. The Tenth Wisconsin now moved on our right, and First Michigan Battery, with companies B and H of my command, also on our right. This position was hardly taken when the enemy charged down on our front, driving in skirmishers and advancing in heavy column. Fire was immediately opened by the whole line and battery, momentarily checking the advance. But they again pressed forward with such vigor, while raking both fronts of the brigade with an enfilading fire of musketry, that the left was compelled to fall back, which was soon followed by the whole line, the enemy meantime having charged in heavy force up the hill and into the right and center of my command, which gave way under the pressure, not, however, without suffering much loss in killed, wounded, and prisoners. In passing to the rear I found no troops to rally with, and did not get my command together until nearing the Chattanooga road. [*O.R.*, XXX, Part I, p. 290.]

Return to your car. Resume driving in the same direction on BROTHERTON ROAD to the "T" intersection (about 0.7 mile). TURN LEFT onto JAY's MILL ROAD and drive to the "T" intersection with REED'S BRIDGE ROAD. TURN LEFT onto that road and drive slightly less than 1.0 mile to the parking area on your right at the crest of the hill. PARK there and dismount. CROSS THE ROAD. Go to the second marker on your left (Vanderveer's Brigade). BE VERY CAREFUL! This road carries high-speed traffic.

STOP 3 – VAN DERVEER SAVES THE UNION LEFT FLANK

You are standing in the right part of Van Derveer's line at midmorning. The line ran from your position to the left and faced south and southeast. The artillery supporting the brigade was positioned where you are and 400 yards to your left.

When Brannan moved his division forward from the La Fayette Road at about 7:30 a.m., he deployed two brigades on line. Croxton's brigade, which featured in the action at Stop 1B, was on the right, Van Derveer's brigade was on the left, and Connell's brigade was in reserve. Van Derveer's brigade made contact with the right flank elements of *Forrest's* cavalry, who were soon re-enforced by *Ector's* brigade. Here Van Derveer fought a two-phased action, first facing south, then facing north to meet a Confederate flanking attack.

Report of Col. Ferdinand Van Derveer, USA, Commanding Third Brigade, Third Division, XIV Corps, Army of the Cumberland

After a fatiguing march during the night of the 18th, and without any sleep or rest, while halting near Kelly's house, on the Rossville and La Fayette road, I received an order from Brigadier-General Brannan, commanding Third Division, to move with haste along the road to Reed's Bridge over the Chickamauga, take possession of a ford near that point, and hold it. I immediately moved northward to McDonald's house [vicinity of today's Visitor Center], and thence at right angles eastward toward the bridge. A short distance from McDonald's I formed the brigade in two lines, sent skirmishers to the front, and advanced cautiously, though without losing time, 1½ miles. In the meantime brisk firing was progressing upon my right, understood to be maintained by the First and Second Brigades of this division. . . .

Perceiving from the firing upon my right that I was passing the enemy's flank, I wheeled the line in that direction and began feeling his position with my skirmishers.

About this time I received an order stating that the Second Brigade was gradually giving back, and that it was necessary I should at once make an attack. This we did with a will, the first line, composed of the Thirty-fifth Ohio on the right and the Second Minnesota on the left, moving down a gentle slope, leaving the Eighty-seventh Indiana in reserve on the crest of the hill. At this time the Ninth Ohio, which had charge of the ammunition train of the division, had not arrived. Smith's battery [Battery I, Fourth Artillery], composed of four 12-pounder Napoleons, was placed in position in the center and on the right of the line.

The enemy having discovered our location, opened a furious fire of artillery and musketry, which was replied to promptly and apparently with considerable effect; for in half an hour the enemy slackened his fire, and his advance line was compelled to fall back. I took advantage of this moment to bring forward the Eighty-seventh Indiana, and by a passage of lines to the front carried them to the relief of the Thirty-fifth Ohio, which had already suffered severely in the engagement. This movement was executed with as much coolness and accuracy as if on drill.

Scarcely was the Eighty-seventh Indiana in line before fresh forces of the enemy were brought up in time to receive a terrible volley, which made his ranks stagger and held him for some time at bay. The Ninth Ohio, which I had previously sent for, arriving at this moment, I placed it on the right of my line. Still farther to the right a section of Church's battery [Battery D, First Michigan Artillery] and the Seventeenth Ohio, which had been ordered to report to me, were in position.

As the enemy slackened his fire, Colonel Kammerling, chafing like a wounded tiger that he had been behind at the opening, ordered his men to charge. Away they went, closely followed by the Eighty-seventh Indiana and the Seventeenth Ohio, the enemy falling back precipitately. The Ninth in this charge recaptured the guns of Guenther's battery [H], Fifth Artillery, and held them. [O.R., XXX, Part I, pp. 427–428.]

Report of Lieut. Frank G. Smith, USA, Commanding
Battery I, Fourth U.S. Artillery, Third Division, XIV Corps,
Army of the Cumberland

When the action of the 19th began the first section of my battery, under First Lieut. G.B. Rodney, was placed in the front line, between the Second Minnesota and the Thirty-fifth Ohio Volunteers (the Thirty-fifth Ohio Volunteers being on the right), and the second section, under Lieutenant Stephenson, on a hillside 60 yards in rear of the right wing of the Thirty-fifth Ohio Volunteers. The firing began before we had fairly taken our positions, and 4 of my men were disabled before I could open fire on the enemy. After a sharp engagement of half an hour's duration, the firing slackened on both sides. Lieutenant Stephenson's section having suffered severely from the musketry fired at the infantry in his front, and as it was impossible to use canister . . . without injury to our own men, I directed it limbered to the right, with the intention of placing it on the right of the line. At this time, however, the Ninth Ohio Volunteers advanced in line and took position on the right of the Thirty-fifth Ohio Volunteers; the firing recommenced, and Lieutenant Stephenson was obliged to go into action on the same ground. The rebels were soon repulsed, after which the second section was moved to the crest of the hill, 150 yards in rear of the line, and placed on the left of your battery [Battery D, First Michigan Artillery], which had come up a short time previously with the regiment of infantry, under Colonel Connell.

On the completion of this arrangement the rebels renewed the attack; in about twenty minutes they were driven back, closely followed by the Ninth Ohio Volunteers and Seventeenth Ohio Volunteers at a charge. [*O.R.*, XXX, Part I, pp. 437–438.]

Report of Col. James George, USA, Commanding
Second Minnesota Infantry, Third Brigade, Third Division,
XIV Corps

The regiment was placed in position at 10 a.m. on the 19th, on the extreme left of the brigade and next to Battery I, Fourth U.S. Artillery, facing the south.

A few minutes later the enemy approached in line in front to within about 300 yards and opened a heavy fire of musketry, which was returned with such effect as to repulse the attack in about ten minutes. Another similar attack was soon after made and met with a like repulse, the enemy falling back in disorder entirely out of sight. About half past 10 o'clock sharp firing of musketry was suddenly opened at some distance in our left and front, which soon began to approach us. The cartridge-boxes had been replenished, and the regiment was laid down in line to await its time, the men having been admonished to withhold their fire until the enemy should be within close range. There soon appeared, approaching in disorder from the left front, a line of our troops in full retreat and closely pursued by the enemy, who was cheering and firing furiously in their rear. It proved to be the regular brigade [King's Third Brigade of Baird's First Division], the men of which passed over our line and were afterward partially rallied in our rear and on our left.

As soon as these troops had passed us the farther advance of the enemy was checked by a volley from our line. A sharp contest with musketry followed, which resulted in a few minutes in the complete repulse of the late exultant enemy, who fled from our front in confusion. [*O.R.*, XXX, Part I, pp. 432–433.]

Turn around to observe the low ridge approximately 50 yards inside the tree line on the other side of the road.

As additional Confederate infantry units moved into the area between the Reed's Bridge Road and the Brotherton Road, *Forrest* was able to shift his cavalry farther north. This movement kept *Forrest's* units as the right flank of the Army of Tennessee.

In keeping with his orders, *Forrest* continued to probe for the Union northern flank. At mid-day he moved a brigade north of Reed's Bridge Road and maneuvered to attack Van Derveer's brigade on the left flank and rear. *Forrest* sent *Dibrell's* brigade, dismounted, along the low ground that runs generally west about 200 yards to your front and right front. *Dibrell's* attack came out of that low ground and moved up the high ground that you can begin to see on the north side of the road.

Report of Colonel Ferdinand Van Derveer, USA,
Commanding Third Brigade, Third Division, XIV Corps,
Army of the Cumberland (Continued)

In the meantime the enemy, massing his forces, suddenly appeared upon my left and rear. He came forward, several lines deep, at a double-quick, and opened a brisk fire, but not before I had changed my front to receive him. My new line consisted of the Second Minnesota on the right, next one section of Smith's battery, . . . then the Eighty-seventh Indiana, flanked by Church's and the other section of Smith's battery, and on the extreme left the Thirty-fifth Ohio. The two extremities of the line formed an obtuse angle, the vertex on the left of the Eighty-seventh Indiana, and the opening toward the enemy. The Second Minnesota and the Eighty-seventh Indiana lay on the ground, and were apparently unobserved by the enemy, who moved upon the left of my lines, delivering and receiving a direct fire, Church opening with all his guns and Smith with one section.

He advanced rapidly, my left giving way slowly until his flank was brought opposite my right wing, when a murderous and enfilading fire was poured into his ranks by the infantry, and by Rodney's section shotted with canister. Notwithstanding this he steadily moved up his second and third lines. Having observed his great force as well as the persistency of his attack, I had sent messenger after messenger to bring up the Ninth Ohio, which had not yet returned from its charge, made from my original right. At last, however, and when it seemed impossible for my brave men longer to withstand the impetuous advance of the enemy, the Ninth came gallantly up in time to take part in the final struggle, which resulted in his sullen withdrawal.

In this last attack his loss must have been very severe. In addition to the heavy fire of the infantry, our guns were pouring double charges of canister in front and on his flank, at one time delivered at a distance not exceeding 40 yards. During the latter part of the contest re-enforcements had arrived, and were by General Brannan . . . formed in line for the purpose of supporting my brigade, but they were not actively engaged at this time. [*O.R.*, XXX, Part I, pp. 428–429.]

Notice the walking trail that goes north from the parking area. If you follow this trail north for about 100 yards you will be in the vicinity of the center of the Thirty-fifth Ohio's line that was facing east. The marker is off the trail to the west. East of the trail and back slightly toward the main road was the position of the section of Battery I, Fourth Artillery and Battery D, First Michigan Artillery.

Report of Lieut. Col. Henry V. N. Boyton, USA,
Thirty-fifth Ohio Infantry, Third Brigade, Third Division,
XIV Corps, Army of the Cumberland

The next move of the enemy was an attempt to flank our position on the left. The regular brigade, which had been engaged on our right and to the front, were driven across our line, which was placed as a support to the Fourth Regular Battery, Lieutenant Smith commanding. Seeing this rapid approach of the enemy in four lines, the front of my regiment was immediately changed to the left, though without orders from the colonel commanding the brigade, it being perfectly apparent that this alone could save the battery.

The assault of the rebel lines proved terrific, but so soon as the confusion attending the passage of the regular brigade had in part subsided, the Thirty-fifth faced, advanced, and by a few moments of close fighting, in connection with the well-directed fire of Lieutenant Smith's double-shotted guns, repulsed that portion of the rebel line opposed to our immediate front. This closed the fighting of the day, it having continued for four hours with great fury. . . . Together with the other regiments of the brigade, we bivouacked upon the battlefield without blankets or tents, and although a white frost covered the ground, and being in an open field, we passed the night without fires as best we could. . . . The regiment went into the fight with a total of 391 officers and men. Of this number 9 were killed, 97 wounded, and 4 reported missing. [*O.R.*, XXX, Part I, pp. 434–435.]

Report of Brig. Gen. J.M. Brannan, USA, Commanding
Third Division, XIV Corps, Army of the Cumberland

About this period, at my repeated and earnest request for reenforcements, General Thomas sent the First Division to my support, and the greater portion of that command advanced to my center to arrest the movements of the enemy in that quarter. In this, however, the First Division failed, the troops retiring with some precipitancy, leaving the battery of the regular brigade in the hands of the rebels, and communication entirely cut off between my extreme flanks. I however succeeded in preventing the rebels from following up their advantage at this point by a charge of portions of the First and Third Brigades, during which the battery of the regular brigade was retaken at the point of the bayonet by the Ninth Ohio Infantry (Col. Gustave Kammerling commanding).

The enemy, however, continued to press heavily on the center, and finding it impossible to re-establish and hold communication between my flanks, I withdrew to a ridge about half a mile from the La Fayette road, removing my dead and wounded, and formed line there, without molestation, at about 2 p.m.

About 3 p.m., by direction of Major-General Thomas, I moved the First and Third Brigades to the right in rear of the Second Brigade, and subsequently, in accordance with orders . . . withdrew my entire division to the right, on the La Fayette road. . . . [*O.R.*, XXX, Part I, p. 401.]

Return to your car. Resume driving on REED'S BRIDGE ROAD for 1 mile to the stop light. TURN LEFT onto the LA FAYETTE ROAD. Drive 0.3 mile and TURN LEFT again onto the ALEXANDER BRIDGE ROAD. Drive 1.3 miles to the BROTHERTON ROAD. TURN LEFT onto this road and immediately TURN RIGHT into the parking lot. Dismount, CROSS THE ALEXANDER BRIDGE ROAD, and walk about 200 yards on the BROTHERTON ROAD to the historical marker on the right for *Maney's* brigade. Position yourself in front of the marker.

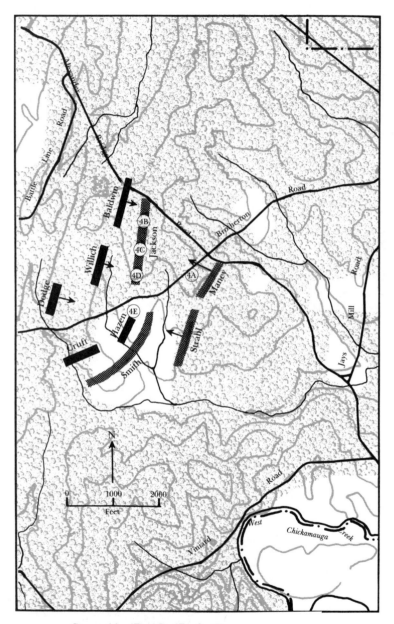

Stops 4A, 4B, 4C, 4D, & 4E
Situation Early–Mid Afternoon
September 19, 1863

THE BATTLE MOVES SOUTH
Noon to 3 P.M. September 19, 1863

STOP 4 POSITION A – JACKSON ATTACKS

While the initial contact of the morning was being fought between the Reed's Bridge and Brotherton Roads, Rosecrans and *Bragg* were both moving ever increasing numbers of troops in a northerly direction. *Bragg* was attempting to envelop the Union left flank, while Rosecrans was re-enforcing that flank to secure his line of communication to Chattanooga. As units moved north they were committed on the southern flank of engaged units. Thus the battle developed in a southerly direction.

When *Liddell's* division was repulsed, it retired in an easterly direction to recover and reorganize. Around noon, the battle picked up in this area and was extended to the southwest by *Cheatham's* division, with three brigades deployed on line and two brigades in reserve, moving across this position and attacking to the northwest. The right flank brigade – *Jackson's* – crossed the road near here and moved in the direction you now face, to a low ridge located perhaps 200 yards down the trail.

Report of Brig. Gen. John K. Jackson, CSA, Commanding Brigade, Cheatham's Division, Army of Tennessee

On September 19, 1863, at about 7 o'clock in the morning, the brigade . . . being the advance of *Major-General Cheatham's* division, crossed Chickamauga Creek at Hunt's or Dalton's Ford, about a mile below Lee and Gordon's Mills. . . . At about 9 a.m. moved by the flank in a northwestern direction and formed line in the rear of *Major-General Buckner's* right as his reserve. Remained in this position about an hour, when an order was received to move still farther to the right to the support of *Major-General Walker*. Passing rapidly about half a mile northward by the right flank, the brigade reached the road leading from Alexander's Bridge, and proceeded thence westward about half a mile.

Here the line of *Major-General Walker's* troops was reached. My brigade was immediately placed in line of battle and ordered to advance. The order was promptly and cheerfully obeyed, and the advance continued about 150 yards, when the enemy opened fire upon my left and center. The brigade returned the fire, which soon became general. A charge being ordered, the troops responded with great intrepidity, driving the enemy before them from half to three-quarters of a mile, capturing 3 pieces of artillery, which were immediately sent to the rear; also a large number of knapsacks, from which the enemy had been driven. At this point the enemy, being heavily re-enforced and having the advantage of breastworks, checked the advance of the brigade and stubbornly held their ground.

Seeing troops on the left retiring, I sent to inquire the meaning of it, and was informed that it was part of *Brig. Gen. Preston Smith's* brigade, which had been pressed back by superior numbers, thus leaving my left flank entirely exposed. Soon afterward my left fell back under the false impression that a retreat had been ordered, but were immediately rallied and reformed, and promptly retook their original position. [*O.R.*, XXX, Part II, pp. 83–84.]

Move to the trail a few yards behind the historical marker. Follow the center of *Jackson's* brigade along the trail to the northwest for about 300 yards to the historical marker for *Cleburne's* division.

POSITION B – JACKSON'S FIGHTING LINE

You are in the location to which *Jackson's* attack carried his brigade. The brigade was deployed along the trail that runs to your left and right. The six foot high monuments are to the regiments of *Jackson's* brigade. The shorter three foot monuments are for the regiments of *Maney's* brigade.

Scogin's battery, on your right, was deployed in the center of *Jackson's* line. The Fifth Mississippi was deployed to the right of this battery.

Report of Maj. John B. Herring, CSA, Commanding Fifth Mississippi Infantry, Jackson's Brigade, Cheatham's Division, Army of Tennessee

Having formed line of battle at the place assigned us, a little in advance of the road, we advanced to attack the enemy about 12 m. There were no skirmishers in front of the line, and I supposed from this fact that we constituted a second line. We advanced not more than 100 yards when we were attacked by the enemy directly in front, who were also advancing. We returned the fire vigorously, and after a few minutes the enemy's line gave way and we drove them back about 1 mile. During this whole charge we were exposed to a continuous retreating fire.

The enemy at last made a stand, from which we failed to move them, owing to the want of ammunition on the part of some and the bad condition of guns on the part of others. The regiment, however, maintained its position gallantly, though exposed to a galling fire from the enemy, until *Lieutenant-Colonel Skyes*, observing that the line had retired on the left, gave the command to fall back. We fell back about 100 yards, faced about, and renewed the fight. In a short time we fell back about 100 yards farther simultaneously with the Eighth Mississippi, which up to this time had not moved from its most advanced position, and having formed a new line we held the enemy in check, though hard pressed. Here fell *Lieutenant-Colonel Skyes*. . . .

I assumed command of the regiment and ordered an equal distribution of what ammunition remained on hand. Here I received a message from *Colonel Wilkinson* that if I should be forced to fall back to notify him of the fact. I replied that my action would be influenced by his. We held this position and stopped the advance of the enemy I suppose half an hour. The Eighth Mississippi then falling back, I ordered a retreat as previously agreed upon. We had gone but a short distance before we fell in with *General Jackson*, who ordered a halt, and directed us to move back by the left flank and form line of battle near the road a little in rear of the position from which we moved to bring on the attack. The enemy advanced and attacked us in this position, but was soon repulsed. [*O.R.*, XXX, Part II, pp. 91–92.]

The fighting became so severe that *Jackson*, with both flanks threatened and nearly out of ammunition, sent to *Brig. Gen. George Maney* for assistance.

Walk about 85 yards to your left along *Jackson's* line on the intersecting trail until you come to the Park Service marker for *Maney's* brigade.

POSITION C – MANEY RELIEVES JACKSON

You are currently in the right center of *Brigadier General George Maney's* brigade's position when he moved forward to relieve *Jackson's* brigade. *Maney's* line ran from your right to your left and was generally along and in front of the ridge. About 200 yards to your left are the Brotherton Road and an open area called Brock Field, a portion of which was planted with corn.

Report of Brig. Gen. George Maney, CSA, Commanding Brigade, Cheatham's Division, Army of Tennessee

I was . . . ordered to enter action by relieving *Jackson's* brigade, my information at the time being that *Strahl's* brigade would be in line on my left. The position pointed out to me as the one at which I was to relieve *Jackson's* command was a ridge well wooded, where the right half of my command rested, but from the center to my left the timber on the side of approach had been newly felled and presented some difficulty to easy passage in line. In extension to my left there was an open corn-field, a narrow strip of woodland intervening. My line commenced engaging instantly on reaching the top of the ridge described, and in a few moments afterward I was informed by a messenger from *General Forrest* that there was nothing on the right but his cavalry, and that he was unable to sustain himself against the strong force of the enemy which was pressing him. *Strahl's* brigade was not at this moment in line with me on the left, it having, as I afterward learned, become earlier engaged and fallen back to reform. My own line numbered less than 1,000 guns. My battery was just in rear of my center, but the ground was not favorable to its advantageous engagement.

About 300 yards in my rear there was a hill top in open woods — a most favorable position in many particulars for a battery. *Lieutenant Turner* was ordered to leave one piece in position to be used in any emergency which might arise, and retire the remaining three to this hill top and there take position and await further orders. Some moments after this I heard a battery open in rear of the right of my line, and, hastening to it, I found that *Forrest* had been forced in on my right. *General Forrest* in person was with the battery, which was firing obliquely to the front and right, and, as I thought, too much in range with two companies of my right regiment, which had been thrown out as flankers to this part of my line. *General F[orrest]* was apprised of this fact and requested to oblique his guns more to the right, which he did and continued firing, as he informed me the enemy was certainly approaching in force from that direction.

The firing was now constant along my entire front, and the enemy's [firing] indicated that his line extended far beyond my left.

Forrest's battery was some protection to my right flank, and my single Napoleon, while it could not fire with any effect over the ridge in front, was in position to rake the open [Brock] field to the left and rear of my line, and to this extent prevent the enemy coming behind us, unless it should first be driven off by sharpshooters lodged on the ridge top under cover of the woods between my line and the field. [*O.R.*, XXX, Part II, pp. 94–95.]

Report of Col. Hume R. Feild, CSA, Commanding First and Twenty-seventh Tennessee Infantry, Maney's Brigade, Cheatham's Division, Army of Tennessee

We halted on the crest of a hill with a gradual slope to the front of some 300 or 400 yards of clear open woods. My regiment being on the right of the brigade, I detached the two right companies to check and advise me of any attempt to turn my right flank, this disposition being made under a heavy fire. In a few moments the two companies, under *Captain Atkeison*, were driven back upon the regiment by a charge of a brigade of the enemy on my right flank, which compelled my right wing to be thrown back at a right angle with my left. In this position we held the ground for two hours, I think, battling with as many of the enemy as could possibly be brought to bear upon us. We occupied the position after our ammunition was completely exhausted, and then did not retire until the left wing of the brigade had been driven from the field by a movement of the enemy upon its left flank, compelling me to retire with my command. [*O.R.*, XXX, Part II, p. 99.]

Narrative of Private Sam R. Watkins, CSA, First Tennessee Infantry, Maney's Brigade, Cheatham's Division, Army of Tennessee

Forward, guide center, march, charge bayonets, fire at will, commence firing. We debouched through the woods, firing as we marched, the Yankee line about two hundred yards off. . . . It was a sort of running fire. We kept up a constant fire as we advanced. In ten minutes we were face to face with the foe. It was but a question as to who could load and shoot the fastest. . . .

We held our position for two hours and ten minutes in the midst of a deadly and galling fire, being enfiladed and almost surrounded, when *General Forrest* galloped up and said, "*Colonel Feild*, look out, you are almost surrounded; you had better fall back." The order was given to retreat. I ran through a solid line of blue coats. As I fell back, they were upon the right of us, they were upon the left of us, they were in front of us, they were in the rear of us.

It was a perfect hornets' nest. The balls whistled around our ears like the escape valves of ten thousand engines. The woods seemed to be blazing; everywhere, at every jump, would rise a lurking foe. But to get up and dust was all we could do. I was running alone by the side of Bob Stout. *General Preston Smith* stopped me and asked if our brigade was falling back. I told him it was. He asked me the second time if it was *Maney's* brigade that was falling back. I told him it was. I heard him call out, "Attention, forward!" One solid sheet of leaden hail was falling around me. I heard *General Preston Smith's* brigade open. It seemed to be platoons of artillery. The earth jarred and trembled like an earthquake. [Samuel R. Watkins, *"Co. Aytch," Maney Grays, First Tennessee Regiment*; or *A Side Show of the Big Show* (Jackson, Tennessee: McCowat-Mercer, 1952) pp. 115–116.]

Continue along the Confederate line. At about 80 yards you will pass the six foot tall stone monument to the Fifth Georgia Infantry. Continue another 30 yards to the smaller monument to the Sixth and Ninth Tennessee.

POSITION D – THE THREAT TO MANEY'S LEFT

Report of Col. George C. Porter, CSA, Commanding
Sixth and Ninth Tennessee Infantry, Maney's Brigade,
Cheatham's Division, Army of Tennessee

My position in the brigade was on the extreme left. . . . The command rested on a skirt of felled timber covering the entire front of my regiment. Remaining in this position for a short time, the enemy's shell coming in quick succession through our ranks, we were ordered to make a direct charge upon the enemy, we at this time constituting the front line. The ground over which my command had to pass was badly adapted to this move, especially as the regiment had to march at a right oblique. The ground was thickly covered with felled timber and piles of wood . . . . [and] I found it impossible to keep a correct line of battle. There were, unavoidably, gaps and groups along the whole line.

Having moved forward in this manner about 250 yards with a steady and determined step, we passed about 75 or 80 yards beyond a slight elevation of ground, when a most deadly concentrated fire, both of small-arms and artillery, was poured into our ranks, my regiment at the time being in full view and at short range of the enemy's guns. There being no forces engaged on my left, my command occupied the greater portion of the enemy's attention, necessarily, who had previously acquired the exact range of this position. I soon found it impossible to proceed farther in this direction. The enemy were almost entirely secluded from our aim, being concealed in a thick covering of timbered land projecting in an angular shape into this open section of country. Here the contest commenced in earnest, and with a spirit and daring not often excelled by any troops. A constant and incessant firing was here kept up on both sides, but with what effect upon the enemy I have been unable to learn. . . . We, however, held this position for nearly an hour, during which time our supply of ammunition was quite exhausted.

About this time the enemy, having received fresh troops, made a rapid advance upon my line both in front and flank, and, as the sequel proved, would have killed or captured the whole command had I not deemed it proper and right under the circumstances to abandon the position and fall back. This was done in tolerable good order. . . .

Having retreated but a short distance, I met with *Brig. Gen. George Maney*, who inquired of me the cause of this retrograde movement on my part of the line. I told him that my position was no longer tenable; that I was out of ammunition; that two-thirds of my command were either killed or wounded, and the enemy was near at hand and advancing in overwhelming numbers. He, seeing our imminent peril . . . ordered me to fall back in rear of *Brigadier-General Smith's* lines and reform my command, which was done. . . .

In this day's engagement . . . . twenty-five were left dead on the field; 155 were wounded, 17 of which number have since died. [The regiment's total strength at the start of the battle was 335.] [*O.R.*, XXX, Part II, pp. 101–103.]

Continue in the same direction through the undergrowth for 150 yards to the edge of BROCK FIELD. Cross the BROTHERTON ROAD and walk to the near edge of the field. Face left.

POSITION E – JOHNSON TURNS THE TIDE

Report of Brig. Gen. George Maney, CSA, Commanding Brigade, Cheatham's Division, Army of Tennessee (Continued)

The action increased in fury, especially on the left, and I was soon convinced that my command was greatly overmatched in numbers. A staff officer was sent with this information to the division general, and another to my left and rear in search of *General Strahl*, with the request for him to move up in line with me on the left. Passing myself to the ridge top to the left of my line, I discovered the enemy but a short distance from my left advancing by the flank boldly and evidently with the purpose of passing through the skirt of wood at right angles with my line, and thus gain my rear and control of my left flank. The emergency was critical, and, being without a staff officer, I hastened in person to *General Strahl*, who I found had received my message and was aligning for advance. To avoid delay, I asked him to move forward a single regiment to hold the interval between my left and the open field, and he ordered his right regiment (*Colonel Walker's*), and perhaps another, to advance immediately. This force made a gallant drive forward and the enemy gave [way] before them. I had about this time received the order to fall back and form behind *Smith's* brigade, which was in line with my guns on the hill top in the rear. My line was retired in as good order as its shattered condition would admit of. [*O.R.*, XXX, Part II, p. 95.]

Jackson's and *Maney's* brigades had been in contact with the Second Division of XX Corps which had been moved north to reenforce Thomas' XIV Corps.

Report of Brig. Gen. Richard W. Johnson, USA, Commanding Second Division, XX Corps, Army of the Cumberland

I received an order from the major-general commanding the corps to move forward and report to Major-General Thomas. . . . The instructions I received were to move in the direction of the cannonading. Arriving near the battlefield, I met Major-General Thomas, who ordered me to form line of battle and move forward and attack. My division was formed with Willich's brigade on the right and Baldwin's on the left, with Dodge in reserve. In this order the command moved forward, though oblique to the general line.

Soon the skirmishers became heavily engaged and the enemy forced back. General Hazen's brigade at this time on my right, was reported heavily pressed, and I ordered Dodge's brigade to his relief. The brigade moved forward at double-quick, and soon engaged the enemy. [*O.R.*, XXX, Part I, pp. 534–535.]

Baldwin's brigade attacked into the northern half of *Jackson's* and then *Maney's* position, while Willich's attack carried him into the southern portion of those two brigades. The troops *Maney* reported as turning his line on the left were from Dodge's brigade, assaulting through the area where you now stand and moving east over the ground south of the Brotherton Road to a position just across the Alexander Bridge Road.

Report of Col. Joseph B. Dodge, USA, Commanding Second Brigade, Second Division, XX Corps, Army of the Cumberland

My brigade, being on the left of the division, was . . . deployed into column . . . in rear of the First and Third Brigades, and [I was] ordered to govern myself by their movements, and to support them.

After moving in this manner a short distance, I received an order to move to the right, until I reached General Hazen's brigade of General Palmer's division, and relieve him, as his men were getting short of ammunition. I accordingly moved my whole command by the right flank about 400 yards, when I found a very brisk engagement going on, and the enemy's line formed in an oblique direction to the one I was in. I immediately changed front forward with my first line, and seeing that the enemy were well sheltered, while my command was badly exposed to their fire, and my men being comparatively fresh, I ordered a charge. . . . The whole column had previously deployed into line. . . .

The order was most gallantly obeyed by both officers and men, and the enemy gave way in utter rout and confusion. In this charge the Twenty-ninth Indiana was on the right, the Seventy-seventh Pennsylvania next, the Seventy-ninth Illinois next, and the Thirtieth Indiana on the left. We drove them in this manner nearly . . . 1 mile when, finding that my line was getting broken in consequence of losses in killed and wounded, and that I had no support on either flank, I ordered a halt. On this charge my command passed some 30 or 40 yards to the right of a battery belonging to the enemy, which was nearly deserted by them, and a part of which was captured by one of the other brigades to my left (General Willich's, I believe). I then reformed my command in its original order and moved about 400 yards to my left and rear and formed a connection with the right of General Willich's brigade, refusing my right slightly, so as to protect my flank as much as possible, and threw out a heavy line of skirmishers in my front and on my flank. There was no force (of ours) on my right in sight, and I was fearful that the enemy would attack us on that flank. [*O.R.*, XXX, Part I, pp. 554–555.]

Return to the BROTHERTON ROAD. TURN RIGHT, and follow the road to the ALEXANDER BRIDGE ROAD intersection. Dodge consolidated and tied in with Willich's brigade in the area to the right of the intersection. Continue about 120 yards on the BROTHERTON ROAD beyond the intersection to the marker on the right for Willich's brigade.

POSITION F—WILLICH'S FORWARD PROGRESS

After pushing *Jackson's* and *Maney's* brigades off the low ridge to your rear, the three brigades of Johnson's Second Division, XX Corps, continued to move forward. Brigadier General August Willich's First Brigade was in the center as he pressed his attack to this position. The Thirty-second Indiana and Eighty-ninth Illinois were on your right, the Forty-ninth Ohio and Fifteenth Ohio on your left.

Report of Brig. Gen. August Willich, USA, Commanding First Brigade, Second Division, XX Corps, Army of the Cumberland

On the 19th . . ., the brigade marched . . . to the support of General Thomas. . . . The ground being wooded and hilly, it would not allow free maneuver for artillery, and I gave Captain Goodspeed instructions to keep his battery out of musket-range and in the rear of the infantry until further orders. As soon as the Third Brigade of this division [Col. William W. Berry] was formed on my left, both brigades advanced, under directions from General Thomas, in a direction which diverged from the advancing line of troops on my right at an angle of about 45 degrees.

My skirmishers soon engaged the enemy, who opened with shell and then with canister from a point right in front, so that the fire did not reach the Third Brigade. After having re-enforced the skirmish line, and having brought to bear two sections of my battery, and having sufficiently shaken the enemy's infantry line, I ordered a bayo-

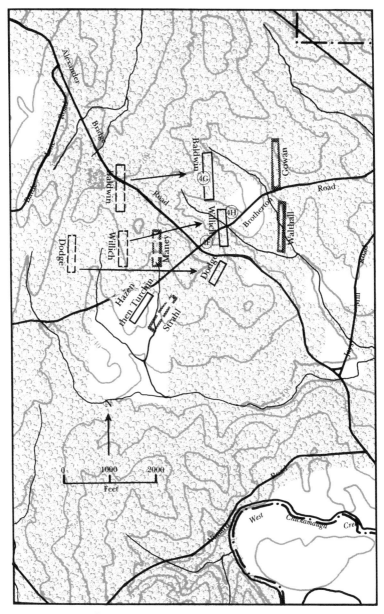

Stops 4F, 4G, & 4H
Situation Mid Afternoon
September 19, 1863

net charge, and took the Eighty-ninth Illinois into a line with the Forty-ninth Ohio and Thirty-second Indiana, keeping the Fifteenth Ohio in reserve. The charge was executed in splendid order, and with such energy that everything was swept before it for about a mile. Five pieces of the enemy's artillery, which had done us much damage, were taken. . . . Fearful to lose all connection with the other troops, I halted my brigade in a good position, and endeavored to find that connection. The Third Brigade was on my left; on the left of the Third Brigade was nothing. [*O.R.*, XXX, Part I, pp. 538–539.]

Continue about 250 yards along the BROTHERTON ROAD to the edge of WINFREY FIELD. TURN LEFT at the edge of the field and walk about 125 yards to the BALDWIN MONUMENT. Face toward the field.

POSITION G – THE CULMINATING POINT

Colonel Philemon P. Baldwin's brigade formed the left flank of Johnson's division. Baldwin's brigade attacked the northern half of the low ridge occupied by *Jackson's* brigade and then *Maney's* brigade. Pushed out of position, *Jackson's* and *Maney's* brigades fell back to a position southeast of this location. Baldwin's attack continued east, came through the woods to your rear, and halted along the edge of Winfrey Field. From this position the Union troops could look out across the field and see *Walthall's* and *Govan's* brigades in the opposite tree line. These brigades had attacked over this area in the morning, been forced back, regrouped, and were now prepared to re-enter the fight.

Report of Col. William W. Berry, USA, Commanding
Third Brigade, Second Division, XX Corps, Army of the
Cumberland

At this point, with an open field in our front, the brigade was halted, maintaining its original formation. Scarcely half an hour elapsed before the enemy advanced with infantry and artillery and attacked with his usual vigor. So far outflanked that we were almost enveloped, Colonel Baldwin ordered the Ninety-third Ohio to deploy on the left of the Fifth Kentucky. In a few moments Col. Stong [Ninety-third Ohio] was wounded. The Ninety-third staggered slightly under the blow, when Colonel Baldwin, riding up with the cry, "Rally round the flag, boys!" seized the colors and ordered the regiment to charge, which was done with a will, and so effectually that the enemy fled, leaving two guns in our possession, one of which was brought away by the Ninety-third Regiment, but the other was so knocked to pieces by Simonson's shells that it was impossible to move it. The Fifth Kentucky and First Ohio, standing stock-still, swept their front as with a broom. In the meantime the Sixth Indiana, having been deployed on the left of the original line, moved up on the double-quick, and successfully engaged the enemy, who was thus driven entirely from our portion of the field. [*O.R.*, XXX, Part I, p. 564.]

Report of Brig. Gen. Edward C. Walthall, CSA, Commanding Brigade, Liddell's Division, Army of Tennessee

Lieutenant-General Polk directed me to move by the right flank in extension of *Major-General Cheatham's* line, taking my position on the right of *Brigadier-General Jackson*. This was done under the enemy's fire, whose purpose seemed to be to turn *General Cheatham's* right flank. *Colonel Govan's* brigade took position on my right, whereupon the brigadier-general commanding ordered his line to advance. My command moved forward some 300 or 400 yards, the enemy contesting the ground, but falling back until the crest of a ridge in front of me had been gained. Here the enemy, strongly posted, delivered a very heavy fire of artillery and small-arms. The advance was checked, and in the course of ten or fifteen minutes my line was forced to retire to its original position on *Brigadier-General Jackson's* right, and I was directed . . . to remain there until further orders. [*O.R.*, XXX, Part II, pp. 273–274.]

Report of Lieut. Col. Bassett Langdon, USA, Commanding First Ohio Infantry, Third Brigade, Second Division, XX Corps, Army of the Cumberland

I halted my regiment, agreeably to orders, in an open field of weeds, with my right near the woods and my left advanced diagonally across the field fronting to the east, with from 100 to 300 yards of open descending ground in my front, terminating in a ravine, beyond which was an open forest into which my skirmishers had followed the enemy. Colonel Baldwin shortly afterward ordered me to change front to the rear on the first company and retire behind the fence on my right, information having been received from Major Stafford, in command of the skirmish line (now strengthened by the remaining platoons of the two flank companies), that the enemy was moving to our left.

But a short time elapsed after this disposition was made till the enemy precipitated a heavy force upon the regiments on our left, closely followed by an attack in our front and upon the brigade on our right. I opened fire by file as soon as our own skirmishers were clear of our front, and soon drove the enemy back from the open field and well into the woods, when, finding myself free from fire, and that the enemy was directing his whole attention to the regiments on my right and left, I sounded the signal to cease firing and again moved into the open field where my fire would be more effective against the enemy.

This position was held till the enemy was repulsed all along the line and had fallen back beyond our fire, when, by order of Colonel Baldwin, I again took position behind the fence, and strengthened it by a hastily constructed barricade of rails. Major Stafford was again sent forward with skirmishers into the woods beyond the open field. . . . Information was sent me that the enemy were now moving to our right, which was promptly communicated to Colonel Baldwin. [*O.R.*, XXX, Part I, pp. 571–572.]

Return along the wood line to the Brotherton Road.

POSITION H – THE LINES ARE STABILIZED

This is about where the right flank of Baldwin's brigade tied in to the left flank of Willich's brigade.

Report of Brig. Gen. August Willich, USA, Commanding First Brigade, Second Division, XX Corps, Army of the Cumberland (Continued)

After some hours of light skirmishing in front, Colonel Baldwin, commanding Third brigade, communicated to me that the enemy was turning his left flank toward the rear. I advised him to take his two rear regiments and charge to the rear and left; at the same time I threw the Forty-ninth Ohio Volunteers along the fence inclosing the open field on the right of the First Ohio Volunteers (Third Brigade). As soon as the enemy entered the open ground he received a murderous fire, which he could not stand; at the same moment Colonel

Baldwin attacked his right, and drove the enemy with great slaughter before him, capturing two pieces of artillery. The particular feature of this attack and repulse of the enemy on our left flank and rear was that it took place directly in front of that division of our army which had to make connection with our left, but which did not move along with us in our first advance, and thereby created an opening of 1¼ to 1½ miles between their front and our own. As we had discovered the flank of the enemy in our first forward move, the great consequence for the success of the day presents itself to every military mind which would have resulted from a spontaneous advance of the division to our left with our own advance, and by which we could have attacked the enemy's broken flank by changing front to the right. As it was, all I could do was to keep my position and be on the lookout for other attacks in the flank and rear. [O.R., XXX, Part I, p. 539.]

In the late afternoon the fighting around Winfrey Field died out. However just at dusk a night attack was begun by *Cleburne's* Confederate division. (See below, pp. 122–23.) Union units in this area were pushed back by *Cleburne's* attack, and eventually they broke contact and retired to the vicinity of Kelly Field. Here they regrouped and went into defensive positions.

Return to your car. TURN LEFT as you leave the parking lot. CROSS THE ALEXANDER BRIDGE ROAD and drive about 0.3 mile to BROCK FIELD. Park in the Turnout on the left. Dismount and walk to the plaque for Hazen's brigade in the center of the field.

STOP 5 – THE UNION LINE RE-ENFORCED

The last time you were in this vicinity (Stop 4, Position E) it was to look at the action by *Jackson's* and *Maney's* brigades of *Cheatham's* division. Now the fighting involves *Cheatham's* other three brigades and a different Union division.

Report of Maj. Gen. John M. Palmer, USA, Commanding Second Division, XXI Corps, Army of the Cumberland

About noon I received orders to move my whole division to the assistance of our troops then engaged. . . . After marching quickly for perhaps a mile and a half, guided by the sounds of the firing, and

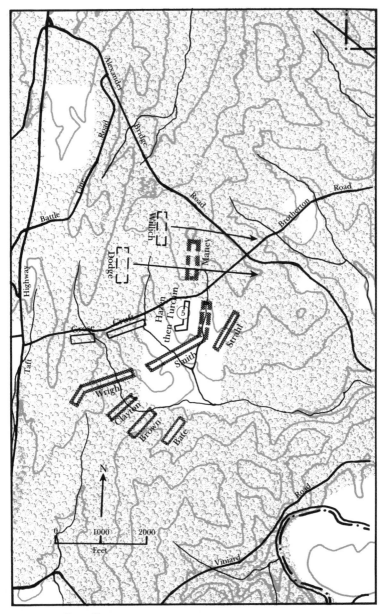

Stop 5
Situation Early–Mid Afternoon
September 19, 1863

forming lines to the right of the [La Fayette] road, [I] ordered Hazen, who was on the left, to march in the direction of the firing, Cruft to keep well closed up to him on his right, and Grose in reserve re-enforcing the right and [to] engage as soon as possible.

At this moment I received a note from the general commanding the army, which led to a slight, but what turned out to be a most advantageous, change of formation. He suggested an advance *en eche-lon* by brigades, refusing the right, keeping well closed up on Thomas. This suggestion was adopted. The brigades, at about 100 paces intervals, pushed forward and engaged the enemy almost simul-taneously. At once the fight became fierce and obstinate. From the character of the ground, but few positions could be found for the effective use of artillery; my batteries were used as well as was pos-sible, but the work was confined mainly to the musket. [*O.R.*, XXX, Part I, p. 713.]

As you face south across the field you are looking at the center and right portion of *Brigadier General Preston Smith's* brigade line as it moved out of the low ground in your front to attack the left elements of Palmer's division, which was also in motion. *Smith's* right flank regiment, the Thirteenth and One hundred fifty-fourth Tennessee, was located near the small stone marker to your front. To your right front, at a distance of 350 yards and on the next rise, was *Scott's* (Tennessee) battery, to your right the Twelfth and Forty-seventh Tennessee and farther to your right the remain-ing regiments—the Eleventh Tennessee and the Twenty-ninth Tennessee.

Report of Col. Alfred J. Vaughn, Jr., CSA, Commanding Smith's Brigade, Cheatham's Division, Army of Tennessee

The division . . . [had] formed line . . . in rear of *Buckner's* corps [and] remained in this position a short time when we received orders to move by the right flank in double-quick to the support of *General Walker*, who for some time had been actively engaging the enemy. On arriving at the scene of action we found *General Walker* stoutly resisted, and his command much exhausted from long and continued action. We were ordered to form line immediately . . . on [the] left of *General Jackson's* brigade.

As soon as formed we were ordered to advance and engage the enemy. We advanced but a short distance before we met the enemy advancing. We engaged him at once, and furiously drove him before us 600 or 800 yards, forcing him to take shelter behind the breastworks from which he had advanced in the morning. We moved steadily forward until within musket range of their works, and notwithstanding we were subjected to a severe and concentrated fire, both of musketry and artillery, the brigade kept up a steady and determined fire until the supply of ammunition was nearly exhausted. *General Smith* being apprised of this, immediately informed *General Cheatham* . . . at the same time assuring him he was able to hold the position until he could forward a brigade to his relief. Whereupon *General Strahl* was ordered forward, and as soon as he occupied *General Smith's* position, *General Smith* withdrew his brigade and moved some 400 yards to the rear and reformed his line. . . . *Scott's* battery . . . advanced with the brigade and took position as ordered, under a heavy and destructive fire of the enemy, so much so that a number of men and horses were disabled before the battery was placed for action. Immediately a rapid and well-directed fire was opened upon the enemy with telling effect upon his ranks. This fire was vigorously maintained until the brigade was relieved and ordered to the rear. [*O.R.*, XXX, Part II, pp. 106–107.]

Report of Col. William M. Watkins, CSA, Commanding Twelfth and Forty-seventh Tennessee Infantry, Smith's Brigade, Cheatham's Division, Army of Tennessee

Under orders from *Brig. Gen. Preston Smith*, I formed my regiments on the left of One hundred and fifty-fourth and Thirteenth Tennessee, having the Eleventh Tennessee on my immediate left. In this order at 12 noon we began the advance, and moved forward to a position about 400 yards from the enemy, who seemed to [be] intrenched, having an open field between us, except a few yards of timber next to the enemy's line. Here the One Hundred and fifty-fourth and Thirteenth Tennessee, by a wheel on its right pivot, separated from my command, while my command and Eleventh Tennessee moved straight forward, the Eleventh Tennessee halting in a drain, by which it was to some extent protected from the enemy's fire.

My regiments were moving forward to the enemy when I was ordered . . . to fall back to the fence, which I endeavored to do, but before my regiments were quite back to the fence, I was ordered . . . to move forward, and I was moving forward to the position on prolongation of the line of the Eleventh Regiment when I was ordered by *General Smith* to fall back to the fence, which I did, and here held my regiments, protected in a measure by the low fence, until *General Strahl's* brigade passed before us and we were ordered to retire. All these movements were executed under a very heavy fire both of musketry and artillery. . . .

After retiring near a half mile from the field, other efforts to dislodge the enemy proving ineffectual, the enemy advanced upon our lines, and my regiments were held in position to check the advance of the enemy. [*O.R.*, XXX, Part II, p. 111.]

Brigadier General William Hazen's Second Brigade, on the left of Palmer's line, was moving east across the Brotherton Road and made contact with the right of *Smith's* brigade.

Report of Brig. Gen. William B. Hazen, USA, Commanding Second Brigade, Second Division, XXI Corps, Army of the Cumberland

On reaching McNamara's house, on the La Fayette and Rossville road, the brigades of the division were formed in two lines facing the east, the second line being doubled by regiments on the center. My brigade was on the left of the division, General Cruft being on my immediate right.

The line was then moved forward *en echelon* by brigades, my brigade commencing the movement. The enemy was struck after advancing about three-quarters of a mile, when a terrific contest here was added to the already severe battle on our left. The enemy gave ground freely, and the left at this juncture making an advance, all the ground desired on the left was carried, extending to the right as far as the *echelons* of the Second Division had been placed. [*O.R.*, XXX, Part I, pp. 761–762.]

Your position in the center of Brock Field is in the right portion of Hazen's battle line: the left was about 100 yards to your left and in the vicinity of the road. The right of the line was 200 yards to your right front. Regiments were initially deployed from left to right: Ninth Indiana, One hundred twenty-fourth Ohio, Forty-first Ohio, and the Sixth Kentucky in reserve. Battery F, First Ohio Artillery was located next to the road 75 yards to your left rear.

Report of Maj. James B. Hampson, USA, Commanding
One hundred twenty-fourth Ohio Infantry, Second Brigade,
Second Division, XXI Corps, Army of the Cumberland

The forward was . . . sounded, and we had advanced but a short distance when the firing commenced in our front, and the regiment was deployed into line of battle under a heavy fire of musketry from the enemy. After lying down in this position for some time on a gentle rise of ground, exposed to a severe fire and meeting with some losses, orders were received to move the regiment by the left flank and form a continuation of the line of battle of the Forty-first Ohio Volunteer Infantry. It was at this time, when confused by a galling fire from the enemy, that Companies A and H and a part of D, not understanding the order from the commanding officer, became detached, and they were unable to rejoin the regiment until late in the afternoon, having in the meantime done gallant service on the right of the Sixth Kentucky. After moving by the left flank about 400 paces, we were moved by the right flank with Company B . . . deployed to the front as skirmishers, the enemy's fire, which had now become very heavy, telling fearfully in our ranks. The colonel at this time fell severely wounded and was carried to the rear.

The firing had now become so heavy in my immediate front that I ordered my skirmish line to assemble on the left of the regiment, and fired by volley until the cartridges were nearly expended, when I was temporarily relieved by the Ninety-second Ohio. After refilling cartridge boxes, the regiment immediately retook position in the front, relieving the Ninety-second and remaining under a severe fire for nearly an hour, when, after a very heavy loss, we were again relieved by one of General Turchin's regiments and ordered to join our brigade, which had been moved to the right. [*O.R.*, XXX, Part I, pp. 775–776.]

Report of Col. Aquila Wiley, USA, Commanding Forty-first
Ohio Infantry, Second Brigade, Second Division, XXI Corps,
Army of the Cumberland

About 1 p.m. we advanced in line of battle to the attack, being on the right of the first line of the brigade, with two companies deployed as skirmishers. Passing through an open wood, our skirmishers soon became engaged with those of the enemy and drove them. On emerging from the wood, we came to an open field about 400 yards in width, with another skirt of woods beyond. Through this woods the enemy started in line across the field to meet us. Near the middle of this field, and a little to our left, was a narrow strip of timber. The enemy had advanced but a short distance when he delivered his fire, and then sought to gain the cover of this strip of timber. We were too quick for them, gaining it first, and delivering our fire by battalion at short range, sent them back to the woods from which they started. As soon as they began to retreat, a battery, planted in the edge of the wood, opened fire, inflicting considerable loss. As soon as the retreating forces gained the cover of the woods a heavy infantry fire was also opened on us. This position the regiment maintained till about 4 p.m., replying to the enemy's fire and repelling three attempts to dislodge us. In repelling the last assault we were supported and assisted by two companies of the One hundred and twenty-fourth Ohio Volunteers. The regiment was then relieved by the Sixth Kentucky, and ordered to retire to procure ammunition and clean their arms. [*O.R.*, XXX, Part I, p. 773.]

Brigadier General Charles Cruft's First Brigade of Palmer's division crossed the Brotherton Road and attacked southwesterly through what is today the woods to your right rear. His report describes both the action and the features of the terrain in 1863.

Report of Brig. Gen. Charles Cruft, USA, Commanding First Brigade, Second Division, XXI Corps, Army of the Cumberland

The effective strength of the brigade on the morning of the 19th instant was . . . infantry 1,280; . . . artillery 128. . . .

All was quiet at the front until about 10:40 a.m., when a discharge of artillery and volleys of musketry off in a northerly direction indicated the commencement of a battle. . . . The Second Brigade (General Hazen) was ordered up by General Palmer, and immediately (at 11 a.m.) my brigade was ordered to follow, bringing up with it the artillery of the division. . . . After having passed along the Rossville road to the house of McNamara, distant about 1½ miles from the mills, the brigade was thrown to the right into an open woods and formed in line, facing the direction of the sound of battle, which was nearly east.

Here General Palmer indicated the order of battle and superintended the formation of his division lines. The Second Brigade (General Hazen) passed me and formed on the left, the Third Brigade

(Colonel Grose) on the right. The division line was to advance *en echelon* by brigades, retiring the right. This order threw the Second Brigade some hundred paces to the front of my left and the Third Brigade the same distance to the rear of my right, and made this brigade for the time being the center of the movement. Skirmishers were thrown out rapidly, and the advance of the division soon commenced in steady line. After advancing about 400 yards, the skirmishers engaged those of the enemy and drove them in. The line pressed steadily up. The Second and First Brigades engaged the enemy nearly simultaneously, at about 12:30 p.m., and the Third Brigade soon also became engaged.

The general orders were to press off in . . . [a] northeasterly course, in the direction of the sound of the battle then progressing, and endeavor to connect on the right of the line of our troops that were fighting. . . .

My command encountered the enemy's line at a point about three-quarters of a mile east of the Rossville [La Fayette] road. The ground between the road and the enemy's line was, at first, an open woodland, with an undulating surface, which terminated in a small ridge, parallel with the road and about half a mile back from it, below which lay a level plateau about a quarter of a mile across. On the east side of this plateau the ground broke off abruptly and disclosed a level, cleared spot of ground, forming a small semicircular cove in our immediate front. At the latter place the enemy made a stand. He had the advantage of position against a line formed on the margin of the plateau. My line was therefore thrown down the side of the bank and rapidly formed on the same level with the enemy. Three of the regiments of the brigade were placed immediately in the fight, the battalion of the First Kentucky for the time being having been placed in support of the artillery of the division. . . .

The brigade was formed in single line, the Second Kentucky on the right, Thirty-first Indiana in the center, and Ninetieth Ohio on the left. Half the battery was opened on the enemy with canister, from the plateau immediately over the heads of the troops, and the other half battery was placed on the ridge, a quarter of a mile to the rear, to shell the woods in our front and flanks. . . .

The fight became very severe in my front at 12:40 p.m. and lasted until 2:20 p.m. . . . with but little intermission in the musketry on both sides. During the action the half battery to the rear was brought up to the left flank of the line, and rendered excellent service by a left oblique fire on the portion of the rebel line which was attacking General Hazen. The enemy made three very obstinate attempts to break my line by charges, and at each time was re-enforced from the woods in their rear. They were on each occasion repulsed, with apparently heavy losses.

My command behaved bravely, and steadily held the line. Not a straggler was observed going to the rear. The file-closers did their duty and every officer and man stood to his work. The cartridges of the men, however, began to fail, and the ill-success of attempts to procure a supply from the rear excited for the moment great apprehension as to our ability to hold the position. A few well directed volleys at the crisis drove the enemy from the front, and at 2:20 p.m. his fire had ceased. Skirmishers were now thrown forward and occupied a margin of the wood, beyond the cleared space, some 300 or 400 yards to our front. A general cessation of the firing now also occurred on the flank, during which ammunition arrived from the rear and was served to the men.

About 3:50 p.m. a very severe attack commenced on what appeared to be our extreme right, and rolled along the line toward the left, apparently concentrating its force on the Third Brigade (Colonel Grose) of this division. His line retired rapidly in direction from my right and occupied the extension of the ridge in a southwesterly direction. This position brought his front to the right and rear of my line.

The fight became momentarily more critical on the right, and orders were now received from General Palmer to move such portion of my command as was possible to Colonel Grose's aid. The Second Kentucky and Thirty-first Indiana were ordered from my front line (leaving the Ninetieth Ohio and battery alone to hold it); their front rapidly changed perpendicularly to the old line, and moved off to the south along the plateau to Colonel Grose's relief at double quick. . . . These two regiments reached Colonel Grose's line only to find it overpowered and giving way, stubbornly, under a most impetuous attack by overwhelming numbers, with its supporting lines on the right wholly gone. They became involved for a moment in the confusion, . . . moved off to the right a short distance to avoid the retreating mass, and engaged the enemy sturdily, checking him sufficiently, perhaps, to prevent a rout.

The moment was critical. Soldiers and officers ran to the rear, mingled with guns and caissons, in much disorder, and the whole plateau was rapidly being commanded by the enemy's musketry. At this time orders reached me to withdraw my command. [O.R., XXX, Part I, pp. 728–731.]

Having been fought to a stand-still by the brigades of Hazen and Cruft, *Smith's* brigade was withdrawn and replaced by the brigade of *Brigadier General Otto Strahl.*

Report of Brig. Gen. Otto F. Strahl, CSA, Commanding Brigade, Cheatham's Division, Army of Tennessee

About 1 p.m. I received an order from *General Cheatham* to move forward, which I did, and took position immediately in rear of *General Smith's* brigade, which was at that time hotly engaged with the enemy and some 200 yards in front of the position I had taken.

Shortly after taking this position *General Smith* sent me word that he was about to be driven back and wished me to come to his support, which I did at once, moving forward over his line to a small elevation some 250 yards in his front, entirely relieving him and engaging the enemy. In a short time after thus engaging the enemy, *General Smith* rode up to me and told me that my left flank was still in rear of *General Wright,* and that my right flank was not supported by any one, and that I was in a position to be flanked by the enemy on my right unless I immediately moved in that direction. Discovering, however, that *General Wright* had retired and that none of our troops were in my front, and knowing the great danger of attempting a flank movement in the presence and under the fire of an enemy, and expecting *General Maney* to come up on my right, I did not move in that direction [to the right] until *General Smith* rode up to me a second time and told me that *General Cheatham* directed that I should close the gap between myself and *General Jackson* by moving to the right. . . . I therefore immediately gave orders to move . . . but had hardly commenced the movement before the enemy met the front of my column with a murderous and destructive fire, enfilading nearly the whole of my line, and moving in such a direction as soon to be in the rear of my right if I attempted to hold the position I then had.

The position of the two lines were about as is shown below:

Yankee Line
_____

Rebel Line
_____

Strahl's Brigade

Yankee Line

Therefore, not knowing whether I was to receive support on my right, and having no time for delay, I immediately gave orders for my line to retire and at once moved back to a position where I hoped to be able to prevent the enemy from flanking me. I gained this position with my left in good order, my right being thrown into confusion by the heavy fire they were receiving both from the front and on their flank. The officers, however, all acted with great gallantry and coolness and immediately rallied their men as soon as they arrived at positions where they could do so and not be in immediate danger of being flanked. In this movement we were compelled to leave most of our killed and wounded on the field. . . .

Our loss while placed in this unfortunate position was near 200, and among that number some very valuable and gallant officers. Most of the field officers on my right were dismounted by having their horses shot under them. . . .

During this short encounter . . . the Nineteenth Tennessee Regiment was on my right, and was, therefore, much more exposed, and consequently met with a much heavier loss than any other in the brigade. But its field officers — *Col. F.M. Walker* and *Lieut. Col. B.F. Moore* — acted with such coolness and gallantry that they inspired their men with courage and confidence, and prevented that demoralization which might have been expected under such trying circumstances.

It was now, while engaged in reforming my line, that *General Maney* came up and pressed the enemy back for some distance on my right, and soon became hotly engaged. As soon as my line was reformed, I moved forward to his support, and arrived on a line with his left just in time to meet the enemy, who were advancing rapidly and pressing his line back. My three right regiments . . . were thrown forward in advance of the left of my brigade, and took possession of a small skirt of woods, which they held until the line on their right had fallen back so far that they were again exposed to a severe enfilading fire, when I again ordered them to retire to the position where they first rallied, in order to prevent the enemy from swinging around my right and thus getting in my rear. Here I reformed my whole line, but learning that *General Smith's* brigade was in line just on my right and but a short distance in my rear, and being without support on either flank, I deemed it advisable to move back and form on him . . . and remained in this position until dark. . . .

The ground over which we had been fighting during the afternoon was of such a nature that it would not admit of the use of artillery, and especially of a rifle battery; therefore, I was compelled to meet every advance of the enemy with my infantry alone, although their batteries were playing on me the whole time, and from positions that made their fire very effective. [*O.R.*, XXX, Part II, pp. 130–132.]

Return to your car. Continue on the **BROTHERTON ROAD** about 0.4 mile to the monument bearing *Bushrod Johnson's* profile on your left. Pull over to the side of the road and stop.

PENETRATION AND COUNTERATTACK IN THE CENTER

Mid-Afternoon September 19, 1863

STOP 6 – THE CONFEDERATE OPPORTUNITY

The ground you have just driven over was crossed by Cruft's brigade in mid-afternoon, pushed back from its position to the west of Brock Field. To Cruft's right was Colonel William Grose's Third Brigade of Palmer's division, which faced south and southeast along the high ground to your left. Grose's line then turned so that the right portion faced east. The entire brigade line was on the south side of the Brotherton Road.

Along the continuation of this high ground, running south and parallel to the La Fayette Road, and at right angles to the Brotherton Road, were Beatty's and Dick's brigades of Van Cleve's Third Division, XXI Corps, which, along with Grose's brigade, had been in contact with the left portion of *Cheatham's* line. Between 1:00 and 2:00 p.m. *Cheatham's* left brigade, *Wright's*, was withdrawn and replaced by the division of *Major General Alexander Stewart*.

Stewart began a succession of attacks first with *Clayton's* brigade, followed by *Brown's* brigade and finally *Bate's* brigade. By 3:30 these had pushed Beatty's and Dick's brigades across the La Fayette Road to the high ground just south of the Brotherton house.

Grose's brigade, which was driven back by *Bate's* brigade, crossed the Brotherton Road in this general vicinity.

Report of Col. William Grose, USA, Commanding Third Brigade, Second Division, XXI Corps

My brigade was formed in double lines, the Twenty-fourth Ohio . . . and the Twenty-third Kentucky . . . in the front line; the Thirty-sixth Indiana . . . and the Eighty-fourth Illinois . . . in the rear line; the Sixth Ohio . . . in reserve.

On meeting the enemy with the front line the troops on the right of my brigade gave way, and the Thirty-sixth Indiana was immedi-

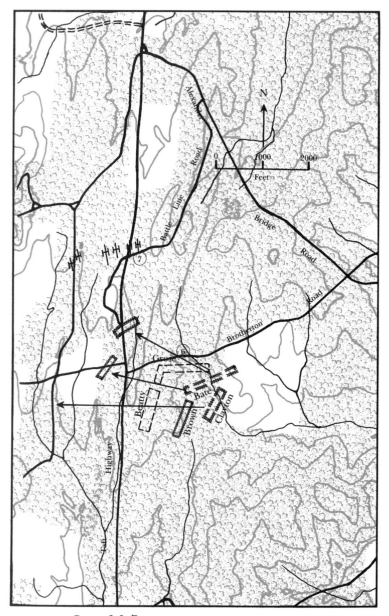

Stops 6 & 7
Situation Mid–Late Afternoon
September 19, 1863

ately changed to the right to defend the flank, and in a very few minutes the enemy passed so far to my right and rear that the Sixth Ohio, as well as the Thirty-sixth Indiana, Twenty-fourth Ohio, and Twenty-third Kentucky, were all desperately engaged and so continued for two long hours. Here was the best fighting and least falling out (except the killed and wounded) that I ever witnessed. Finally the ammunition of these four regiments gave out, and there being none at hand (bad luck) they had to be retired.

Now came the time for the Eighty-fourth Illinois to come into the breach. The colonel changed front to the right, and with his brave and hitherto-tried regiment contested every inch of ground until compelled to give way before overwhelming numbers, the enemy having reached his then right flank (our former rear). All was retired in tolerably good order, which ended my fighting for the day. [*O.R.*, XXX, Part I, pp. 780–781.]

Bate's attack continued to press to the northwest through the woods until his right was in the vicinity of Poe Field and his left had crossed the La Fayette Road and was northwest of the Brotherton house.

Continue along the BROTHERTON ROAD for 0.2 mile to the "T" intersection. The Brotherton house is directly to your front. TURN RIGHT onto the LA FAYETTE ROAD. Drive 0.4 mile, and then TURN LEFT onto POE ROAD. Drive a few yards to the turn-out on the left opposite Battery M, Fourth U.S. Artillery. Dismount and cross the LA FAYETTE ROAD to the battery along the park road in POE FIELD (Battery H, Fourth U.S. Artillery). BE EXTREMELY CAREFUL WHEN CROSSING THE LA FAYETTE ROAD!

STOP 7 – THE SHOULDER OF THE PENETRATION

When you reach the position of Battery H, Fourth U.S. Artillery, face to your right. You are now at the northern end of Poe Field. The right portion of *Bate's* brigade entered the field from the far wood line about 350 yards to your front. *Bate's* left crossed the La Fayette Road and extended at an angle back through the woods on this side of the Brotherton house. The artillery that you see at the south end of the field marks a unit that was there late in the next afternoon.

Report of Brigadier General William B. Bate, CSA,
Commanding Brigade, Stewart's Division, Army of Tennessee

"My command . . . formed line of battle in rear of *Brigadier-Generals Brown's* and *Clayton's* brigades, the whole under command of *Major-General Stewart* . . . At 3 p.m. *Brigadier-General Clayton's* and *Brown's* brigades successively engaged the enemy. In about thirty minutes I was ordered by *Major-General Stewart* to advance, *General Clayton* having withdrawn and *Brown* also passed to the rear. My line of battle was organized by placing *Caswell's* battalion of sharpshooters (Fourth Georgia) on the right, and in succession from that wing were the Twentieth Tennessee . . . Thirty-seventh Georgia [whose farthest advance marker you can see in the far wood line]; . . . Fifty-eighth Alabama . . . and Fifteenth and Thirty-seventh Tennessee . . . constituting the supporting line.

I had thrown out no skirmishers. The whole command moved forward with spirit and zeal, engaging the enemy hotly before it had proceeded 200 yards, his lines extending in front and to the right and left of us. A battery in front of my extreme right played constantly and with terrible effect upon that wing until my right pressed within less than 50 paces of it, when it was rapidly removed to prevent capture. Another revealed its hydra-head immediately in rear of this, supported by a second line, hurling its death-dealing missiles more destructively, if possible, upon our still advancing but already thinned ranks.

Having driven the first line back upon its support, a fresh battery [your present location] and infantry were brought to play upon my right, which, by its advanced position had become subject to an enfilade fire, and gave way, but not until . . . the three officers commanding . . . the three right battalions, were wounded, and at least 25 per cent of their numbers killed and wounded. [*O.R.*, XXX, Part II, pp. 383–384.]

Report of Brig. Gen. William B. Hazen, USA,
Commanding Second Brigade, Second Division,
XXI Corps, Army of the Cumberland

I was at this time relieved by General Turchin and ordered back to the [La Fayette] road to fill my boxes with ammunition, already twice exhausted, and take charge of some batteries left there without supports. This I had just accomplished when a vigorous attack appeared to be going on upon that part of our lines immediately to the right of the ground fought over by the last *echelon* [Grose's brigade] of our division. I at once moved my brigade to the right, and forming it so as to face the sound of battle, moved forward and placed it in position as a support to some troops of General Reynolds, my left resting on the La Fayette and Rossville road near a small house [Poe's], the right thrown forward, forming an angle at about 45 degrees with the road. The battle neared my position rapidly. . . . The enemy continued to advance steadily, and the line in my front gave way. My men then advanced to the top of the crest, and withstood the shock until they were completely flanked upon their left, then obliqued well to the right and took position upon a high elevation of ground confronting the left flank of that portion of the enemy which had broken our center.

The advance of the enemy was now steady, and northward nearly in the direction of the La Fayette and Rossville road. I found myself the only general officer upon that part of the field, and to check the farther advance of the enemy was of the utmost importance. I hastily gathered and placed in position all the artillery then in reach . . . in all about twenty pieces, and with the aid of all the mounted officers and soldiers I could find, succeeded in checking and rallying a sufficient number of straggling infantry to form a fair line in support of the artillery. My brigade could not be brought into position in time, there being but about two minutes to make these dispositions before the blow came, when the simultaneous opening of all the artillery with grape checked and put to rout the confronting columns of the enemy. [*O.R.*, XXX, Part I, p. 762.]

By 4 p.m. the Union situation at this position and farther south had reached a critical stage. Confederate infantry had created an opening in the Union center and were attempting to widen the breach and exploit their initial success. On the northern edge of the penetration it was the deadly fire of artillery at close range that was responsible for stopping the Confederate infantry until re-enforcements could be deployed. Reports of the Union artillery commanders in this area give an excellent account of artillery's capability against infantry at close range.

You are in the location of the left portion of the massed batteries that were used to stop the attack across Poe Field.

Report of Lieut. Harry C. Cushing, USA, Commanding
Battery H, Fourth U.S. Artillery, Second Division,
XXI Corps, Army of the Cumberland

On the morning of the 19th . . . I moved [my battery] from its temporary position . . . and joined Colonel Grose's brigade. I was immediately moved into action. I sent Second Lieut. Robert Floyd, with one section, to the left center of the brigade and took the other to the right myself. Fighting commenced immediately and was very severe. The enemy endeavored to drive our right, but the vigorous action of . . . the Sixth Ohio and a liberal use of short-fused case-shot and canister by my section caused them to retire, and the arrival of General Reynolds' troops completed their discomfiture. This gave me time to refill my limbers, and, fighting being discontinued in our immediate front, we lay quiet about a quarter of an hour, but increased firing in General Reynolds' front decided me to go to his assistance.

At a gallop I took the whole battery and reported to General Reynolds, and took position on the left of his battery. His troops were retiring before the heavy force of the enemy, but the quick and well-sustained fire of these batteries gave the troops time to recover and the enemy was repulsed there. The enemy, foiled there, gained ground to the left and precipitated themselves in tremendous force on the right of these troops and enfiladed our line of batteries.

The whole line was thrown back, and this throwing the batteries back in the hollow, I reported to General Hazen, who was forming a new line across the road. M, of the Fourth Artillery, F, of the First Ohio, and my battery were massed obliquely across the road covering the rebel approach. Their appearance was the signal for a most rapid and destructive fire from these batteries and driving the rebels. This closed the fight for me that day, my ammunition being totally exhausted. [*O.R.*, XXX, Part I, p. 799.]

Narrative of Lieut. A.G. Bierce, USA, Topographical
Engineer, Second Brigade, Second Division, XXI Corps,
Army of the Cumberland

The forest was so dense that the hostile lines came almost into contact before fighting was possible. One instance was particularly horrible. After some hours of close engagement my brigade, with foul pieces and exhausted cartridge boxes, was relieved and withdrawn to the road to protect several batteries of artillery—probably two dozen pieces—which commanded an open field in the rear of our line. Before our weary and virtually disarmed men had actually reached the guns the line in front gave way, fell back behind the guns and went on, the Lord knows whither. A moment later the field was gray with Confederates in pursuit.

Then the guns opened fire with grape and canister and for perhaps five minutes—it seemed an hour—nothing could be heard but the infernal din of their discharge and nothing seen through the smoke but a great ascension of dust from the smitten soil. When all was over, and the dust cloud had lifted, the spectacle was too dreadful to describe. The Confederates were still there—all of them, it seemed—some almost under the muzzles of guns. But not a man of all these brave fellows was on his feet, and so thickly were all covered with dust that they looked as if they had been reclothed in yellow. ["A Little of Chickamauga," *The Collected Works of Ambrose Bierce*, 10 vols., New York, Gordian Press, Inc. 1966; Vol. I, pp. 271–272. Bierce, later a celebrated journalist and short-story writer, was officially mentioned for good conduct by General Hazen. [*O.R.*, XXX, Part I, p. 98.]

Return to your car. Continue on the POE ROAD until it rejoins the LA FAYETTE ROAD. TURN RIGHT and drive slightly less than 0.2 mile. STOP in the parking lot in front of the Brotherton house. Dismount and walk up onto the open ridge south of the house. Position yourself in the vicinity of Battery B, Twenty-sixth Pennsylvania Artillery (the tallest monument in the field) and face the La Fayette Road.

STOP 8, POSITION A – STEWART'S BREAKTHROUGH

In the woods of the high ground to your front is the position occupied by Grose's brigade and further to the right the positions of the brigades of S. Beatty and Dick. As *Bate's* attack pushed Grose's brigade back across the Brotherton Road and toward Poe Field, *Clayton's* attack in conjunction with the right elements of *Brigadier General Bushrod Johnson's* division drove S. Beatty's and Dick's brigades back across the road.

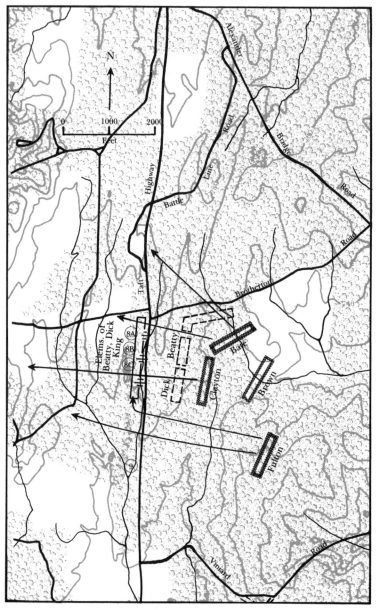

Stops 8A, 8B, 8C, & 9
Situation Mid–Late Afternoon
September 19, 1863

Report of Brig. Gen. Henry D. Clayton, CSA, Commanding
Brigade, Stewart's Division, Army of Tennessee

I again moved forward about 4 o'clock, the brigades of *General Brown* and *Bate* having successively advanced and engaged the enemy. Passing *Bate's* brigade, then in front, my line continued steadily forward with promptness and spirit, accompanied nearly to the Chattanooga [La Fayette] road by the Fifty-eighth Alabama Regiment, . . . and a small portion of another regiment which I did not recognize, both of *Bate's* brigade.

The enemy continued to retreat to and beyond the Chattanooga road, near which my brigade captured two pieces of artillery, which were brought off . . . by my regimental commanders. . . . My brigade continued the pursuit of the enemy one-half mile beyond the road, when a staff officer reporting the enemy advancing in strong force from the right, and it also having been reported to me, through my assistant adjutant-general by a staff officer whom he did not recognize, that the enemy's cavalry had been seen in force upon the left as if preparing to advance, my brigade fell back across the road at leisure, where I halted and reformed it in connection with the portion of General *Bate's* brigade already referred to. [*O.R.*, XXX, Part II, p. 402.]

Report of Col. Bushrod Jones, CSA, Commanding
Fifty-eighth Alabama Infantry, Bate's Brigade,
Stewart's Division, Army of Tennessee

At 3 p.m. we were ordered forward to relieve the brigade *[Brown's]*, then retiring, and in a few moments the fire of small-arms was brisk and active. My command was the third battalion of the brigade in line of battle, and stationary during the first half hour of the firing; the battle-field, an open, woody country. The enemy advanced to within 200 or 300 yards, but could not be plainly seen on account of the smoke, trees, etc. After the firing had been continued about thirty [minutes] *Clayton's* brigade was moving forward to engage the enemy and to our support. The noise of battle was so great I could not hear any command; but thinking it an opportune moment for a charge, and seeing some of the brigade on my right move forward, I advanced to the front of my command and ordered a forward movement.

The men and officers promptly and gallantly obeyed the command. The movement began at the moment when the Thirty-sixth

Alabama Regiment . . . was in the act of passing over my command in the charge, and the two regiments, commingled, charged in a run with loud and enthusiastic cheers. The enemy gave way and fled in confusion. We pursued them through the woods about a mile.

I halted the regiment a short distance before reaching the field in front, after repeated unsuccessful efforts, on account of the impetuosity of the men. I ordered the halt, thinking farther pursuit fruitless and hazardous, as we had already gone far in advance of the general line of battle, and were exposed to an enfilade fire of grape from the right.

The officers of the left wing not hearing the command "halt," on account of the noise and excitement, continued the pursuit several hundred yards farther, capturing 20 or 30 prisoners and passing a battery of three guns that had been abandoned by the enemy. . . . Having halted the regiment and formed line, I waited about a half hour for the return of those who had gone ahead of the line and for support on the right and left. But believing the enemy were again advancing, I retired slowly and in good order about a quarter of a mile, where I found *General Clayton* and *General Bate* reforming their respective brigades. I reported to *General Bate* what I had done and he replied, "You have done right; I take off my hat to your regiment." The engagement of my command with the enemy began at 3 p.m. and lasted until nearly 5. [*O.R.*, XXX, Part II, pp. 388–389.]

Report of Col. Alexander M. Stout, USA, Seventeenth Kentucky Infantry, First Brigade, Third Division, XXI Corps, Army of the Cumberland

We move quickly to the scene of conflict. . . . Arrived there, the brigade was formed in two lines, the Seventy-ninth Indiana Volunteers on the right in the first line, and the Nineteenth Ohio Volunteers on the left, the Seventeenth Kentucky Volunteers on the right in the second line, the Ninth Kentucky Volunteers on the left. The first line at once engaged the enemy. The Seventy-ninth Indiana . . . finding a battery of the enemy in its front, charged upon it and silenced it, but was almost immediately repulsed by the enemy and driven back through my regiment, which at once opened upon the enemy, who was partially concealed by a dense cover of underbrush.

The firing on both sides was very severe, and continued for near a half hour, when the enemy fell back, still leaving the battery. . . . An order was then received . . . to advance. And I did advance to within 50 paces of the battery, when seeing that the regiment on my left had halted, my own was halted also. But a little before this advance, and after the firing had ceased, some officers and men of the Seventy-ninth Indiana advanced to take the captured artillery to the rear, when a portion of my command did likewise, and wheeled two of the pieces with the flag of the battery to the rear through my lines. . . .

In the meantime, the enemy were seen and heard moving to my right, as if to turn it, and two or three regiments from some other brigade moved from our rear to my right, when the enemy attacked them with great fury, and almost immediately turned their right, advancing and firing with great rapidity; they broke to the left and rear in great disorder. My regiment at once felt the enemy's fire upon the right flank and rear, and to escape capture fell back to the left and rear by companies; the first company first, then the second, and so on, until all were in retreat to the left and rear, the enemy in greatly superior numbers advancing and firing with great rapidity. . . . We fell back through a dense wood to a small open field of high ground, from which one of our batteries [Twenty-sixth Pennsylvania] was playing upon the advancing enemy, and there we ourselves confronted him in support of the battery. We, with the aid of others, succeeded in checking his advance in our front, but we hardly had time to become aware of this success before we felt the fire right across the battery upon our right and rear.

Being again compelled to retire, we pursued the same course as before, until we reached a high and commanding ridge about 1 mile from the battlefield, where the brigade formed again. . . . [*O.R.*, XXX, Part I, pp. 815–816.]

S. Beatty's and Dick's brigades, both of Brigadier General Horatio Van Cleve's Third Division, XXI Corps, had been deployed on the wood line on the east side of the La Fayette Road sometime around 1 p.m. These two brigades and the right part of Grose's brigade stopped the initial attack of *Stewart's* Confederate division.

When *Stewart* regrouped and recommenced his attack at 3 p.m., his brigades, with the assistance of the right brigade of *Johnson's* division, were successful in forcing the Union brigades off the high ground to your front and back west across the La Fayette Road. Here parts of S. Beatty's, Dick's and E. King's brigades attempted to halt the Confederate attack.

Continue south along the high ground to the monument marking the position of the Seventh Indiana Battery, which was firing in support of Dick's brigade.

POSITION B—THE DEFENSE COLLAPSES

*Report of Capt. George R. Swallow, USA, Commanding
Seventh Indiana Battery, Third Division, XXI Corps,
Army of the Cumberland*

[One] section was detached, and remained with the Third Brigade the remainder of the day. The remaining four guns were ordered to the front with the Second Brigade, took position several times on the right of the road leading from Lee and Gordon's Mills to Chattanooga, but could do no firing, and seeing part of our line falling back I retired, and took position on the left of the road in a small field; had been in position but a short time until our line fell back to, and across, the road. I then opened . . . a rapid fire with canister, and kept it up until two regiments fell back through the battery, in confusion and disorder; part of the Thirteenth Ohio then rallied on my right and rear, but their lieutenant-colonel being killed, they, too, fled in disorder. My canister being exhausted, and the enemy in force in front and on the right, I, with some difficulty, withdrew the battery to the rear . . . [O.R., XXX, Part I, p. 836.]

*Report of Capt. Horatio G. Cosgrove, USA, Commanding
Thirteenth Ohio Infantry, Second Brigade, Third Division,
XXI Corps, Army of the Cumberland*

We joined the remainder of the brigade . . . at 2 p.m. and soon after took position, with the Fifty-ninth Ohio Volunteer Infantry on our right and the Eighty-sixth Indiana Volunteers on our left. Sharp skirmishing took place between our skirmishers and the enemy until 4 p.m., when, the enemy having by a flank movement compelled the regiment on our right to give way, and having completely flanked our position, we were compelled to fall back in some disorder. The regiment was rallied near the road, when, the enemy coming upon us in overwhelming force, we were compelled again to fall back, losing many commissioned officers and men, killed or wounded. . . .

The commanding officer being killed, the command of the regiment devolved upon me, and I formed the regiment on the crest of a hill to the rear of our former position, and lay in line until the morning. . . . [*O.R.*, XXX, Part I, pp. 830.]

The high ground where the line finally held is approximately 750 yards west of your current position. Beyond this high ground the Dry Valley Road runs from Crawfish Springs—the present town of Chickamauga—north to McFarland's Gap and on to Chattanooga. The interdiction of this road by any major Confederate forces would have split the Army of the Cumberland and separated it from its base at Chattanooga.

Report of Lieut. Col. Granville A. Frambes, USA, Commanding Fifty-ninth Ohio Infantry, Second Brigade, Third Division, XXI Corps, Army of the Cumberland

I received an order from Colonel Dick to form my regiment on the right by file into line, with the Forty-fourth Indiana on my left, and to advance in line of battle into the woods, and be sure to keep my left in line with and joined to the Forty-fourth Indiana. I had not advanced over 300 yards when my regiment became engaged with the enemy, well positioned in a depression in the woods. I kept up an incessant fire, and advanced steadily all the time, driving the enemy slowly before me until he reached his second line, when he came to a stand.

I then ordered my regiment forward on double-quick, cheering heartily as we went, which caused the enemy to give way in confusion in my front. I then observed that my line was in advance of the remainder of the line, and my right flank was unprotected by an interval of half a mile caused by the force on my right not connecting with me. I then halted and had to lie down and fire at will.

Shortly after I gave this order I discovered that the enemy was flanking me on my right and the line on my left was falling back rapidly, which left me in great danger of being captured. I then gave the order to fall back. My regiment fell back in order about half way to the road, when I moved it by the left flank a short distance and then forward and joined the Thirteenth Ohio on its right and engaged the enemy vigorously, but my right flank being exposed, the enemy took advantage of it and charged upon us with an overwhelming force, which caused my regiment to fall back with the whole line in confusion. I succeeded in rallying a part of the regiment behind a line of artillery stationed on a ridge in an open field on the west side of the Chattanooga road.

Here we succeeded in checking him by the aid of artillery and the stubborn fighting of the fragments of several different regiments for some time, but was finally forced to give way. I then fell back to the Crawfish Spring [Dry Valley] road, about a half mile, where . . . the brigade . . . camped during the night. [*O.R.*, XXX, Part I, p. 833.]

Continue south along the high ground to the monuments to the Nineteenth Battery, Indiana Artillery of Colonel Edward King's brigade and the Ninety-second Illinois Mounted Infantry of Colonel John Wilder's brigade. Face southeast.

POSITION C – OUTFLANKED

Colonel E. King was killed the next day and there are no surviving reports from his regimental commanders. However, from reports of commanders of the battery and the mounted infantry regiment supporting King's brigade, one can piece together what happened here. The Confederate force attacking in this area was *Johnson's* brigade, the right brigade of *Brigadier General Bushrod R. Johnson's* division.

Report of Col. John S. Fulton, CSA, Commanding Johnson's Brigade, Johnson's Division, Army of Tennessee

The command to move forward was given. . . . We did not advance exceeding 700 yards when the enemy opened fire upon us and we became hotly engaged. The enemy had planted a battery . . . which opened upon our advancing lines, throwing in rapid succession grape and canister, and supported by infantry, whose fire of small-arms was heavy, well-directed, and disastrous.

The entire brigade now became hotly engaged, . . . which lasted nearly an hour, the enemy making a stubborn resistance, gradually retiring, he having the advantage of both undergrowth and ground, but finally was driven across the Chattanooga and La Fayette road. The Seventeenth Tennessee Regiment, on approaching the road was halted and opened fire on the enemy in its front, distant about 200 yards in a woodland. The undergrowth having been cut out, the enemy were in full view. The Forty-fourth Tennessee [on the brigade right] was still engaging the enemy. The Twenty-fifth and a portion of the Twenty-third Tennessee regiments crossed the road . . . and gained the cover of the woods and moved to the flank of the enemy's battery (still firing upon the right of our line) at right angles with my present line, gaining a fence, under which they opened fire. Delivering several volleys, [we] ceased firing, reloaded, and charged the battery, driving the enemy's gunners from their guns and killing several horses. The caissons were moved off by the enemy, leaving their pieces on the field. . . .

Lieutenant-Colonel Tillman, of the Forty-first Tennessee, *Gregg's* brigade, rode up to me at this time, stating that the enemy was moving down the road to my left and would soon be in my rear. Doubting the report, I suggested that our lines were connected on our left and that a flank or rear movement could not, therefore, be made by the enemy. I, however, found that but two regiments of *Gregg's* brigade had moved up with my line, and they had retired. . . .

I started to the road to satisfy myself as to the correctness of this report. I had gone but a short distance when I discovered a column of the enemy moving by the flank in direction of the Seventeenth Tennessee Regiment, which rapidly gained its rear. I heard distinctly the commands "halt," "front," and immediately their fire was pouring upon our flank and rear. Here a general stampede ensued, so suddenly and unexpected was the movement. We fell back 200 yards in rear of the Chattanooga and La Fayette road and reformed. In this flank movement of the enemy, the Seventeenth Tennessee Regiment lost 11 officers, including their gallant major . . . and about 60 men taken prisoners. The brigade built temporary breastworks, behind which it remained during the night in line of battle. [*O.R.*, XXX, Part II, pp. 473–474.]

Report of Capt. Samuel J. Harris, USA, Commanding Nineteenth Indiana Battery, Fourth Division, XIV Corps, Army of the Cumberland

About 3 p.m., the brigade having been sent forward, the battery was ordered to take position on a ridge running parallel to the Chattanooga road, separated therefrom by a thin growth of timber, and covering all the space intervening. About 3:30 we commenced the action by projecting spherical case over the heads of troops belonging to Van Cleve's division, who were now falling back, and when we could do so without endangering the lives of our own men, used canister, I think to good advantage.

At 4:15 the battery and parts of batteries on our right and left having all retired, and receiving a close and destructive fire on my right, I ordered the piece on the right to retire, with the purpose of changing the front of the right half battery, so as to enable me to meet the fire of the enemy.

These instructions were misapprehended. While endeavoring to execute this movement I was disabled by a contusion received on my right side. . . . and being unable to meet the flanking movement of the enemy . . . and receiving no support from the infantry detailed for that purpose, the battery fell back . . . with the loss of one 12-pounder smoothbore, which was unavoidably left on the ground, in consequence of the number of horses killed and disabled . . . and the close proximity of the enemy. [*O.R.*, XXX, Part I, p. 471.]

Report of Col. Smith D. Atkins, USA, Commanding
Ninety-second Illinois Mounted Infantry, First Brigade,
Fourth Division, XIV Corps, Army of the Cumberland

At about 1 p.m. [I] was ordered by General Reynolds to hitch all my horses in the woods, which I did, and moved up to and on the right of a battery planted by General Reynolds in reserve to King's brigade. [I] had just got into position when I was ordered by General Reynolds to the support of Colonel King's brigade, and immediately moved forward by the flank, a captain being sent to show me the way. He went to the road with me and told me to "keep down the road", when he left me. We were then moving by the right flank down the road in front of our first position, with timber and underbrush on the left of the road. King's brigade had already been pressed back, and the fire of the enemy was directly on my left flank from the timber; in front of me the enemy were pressing over the road.

I ordered the head of my column to the right along a fence facing the timbered hollow into which the enemy were pressing. When two companies had filed to the right some mounted officer rode up and ordered my regiment to "get out of the road," which the regiment did by a right flank, and under fire the regiment fell back over the open ground to its old position on the hill.

Here we reformed our line, not without some difficulty, as the center of the regiment was crowded by previous movements, and some confusion was occasioned by the coming in of some of King's brigade, leading to the fear that we were firing on our own men. Order was soon restored, and my regiment lying down cooly received the fire of the enemy and returned it, gallantly maintaining our ground, until I perceived that the other regiment supporting the battery had given way, and men falling back from other regiments were taking our horses hitched in the rear, and that both batteries had limbered up and were leaving, while the enemy pressing up the wooded ravine to my right had completely flanked my regiment, subjecting it to an enfilading fire, when I ordered my regiment to fall back and mount their horses. The engagement lasted only a few minutes, and my loss was about 25 in killed and wounded. . . . [O.R., XXX, Part I, p. 456.]

Return to your car. Continue on the LA FAYETTE ROAD for about 0.6 mile to a turnout on the right shoulder. STOP and dismount. Walk forward along the LA FAYETTE ROAD about 100 yards, then turn right and walk 20 yards toward the small stream. You will be facing west, toward the Wilder Tower. You should be able to look over the field beyond the stream and see the wood line at the top of the rise to the southwest.

The marker you see on the high ground in the field, short and to the right of the Wilder Tower, is to the Thirty-ninth North Carolina and Twenty-fifth Arkansas Regiments of *McNair's* brigade, *Johnson's* division. The Brock family cabin was near this marker.

STOP 9 – JOHNSON'S BREAKTHROUGH

When *Johnson* began his attack in mid-afternoon, he initially deployed *Johnson's (Fulton's)* brigade on the right, *Gregg's* brigade on the left and *McNair's* brigade in reserve behind *Gregg's*. The portion of the La Fayette Road that you just drove down was crossed by *Fulton's* brigade as it conducted the flanking movement against Union troops in Brotherton Field. From your current position you can understand what happened to the regiments in the left and left center of *Johnson's* division.

Report of Brig. Gen. Bushrod R. Johnson, CSA,
Commanding Provisional Division, Army of Tennessee
attached to Longstreet's Corps, Army of Northern Virginia

About 2 p.m. the enemy in my front advanced and drove in my skirmishers. I ordered *Bledsoe's* and *Everett's* batteries to open fire, and *Culpeper's* battery was brought into action on the left of *Gregg's* brigade. These guns all fired in a direction bearing toward Vineyard's house, from which direction the attack seemed mainly to come. The right of *Gregg's* and the left of *Johnson's* brigades repulsed the attack in that vicinity, but the engagement still continued on the left of *Gregg's* brigade, where the left regiments were suffering severely. The Fiftieth Tennessee Regiment lost 12 killed and 45 wounded before it moved from its position.

About 2:30 p.m., by direction of *Major-General Hood*—having instructed my artillery to move with the infantry and to come into action whenever opportunity permitted, particularly cautioning my command to preserve its connections, to wheel slowly, and to touch to the right—I ordered the division to advance and engage the enemy. This movement did not extend to the division on my left. In front of *Gregg's* brigade the woods presented a thick undergrowth, in which that brigade at once becoming hotly engaged, its progress was impeded, while *Johnson's* brigade advanced some 600 yards before the enemy opened fire upon it. The artillery advanced and fired by section, keeping well up with the infantry. *Gregg's* brigade advanced some 300 yards, obliquing in endeavoring under fire to keep the connection to the right. The connection, however, was broken in the thick woods between the second and third battalions [regiments] the two right regiments preserving their connection with the line on their right, and wheeling with it to the right; the third and fourth regiments, advancing less obliquely, faced more to the south, while the left regiment of that brigade (the Fiftieth Tennessee Regiment . . .) moved more directly to its front, which was in a southern direction, owing to its left having been thrown back to connect with *Preston's* division, and at the same time it stretched out to the right just north of Vineyard's fields to cover the increasing interval, until nearly the whole regiment was deployed in open order as skirmishers. This movement of the Fiftieth Tennessee Regiment was induced by the heavy attack of the enemy on that flank, but it did not succeed in preserving the connection, and it became separated from the brigade. . . .

Two regiments of *McNair's* brigade, the Thirty-ninth North Carolina Regiment . . . and the Twenty-fifth Arkansas Regiment . . . were sent forward between the Fiftieth Tennessee Regiment and the brigade to which it belongs. These two regiments came up to the left of the Seventh Texas Regiment, of *Gregg's* brigade, about 400 yards in front of the position from which my line had moved, and advanced gallantly to the road from Chattanooga to Lee and Gordon's Mills, north of Vineyard's farm, and left still a wide interval on the right of the Fiftieth Tennessee, . . . which . . . continued to present an extended line and to fight gallantly and persistently the heavy forces in front, while its ranks were being continually thinned. . . . The two

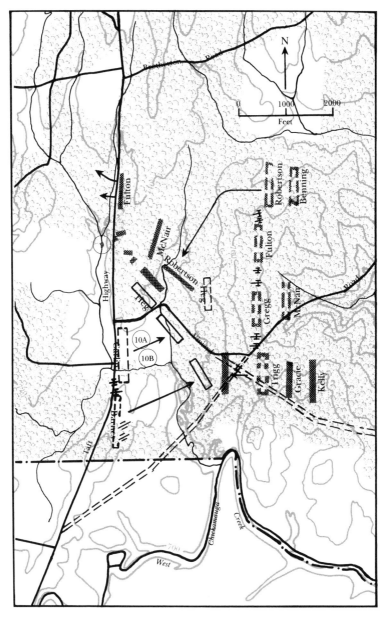

Stops 9, 10A, & 10B
Situation Early–Mid Afternoon
September 19, 1863

regiments from *Gregg's* brigade [Thirty-ninth North Carolina and Twenty-fifth Arkansas] drove the enemy in rapid flight across the Chattanooga road, and passed a small house in a corn-field west of the road and north of Vineyard's house; and . . . here, though the enemy in their front were in flight and broken, those regiments fell back for want of support and on account of re-enforcements received by the enemy and a flank fire on the left. [*O.R.*, XXX, Part II, pp. 453–454.]

The wood line along the southern edge of the open field marks the general location of the left flank of Colonel John T. Wilder's brigade of mounted infantry. It was from this location that the destructive fire was brought upon the flank of the Confederate attack.

Under the heavy flanking fire from the units of Wilder's brigade, which was followed up by an attack north along the La Fayette Road by two regiments of Colonel Charles G. Harker's Third Brigade, First Division, XXI Corps, the two Confederate regiments of *McNair's* brigade were forced to retreat back across the road. This uncovered the flank of the rest of *Johnson's* division and was instrumental in forcing the Confederate retreat.

Return to your car and drive south on the La Fayette Road about 0.3 mile to the small gravel parking area on the right. Park there.

STOP 10 – THE FIGHT AROUND THE VINIARD FARM
Afternoon, September 19, 1863

Walk south beside the road for about 25 yards. This is a high speed road, so please be careful. Turn left, cross the La Fayette Road and walk east along the Viniard-Alexander Bridge Road for approximately 100 yards. Then turn south into the open field and proceed to the crest of the high ground that runs north to south across this field. Position yourself in the vicinity of the Thirty-eighth Illinois monument and face east. Your back will be to the La Fayette Road.

POSITION A – CONFEDERATE RESERVES GO ASTRAY

You are now in the center of the position where bloody fighting occurred during the afternoon of September 19. The combat in this area was characterized by attack and counterattack with musket and artillery fire being exchanged at close range. As reinforcements became available they were committed to the action. By evening Union and Confederate units in this area had fought themselves to exhaustion.

The monuments in this field and north along La Fayette Road can be confusing because they represent the location of Union units for brief periods while the fighting was fluid throughout the area.

In 1863 this area appeared significantly different than it does today. The wood line to your left rear, east of and parallel to the La Fayette Road, was about 50 yards farther to the east. The wood line where the ground falls away to your front was approximately 400 yards farther to the east, and part of the large field was planted in corn. The woods to your right were not there at all, and the field extended for about 350 yards south of the current wood line. Even though the field was much larger, there was a small protrusion of woods at the southeast corner of the field. To your rear, a small metal marker identifies the location of the Viniard home in the small cleared area under the trees just across the La Fayette Road. The thin tree line behind that site was not there, but the small intermittent stream that it marks was there, referred to in reports as a ditch. The field beyond this stream rises to a long wood line. Both are as they were in 1863. The high brush on the north side of this field was not present and there was a clear field of fire and observation into the area to the north.

During the morning hours *Bushrod Johnson's* division had occupied positions east of your present location. *Gregg's* brigade was located 800 yards directly to the east. To *Gregg's* right and 1000 yards northeast of your location was *Johnson's (Fulton's)* brigade. *Johnson* had placed *McNair's* brigade in reserve behind *Gregg. Major General John B. Hood's* division was deployed on *Johnson's* right (north) flank. *Hood's* left brigade, connecting with *Johnson's* right, was *Robertson's* brigade with *Benning* just to the east in a supporting role.

Hood's division was placed in an ideal location to exploit the penetration made by *Johnson's* and *Stewart's* divisions. Around mid-day *Trigg's* brigade of *Brigadier General William Preston's* division moved into position on *Gregg's* left flank. The other two brigades of *Preston's* division were located just behind *Trigg*, but would not be committed to the fight.

Across the La Fayette Road, along the tree line west of the open field, was the mounted infantry brigade of Colonel John T. Wilder. Armed with seven-shot Spencer carbines, this brigade had been performing a covering mission to the east of this position on September 18 and fought the delaying action at Alexander Bridge, two miles to the east. Wilder's troopers had spent the night of September 18th in a position 900 yards east of your position, but during the early morning hours of the 19th they were withdrawn to the high ground across the field.

At mid-day Brigadier General Jefferson C. Davis' First Division of the XX Corps was moved into this area. Colonel Hans C. Heg's Third Brigade was deployed in the woods to your left. Brigadier General William P. Carlin's Second Brigade was deployed generally in this field, on Heg's right. The fighting commenced as Heg's brigade moved east and made contact with *Gregg's* brigade.

Report of Col. John A. Martin, USA, Commanding Third Brigade, First Division, XX Corps, Army of the Cumberland

We marched at 8 o'clock, and at 11:30 o'clock reached a point near General Rosecrans' headquarters. The brigade filed through the woods to the right, and after marching about a mile was rapidly formed in line of battle, the Fifteenth Wisconsin, Eighth Kansas, and Thirty-fifth Illinois being in line, and the Twenty-fifth Illinois a reserve directly in their rear. The brigade then moved three-quarters of a mile to the right, then by the left flank forward. We had not advanced more than a hundred yards when the enemy, concealed in the timber and behind fallen logs, opened a destructive fire on us. The men replied with promptness and effect, and pushed forward vigorously. The roar of musketry at this time was deafening.

The Twenty-fifth Illinois was ordered forward and came gallantly into line. The stream of wounded to the rear was almost unparalleled. Still the brigade held its ground, cheered on by the gallant, but unfortunate, Colonel Heg, who was everywhere present, careless of danger. The enemy was constantly re-enforced, and at last flanked us on the left, pouring a destructive fire down our line. We had then held the ground three-quarters of an hour. Colonel Heg gave the order to fall back, and the men slowly retreated, taking shelter behind the trees, firing at the advancing enemy, and stubbornly contesting every inch of the ground. Fifty yards to the rear they were again formed and again advanced, almost gaining their original ground, but were again compelled by overwhelming numbers to fall back.

Again and again they formed and advanced, only to be driven back. Almost half of the brigade was killed or wounded. Colonel Heg was mortally wounded; but the remnants of the brigade, falling back to a fence a short distance in the rear, held the enemy in check until re-enforcements came up and relieved them, when they fell back across an open field, taking position in the edge of a forest behind a log barricade. What remained of the brigade I reformed here, with the assistance of Captain Morrison, assistant adjutant-general of the division, and again advanced across the field, taking our old position behind the fence, and remaining there until nearly dusk, when the ammunition of the men was exhausted and we withdrew to the barricade in the edge of the woods again. Just at dark we were withdrawn by order of General Davis, and went into bivouac near the battle-field. [*O.R.*, XXX, Part I, pp. 529–530.]

Report of Brig. Gen. William P. Carlin, USA,
Commanding Second Brigade, First Division, XX Corps,
Army of the Cumberland

Under the direction of Brig. Gen. J.C. Davis, commanding the division, the brigade was brought into action on the right of the Third Brigade, Colonel Heg commanding, and in the following order: the Thirty-eighth Illinois . . . on the left; the One hundred and first Ohio . . . in the center; the Eighty-first Indiana . . . on the right; the Thirty-eighth Illinois being in the timber, the other two regiments in an open field. The Twenty-first Illinois . . . was first ordered by General Davis to remain in reserve, and was placed about 100 yards to the right and rear of the Eighty-first, in the edge of a forest which lay directly in front of it. This regiment had no sooner reached the position . . . than an order came from General Davis for it to report to Colonel Heg to support his brigade. . . .

About the same time the general commanding the division ordered me to send a regiment to support the artillery of the division, and . . . the Eighty-first Indiana was detached from my command. The Second Minnesota Battery had previously been withdrawn from my brigade, and was serving under the direction of Captain Hotch- kiss, chief of artillery. My command during the fight was therefore reduced to two regiments of infantry. The incompetency displayed by Captain Boone [commanding the Eighty-first Indiana] early in the action induced me to supersede him by Maj. James E. Calloway, Twenty-first Illinois . . . a gallant and very efficient officer.

When my line was formed, General Davis rode along my regi- ments and ordered them to lie down, without giving me or them additional instructions. The firing then was heavy on my left, and from the enemy. When my line was first formed Colonel Wilder informed me that two of his regiments were on my right in the

timber. Shortly after this I discovered troops in front of my right
swinging around at right angles to my line. Not knowing whose they
were I galloped over to them, under fire from the enemy, and ascertained that they were Colonel Barnes' brigade. They continued their
wheel to the left, until they masked half of the One hundred and first
Ohio, when, to prevent them masking both my regiments, I ordered
Lieutenant-Colonel Messer to advance and half wheel to the left and
open fire into the woods, where the enemy was posted. This movement was completed when a volley from the enemy caused the left of
Barnes' brigade to break, and in doing so they carried away the right
of the One hundred and first Ohio. The Thirty-eighth Illinois maintained its position till the Third Brigade had been driven back, when
that regiment gave way. The One hundred and first Ohio fell back in
better order, fighting over every step. . . . The two regiments fell back
across the road and across the open field west of the road into the
edge of the timber occupied by a part of Wood's division. During this
retreat there were many instances of individual gallantry. . . .

In the open field west of the road I succeeded in rallying men
enough from all the regiments of the Second and Third Brigades, and
some from other divisions, to form a respectable line. This was a very
arduous and very perilous service. . . . With the hope of recovering
the ground we had lost, I led them in a charge across the field to the
road, but the want of regimental organizations prevented me from
getting them farther.

At that moment a brigade of Sheridan's division took the front
but was soon driven back. It was now about sundown, and orders
were received from General Davis to fall back to an open field half
a mile to the rear, and bivouac for the night. [*O.R.*, XXX, Part I,
pp. 515–516.]

Report of Brig. Gen. Jerome B. Robertson, CSA, Commanding Brigade, Hood's Division, Army of Northern Virginia

After having remained in line of battle from daybreak until
nearly 3 p.m., I was ordered to take position on the left of *Colonel
Sheffield*, commanding *Law's* brigade (*General Law* being in command
of the division). This placed me on the extreme left of our line. On
receiving the order to advance and attack the enemy, I was directed to
keep closed on *Law's* brigade. I had not advanced more than 200
yards until the enemy was reported appearing on my left and endan-

gering my left flank. *Colonel Manning*, commanding Third Arkansas, my left regiment, was ordered to change front with two companies and meet them, I believing at the moment that it was a small force sent to make a diversion by threatening my flank.

Before these dispositions were completed, my line had passed the crest of the hill and I discovered the enemy in heavy force on my left, and they opened a heavy fire upon me. I sent a staff officer to inform *General Law* of it. He sent me orders to change front and meet them. This made it necessary for me to change my front forward on left battalion, which was done promptly under a heavy fire. To do this, I had necessarily to detach my brigade from *General Law's*. I sent a courier to inform him of the change.

My line steadily advanced, the enemy stubbornly contesting every inch of ground, until I reached the fence that divides the two fields on the crest of the hill. [This fence was located where the tree line is today, on the east edge of the field.] The thick woods through which my two right regiments (Fourth and Fifth Texas) advanced prevented me from knowing what was on my right, and I was advancing in a direction that separated me from the left of *Law's* brigade, thus leaving a considerable space uncovered and exposing my right flank. I determined to hold this, if possible, until I could be reenforced.

As soon as we reached the hill and drove the enemy from it, he opened upon us with grape and canister from two batteries, both of which raked the hill. Seeing that my force was too weak to hold the hill, with my loss momentarily increasing, I ordered them to fall back just behind the crest of the hill. On seeing this, the enemy pushed forward his infantry to the crest. As soon as they appeared on the hill, they were charged and driven back. In this charge I had three regimental commanders wounded. . . .

Immediately upon reaching the hill, I sent a courier for reenforcements, and a staff officer for a battery. *Brigadier-General Benning* came up promptly with his brigade, and . . . assisted in holding our position until nightfall, when we were moved, by order of *General Law*, to our position on the left of the division, relieving *General Hindman*, where we bivouacked for the night.

I sent three different messengers for a battery, all of whom returned without any. I then went myself, but could not get the officer in command of the only one I could find to bring his battery up. I have no hesitation in believing that if I could have gotten a battery in position we could have inflicted heavy loss on the enemy, as his infantry was massed in heavy columns at the far end of the field from us. [*O.R.*, XXX, Part II, pp. 510–511.]

Walk south 25 or 50 yards farther into the field and face to the east.

POSITION B – A BAD DECISION

Johnson shifted his division in a northwesterly direction, leaving an opening in the Confederate line to your front. As *Benning's* and *Robertson's* brigades moved south and behind *Johnson's* attacking division, which by now had reached the La Fayette Road, *Preston's* division arrived in the area directly east of this field. *Preston* sent *Trigg's* brigade forward to support *Robertson* and *Benning. Preston's* division was the left-most attacking unit of the Army of Tennessee. Although *Trigg's* brigade forcefully attacked, *Preston's* other two brigades were allowed to remain idle at a time when maximum combat power was needed in Viniard Field.

Report of Col. Robert C. Trigg, CSA, Commanding Brigade, Preston's Division, Army of Tennessee

About 12 m., by direction of *General Preston,* I moved my brigade by the right flank and reformed on the crest of a ridge about half a mile north of Hunt's house. As soon as the line was formed I deployed the First Regiment Florida Cavalry, dismounted, . . . as skirmishers, 300 yards in advance, and covering the entire front of the brigade. This regiment soon became engaged with the enemy's infantry in a corn-field and the woods to the right of the field. It kept up quite a brisk fire for more than two hours, when the right was driven in by a destructive fire of grape and canister from a battery in the field.

At this time I was ordered to re-enforce *General Hood* and moved in the direction of the firing. The firing was on my right. I moved by the right flank until met by a staff officer, who came to conduct me to the point where *General Hood* needed support (the position held by *General Benning's* brigade). At his instance I moved by the front. Soon after I was met by another staff officer, who claimed my support for *General Robertson's* brigade. I continued my movement by the front until I came near a corn-field, in which the enemy had a battery protected by earth-works, near the Chattanooga road, and supported by a long line of infantry drawn up in the field and in rifle-pits and woods on the right and left of the battery.

The enemy was advancing when I first discovered him, and had passed about one-third the length of the field. The troops that had won the wooded ridge outside of the field and to my right were falling back in some confusion. The advance of the enemy and the falling back of our troops seemed to effect some change in the mind of the officer conducting me. He requested me to halt until he could learn precisely what position I was to take. While thus halted and under the enemy's fire *General Robertson* appeared, and hurriedly informing me that his line was very much weakened and would be beaten back unless quickly re-enforced, indicated the direction in which I should move. I obliqued to the right until I supposed that my right was opposite to his left. This brought the front of my brigade to the corn-field fence.

All this while I had been under a most destructive fire of the enemy's artillery, and at this time he concentrated upon me the fire of his whole force in the corn-field and in the timber around it. I had not as yet fired a single gun. I reserved my fire until I reached the fence. At the first volley the enemy broke in confusion to the left and rear. Seeing his confusion, I ordered my brigade to charge before he could rally. The Sixth Florida Regiment gallantly responded, leaping the fence and dashing forward to the crest of the ridge, forcing the enemy's broken line to seek the nearest cover on the right, left and in rear.

This regiment regained the ridge [your present location] . . . cleared the corn-field of all the infantry, drove nearly all the gunners from the battery, and would have certainly captured it but for a lamentable interference with my command. When the order to charge was given, I was on the right with this regiment. The order was not promptly conveyed to the other regiments of the brigade, and they failing to conform to the movements of the Sixth Florida, it got from 150 to 200 yards in advance. Having gained the crest of the ridge, I discovered for the first time that the other regiments of the brigade were not up with the Sixth Florida. I immediately started to bring them up, but had gone but a short distance when I perceived them crossing the fence and moving forward in good order. I returned to direct the movements of the Sixth Florida. When these regiments had reached the second fence I discovered that they were being moved by *Brigadier-General Robertson* across the field by the right flank and in rear of the Sixth. Finding that this regiment would not receive support from the rest of the brigade, and it being exposed to a terrible fire from the front and left (the enemy having in part recovered from his panic), I withdrew it below the crest of the ridge, and unwillingly relinquished the capture of the battery. . . . [*O.R.*, XXX, Part II, pp. 430–431.]

To the southeast you can see the right angle intersection of the tree lines. Although these tree lines were not there in 1863, they intersect where a tree line pointed into the open field. The Eighty-first Indiana was detached from Carlin's brigade and deployed to the right of Carlin and to the left of Barnes' brigade. This regiment made initial contact in a position that ran from the juncture of today's tree lines northwest to the vicinity of the small ridge where you are. The forward and rearward movements of this regiment were parallel to the tree line to your right. Because of its position and the length of time that it remained in contact, the report of its commander provides an excellent account of the surging action.

Report of Maj. James E. Calloway, USA, Twenty-first
Illinois Infantry, Commanding Eighty-first Indiana
Infantry, Second Brigade, First Division, XX Corps,
Army of the Cumberland

About 2:30 p.m. on the 19th, . . . while with the Twenty-first Illinois Volunteers, and being hotly engaged with the enemy at a point about 3 miles north of Crawfish Spring . . . east of and parallel to the La Fayette road . . . I received an order to immediately report to Brigadier-General Carlin, commanding brigade. Upon reporting, General Carlin directed me to at once assume command of the Eighty-first Indiana Volunteers, of his brigade. I immediately obeyed the order, and, upon assuming command, found the regiment . . . lying about 50 yards in rear of and supporting the Second Minnesota Battery, the regiment not yet having engaged the enemy. The regiment then numbered, in fighting men present for duty, 15 officers and 240 enlisted men.

About five minutes thereafter I received an order in person from Brigadier-General Davis, commanding division, to move my command about 200 yards to the right and front of the Second Minnesota Battery and support a regiment there severely engaged with the enemy. . . . Upon taking position, the right resting behind and shielded by a point of timber with heavy undergrowth, the left resting on the crest of and being covered by a slight elevation, I had discov-

ered a regiment . . . [Eighth Kentucky of Barnes' brigade] to my right
and a little to my front slowly giving way to the right, and steadily
contesting the ground under a most withering fire from a very heavy
column of the enemy briskly advancing and not over 300 yards
distant.

We immediately opened a well-directed fire, first by volley and
then by file, causing the enemy to recoil and give way in much
confusion, thereby relieving the regiment to our right. The firing had
not yet ceased when a large body of the enemy was seen moving to
our left, and soon attacked the Second and Third Brigades of Davis'
division. The enemy in our front again took courage and advanced
upon our position, but, being shattered, was easily repulsed. The
brigades to our left and the Second Minnesota Battery, together with
the Fifty-eighth Indiana Volunteers, immediately joining the Eighty-
first Indiana on the left, though most stubbornly and bravely resisting
the terrible onsets of most overwhelming numbers, were driven from
their position, leaving the Eighty-first Indiana entirely without support on the left. I had in the meantime made a partial change of front
to the rear by throwing back the left wing of the regiment, and
continued our fire, somewhat enfilading the lines of the enemy and
partially checking his farther progress.

About this time a vigorous attack was made on our front and
right, causing the . . . [Eighth Kentucky] to farther withdraw.

The Eighty-first Indiana Volunteers, owing to the admirable position occupied, was not suffering very greatly, but the position was so
flanked as to endanger my entire command, exposing it to capture. It
was then withdrawn in good order about 200 yards to a thin curtain
of timber covering the road.

After again halting and reopening fire, I was informed by an
officer that 50 yards to our rear and across the road was a fieldwork
that had been hastily constructed of rails. I accordingly faced the
regiment about and took position within the works, when we again
opened and continued a most galling and deadly fire upon the enemy,
who had advanced within short range, and after long and hard fighting he was dislodged from his position with heavy loss.

We immediately followed his retreating forces and retook our
former position . . . and held it during the remainder of the day. The
Fifty-eighth Indiana Volunteers again came up to our left, and about
the same time I observed Brigadier-General Carlin, still to the left of
the Fifty-eighth Indiana . . . most fearlessly moving forward a body of

troops I then supposed to be the remainder of this brigade to the attack of the enemy. . . .

The general and his command made a most gallant and heroic resistance, but being overpowered, were shattered and driven back with fearful loss, leaving the colors of the Twenty-first Illinois . . . in the hands of the color-sergeant, who was shot dead on the field. I immediately ordered the Eighty-first Indiana . . . to open an oblique fire to the left, completely enfilading the lines of the enemy, and repulsing him with immense slaughter, recovering the colors of the Twenty-first Illinois . . . and protecting the One hundred and first Ohio while it most gallantly recovered the Eighth Indiana Battery taken by the enemy. The Third Brigade of Sheridan's division came to the relief of General Carlin, and formed on the left of the Fifty-eighth Indiana Volunteers. . . .

Hearing a heavy roll of musketry and much cannonading on our right, and not knowing who occupied the position, I had fears that my position might be flanked, as the forces seemed to recoil and the firing was growing to our rear. Upon information received, and after making a personal inspection of the right, I learned that a brigade commanded by Colonel Barnes had been repulsed on our right, but the colonel had so posted his battery as to command his front and our right, enfilading the enemy's approach in attempting to turn our position. . . .

During the engagement on that afternoon we fired an average of 54 rounds to each man of my command, and suffered . . . a grand total of 66 killed and wounded. [O.R., XXX, Part I, pp. 523-524.]

Retrace your steps to the Viniard—Alexander Bridge Road and walk back toward the intersection with the La Fayette Road. When you reach the vicinity of the Eighth Indiana battery—marked by two guns—stop and face east.

POSITION C—OVERRUN

Report of Capt. George Estep, USA, Commanding
Eighth Indiana Battery, First Division, XXI Corps,
Army of the Cumberland

We . . . remained quiet till afternoon, when I was ordered by one of Colonel Buell's staff to move with the brigade to the left on the Chattanooga road. . . . Was ordered into position with the brigade on the right of the road, the left half of my battery resting in woods and the right in an open field.

I had been in position but a moment (in battery) till I learned that the enemy were driving our troops (do not know whose they were) back on the line we had just formed. Hurried into position as I was, I feared to fire on account of destroying our own men. I then rode to a battery commander on my right who was in position when we came up, to learn, if possible, the location of the enemy as well as that of our own forces. He told me that he had been firing at a range of 800 yards, but that the distance was growing less very fast. I rode back and ordered the right half to commence firing shell at a range of 700 yards, believing from the information I had received that the shell would not interfere with our troops in front.

A moment after this and the battery was filled with men falling back through it in great confusion. I was compelled to cease firing till our men passed from my front. I thought I would then be able to deal a destructive fire on the advancing line of the enemy, but he was pressing so close upon our line, delivering his fire as he advanced, his shots taking effect on my horses, I was compelled to retire the battery. This I succeeded in doing by leaving one piece of the left section on the field, 5 horses being killed and disabled belonging to the piece. The limber was upset and rendered worthless. The piece was afterward drawn to the rear by hand by my own men and by some of the men belonging to the Twenty-sixth . . . Ohio. . . .

I moved five pieces of the battery to the rear with the regiments of the brigade across the road and field to the timber, and again opened fire with other batteries on my left on the enemy, who did not attempt pursuit over the open field. The brigade suffered severely in killed and wounded. . . . The brigade was soon ordered forward over the field near the position first taken. I was ordered by Colonel Buell to move with it. I did so promptly, got into position, and commenced firing at a range of 90 or 100 yards at the enemy's lines, then lying down in the woods. I am positive that while in this position I did the enemy serious injury, but his musketry fire became so heavy, terrible, and galling that to remain there longer was only to insure me that I would not have a horse left. I gave the order to limber to the rear.

The execution of the order had scarcely begun when the infantry began to fall back, being charged by the enemy *en masse*, who came yelling like devils. Three of my pieces were left on the field, but the enemy was again charged by our troops and my pieces retaken. I then

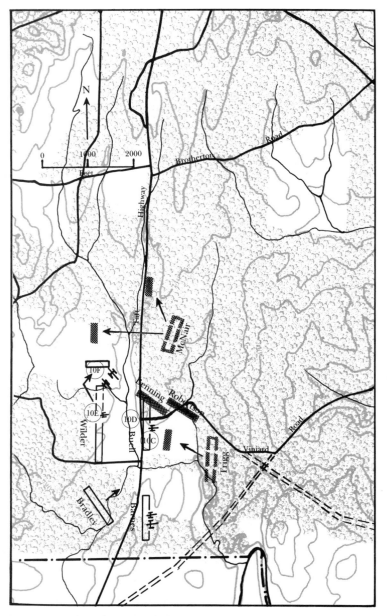

Stops 10C, 10D, 10E, & 10F
Situation Mid–Late Afternoon
September 19, 1863

moved to the rear and worked nearly all night in repairing carriages and harness, and supplying with extras, and from my battery and forge teams, the horses killed and disabled during the day. [*O.R.*, XXX, Part I, pp. 676–677.]

Cross the La Fayette Road. Position yourself opposite the Viniard – Alexander Bridge Road and La Fayette Road intersection facing east and far enough from the road to be safe.

POSITION D – DESPERATE DEFENSE

The casualties suffered by Heg's and Carlin's brigades seriously reduced their effectiveness. At approximately 3 p.m. Brig. Gen. Thomas Wood's First Division, XXI Corps was committed to the battle in this area. Wood deployed Col. Charles Harker's Third Brigade to the left of this location, where elements participated in the attack north along the La Fayette Road into the flank of *Johnson's* division. Col. George Buell's First Brigade was placed in position parallel to the La Fayette Road to reenforce Heg's and Carlin's brigades. A report from one of Buell's regimental commanders vividly describes the fighting.

Report of Lieut. Col. William H. Young, USA,
Commanding Twenty-sixth Ohio Infantry, First Brigade,
First Division, XXI Corps, Army of the Cumberland

At about 2:30 or 3 p.m. . . . when the brigade was ordered to the left on the Chattanooga road, my regiment took the road in the rear of the One hundredth Illinois, and moved with the rest of the brigade at a double-quick some 2 miles to where the battle seemed to be raging with the utmost fury. Arriving at this point, where the conflict seemed fiercest, and the enemy was apparently pushing back our lines, my regiment was immediately thrown into line at double-quick on the right of, parallel to, and about 40 yards off the road, the Eighth Indiana battery being on my right, my left resting in the woods.

In my immediate front, and for 75 yards in front of the prolongation of my line, to the right, was a heavy timber, thickly grown with jack-oak bushes, making it utterly impossible to see what was going on 20 yards distant. Seventy-five yards to my right this timber made a right angle to the front, leaving on its right and in front of the road an inclosed field extending about 500 or 600 yards along the road and

600 to 700 yards to the front, being limited in each direction by timber and thickets. On my left and at my flank the line of timber in my front made a right angle to the rear, crossing the road and forming a dense cover for several hundred yards, and then opening into a half cleared, but bushy and thickly weeded field; 30 to 40 yards in the rear of, and parallel to, my line . . . was the road, and in the rear of this another inclosed field, extending about 400 yards to the rear of, and 600 to 700 yards parallel, with the road toward the right, and being bounded by timber in both directions. This last field descends with an easy slope from the road about 100 to 150 yards to a narrow ditch or gully and then rises with a slight grade to the timber in its rear. The gully varies in depth from 1½ to 3½ feet and in width from 3 to 6 or 8 feet, its border at intervals being slightly fringed with weeds and willows. . . .

I immediately caused my men to lie down and simultaneously received instructions from General Wood that the position must be held. Even while receiving his instructions, and before the men had been allowed a moment to recover their wind after the rapid march, it became manifest the lines in our front were broken and the enemy pressing them rapidly back. In a moment more dozens, then scores, and finally hundreds, of straggling soldiers came rushing through the woods and over my line in the wildest disorder and most shameful confusion, there seeming to be no effort to either check or control the retreat, and at the same time a most galling fire began to reach and take effect upon my men, though lying close upon the ground.

In the meantime, I was holding my fire until our own men should be out of the way, intending, when the rebel line should show itself, to deliver my fire by volley and meet him at a charge with bayonets (previously fixed). As I was about executing this intention, a mounted officer came galloping to the rear calling out, "for God's sake, don't fire; two lines of our own troops are still in the woods." At the same instant I discovered a rapid fire enfilading my line from the timber on the left, most cruelly cutting my command. My horse fell under me pierced . . . with nine balls; my acting major was dismounted and wounded, and the rebel line appeared in front within 20 yards, advancing firing.

I immediately commenced firing and ordered a charge, but the command could be only partially heard, and the charge was not made. The rebel advance in front, however, was momentarily checked and his fire weakened; but the battery on my right had already been withdrawn; a heavy line of rebels were already on my left, and rapidly gaining my rear, making it impossible to hold my position even for a moment longer except with the certainty of capture. I reluctantly gave the command to retire across the road to the fence immediately in my rear. This was done in tolerable order, but under a most galling fire. . . . This conflict was short and bloody, begun at a great disadvantage, kept up with the highest heroism, and the ground only yielded when the bayonet had been freely used and defense had become hopeless.

On retiring to the fence . . . the regiment was in great part promptly rallied, though under a severe direct and cross fire and the loud cheers of the advancing rebels. From this position an effective fire was poured back into the enemy, and he was compelled to retire to the timber for cover.

But now a most terrible fire was concentrated upon us, direct and right and left oblique, there being no support on either of my flanks. The officers and men conducted themselves most heroically . . . disdaining the cover of the low fence and defiantly receiving and returning the concentrated fire of more than twice their front.

Again the enemy was closing up on my left flank not 30 yards from it and rapidly gaining my rear. I still hoped, though I had not seen it, there was some support on the left, and, depending for support for my right upon a rally that was being made around some old buildings 250 yards distant on the prolongation of my right, as well as upon a few brave heroes scattered along the fence between me and those buildings, I determined to hold the fence a few minutes longer; but it seemed of no avail. There was now almost a semicircle of fire around us; it was growing hotter every moment; we were beginning to receive the fire of our own troops rallied in the ditch below us and in the woods beyond. The five left companies had lost from one-half to three-quarters of their numbers. The left center company had but 5 men left from 24, and 1 of its officers was killed. . . . It was a proud thing to have died there with those that were dead; it was duty to save the remnant of the living for still another struggle.

I now gave the command to fall back to the ditch. Many wounded had already sought this as a place of refuge from the storm of musketry, grape-shot, and shell now sweeping the field from the edge of the timber on both sides. Many others had also rallied here from the troops that had retreated over my line. . . . Many of my own men had rallied here when the line first fell back and were fighting bravely from the imperfect cover the shallow ditch afforded.

From this third position another defense was now opened, and for a few moments vigorously and effectually maintained. But this line, like the others, was flanked and raked with a murderous fire. . . . The enemy had not yet attempted to cross the open field. Our own artillery and infantry were already pouring into them an effective fire from the timber in the rear. The troops collected around the old buildings . . . were successfully holding the enemy's left, and under cover of their fire a brave remnant of my command with myself made good our retreat by the right and rear, many others moving directly to the rear through a very storm of bullets.

I immediately proceeded to reform my regiment, and after moving my colors into the open field, succeeded—with the assistance of my officers . . . in rallying the bulk of my surviving men. Supported by a few men of the Thirteenth Michigan bravely rallied around their colors, and another fragmentary regiment of, I think, Davis' division, and a few brave spirits of various regiments under the immediate command of General Wood, we charged across the field under the cover of Bradley's [Sixth Ohio] and Estep's [Eighth Indiana] batteries, but in the face of a galling fire. We were joined . . . by many brave fellows who had staid in the ditch, and a few others who had remained by the fence. . . .

Our little line staggered for a moment under the concentrated fire opened upon it from the woods, but pressing quickly forward firing we entered the woods at the point where the Eighth Indiana battery had formerly stood, and nearly parallel to our original line, driving the enemy steadily before us. We [had] entered the woods 200 yards, when, perceiving a rapid cross-fire on my left flank, I changed front to the rear on my first company, and, taking cover behind the fence at the edge of the woods, soon beat off the enemy in that direction.

At this juncture I perceived a compact rebel line 500 to 600 yards distant advancing across the field from the woods in front of the road. I now changed front to the rear on my tenth company and ordered my men to lie down until the enemy should approach; other troops of our brigade then being on my right, somewhat to my rear, and a strong line of Sheridan's division at the same time coming up in my rear across the field in the rear of the road, this line halted near the road just as the enemy's fire was becoming severe, and commenced firing into my rear.

I promptly moved back to the fence, and taking position under its cover awaited the onset. It was opened with a most murderous fire, driving back upon me a Kentucky regiment (of Sheridan's division, perhaps) which was advancing in line obliquely across my front. The entire line was broken by the shock. I held my command for a few minutes at the fence, but seeing the uselessness of attempting to hold the position, fell back to the ditch, where I rallied a few men. . . . We drew back in tolerable order to the timber, when the regiment was again formed, mustering about 147 men out of 335 who had entered the battle, and 14 officers out of 24. [*O.R.*, XXX, Part I, pp. 668–671.]

To the north and to the northeast you can see the markers to the Georgia regiments of *Benning's* brigade, the flanking force that Lieut. Col. Young mentions in his *Report*.

Report of Brig. Gen. Henry L. Benning, CSA, Commanding Brigade, Hood's Division, Army of Northern Virginia

At about 3 p.m. . . . I was ordered to advance and support *Brigadier-General Robertson*, who was a little to my left. On advancing, I found him with his brigade hotly engaged with a superior force of the enemy's infantry aided by a battery. The place was on the Chattanooga road near a small house, and a smaller out-house with open ground for 150 or 200 yards in front, and stretching to the right and left, through which ran the road from front to rear. Beyond the open ground all was forest, in which, on the right of the road, was the enemy's battery. Thus the missiles from the battery not only swept over nearly all of the open ground, but passed on with effect far into the level wood in the rear.

When we first encountered the enemy they were at the two houses and on the near side of the open ground. After an obstinate contest they were driven from this position and across the open ground into the woods beyond. We then occupied the ground about the houses. My numbers were too few to venture with them alone to follow the enemy into the wood and to the battery. The place we held was much exposed to the enemy's fire, but with little cover furnished by the houses, some stumps, and a few scattered trees, I thought I could hold it till the re-enforcements (every minute expected) should arrive, when a general advance might be made and the enemy swept from the opposite wood. We did hold it for a long time, driving back several charges of the enemy to retake it. No re-enforcements came.

Finally toward sunset the enemy's fire from his battery and from his infantry, protected by the wood, became so heavy, and so many of our officers and men had fallen, that we had ourselves to retire a short distance. We accordingly took up a new position 100 or 200 yards in the rear of the houses, where we remained till the close of the fight.

We felt much . . . the want of artillery to oppose not only to the enemy's artillery but to his infantry; but none came to our aid. None had been attached either to my brigade or to *Brigadier-General Robertson's*.

My loss was very heavy to my numbers. In the Twentieth [Georgia] Regiment 17 officers out of 23 were killed or wounded. In the other regiments the proportion though not so great was very great. The proportionate loss among the men was but little less. The command fought with a dogged resolution. [*O.R.*, XXX, Part II, pp. 517–518.]

Walk west, cross the stream at the footbridge beyond the Heg monument, and proceed to the northwest corner of the field. Here, near the woods, you will find the monument to the Eighteenth Indiana Battery.

POSITION E – THE UNION LINE HOLDS

This was the left flank position of Colonel John T. Wilder's mounted infantry brigade, to which the Eighteenth Indiana battery belonged. From here the guns were able to bring killing fire into the right of *Benning's* line near the La Fayette Road and the ditch.

Report of Capt. Eli Lilly, USA, Commanding
Eighteenth Indiana Battery, First Brigade (Mounted),
Fourth Division, XIV Corps, Army of the Cumberland

I did not become engaged until about 2:30 p.m., when our brigade moved in support of Davis' division, at which time I shelled the enemy's lines to cover the movement. When our brigade was relieved by other troops and returned to its former line I ceased firing.

My position at this time was on the west side of and facing the Gordon's Mills and Chattanooga road, four pieces near the right of an open field, two pieces at the left corner of the same field [your position], all retired in the edge of the timber. A ravine crossed the field parallel to our line two-thirds of the way to the road.

The troops in our front were now falling back, and as it was expected the enemy would fall on our left, the lines were extended in that direction and the four pieces on the right were now moved to a corn-field on the left of the timber we had just left, and in a direct line with our former position. This was no sooner done than the enemy moved to the road in front of our center, when the section posted at the corner of the field opened lively, the pieces being double-shotted with canister. They advanced under this and a strong oblique fire from my pieces on the left, in addition to the fire of the infantry lines, until they reached the ravine, when they fell back in disorder. We remained on this part of the field all night. [*O.R.*, XXX, Part I, pp. 466–467.]

Walk through the small line of brush to the north and proceed about 200 yards into the next field. The white stone marker 350 yards in front of you is the monument to the Thirty-ninth North Carolina and Twenty-fifth Arkansas of *McNair's* brigade, *Johnson's* division.

POSITION F–SPENCERS PROVE THEIR WORTH

From this position heavy flanking fire was placed on the left part of the penetration started by *Johnson's* division. Confederate reports refer specifically to this fire as a major contributing factor in his decision to retreat to the east side of the La Fayette Road.

Report of Col. John T. Wilder, USA, Commanding First Brigade (Mounted Infantry), Fourth Division, XIV Corps, Army of the Cumberland (Continued)

On the morning of the 19th I received orders from department headquarters to take up a position "on the right fighting flank of our army, and keep the department commander advised of events in that vicinity." I immediately occupied the woods at the edge of a field on the west side of the road from Gordon's Mills to Rossville, at a point where the road from Alexander's Bridge and the fords in the vicinity of Napier's Gap intersect that road, being satisfied that the rebels would attempt an advance in that direction.

At about 1 p.m. heavy fighting was heard in my front, and by General Crittenden's order I advanced my line across the road, when, seeing a rebel column in the act of flanking a battery of General Davis' command, I sent two regiments to the right to repel them.

This was done in handsome style by Colonels Monroe and Miller, with their regiments, when my skirmishers reported a heavy rebel column flanking my left under cover of the woods.

I now brought my entire command double-quick back to their original position, changing direction to my left with two regiments, and opened a deadly fire on a dense mass of rebels, enfilading their left flank as they were making their way (across the road to Gordon's Mills) in the open ground in front of Mrs. Glenn's house, first staggering them and soon routing them in confusion, driving them back into the woods east.

In a few moments this or another column of rebels came out of the woods near Vineyard's house, moving obliquely at and to my right, driving General Davis' command before them. General Crittenden at this point came near being captured in trying to rally these troops. I immediately again changed front and enfiladed their right flank with an oblique fire, which soon drove them back with terrible slaughter. General Davis now rallied his men, who gallantly advanced on my right under a galling fire, but were soon driven by overwhelming numbers back again to my right, being followed to the center of the field to a ditch in which the rebel advance took cover. I at once ordered Captain Lilly to send a section of his battery forward on my left to a clump of bushes and rake the ditch with canister. This was promptly done, with terrible slaughter, but very few of the rebels escaping alive.

In these various repulses we had thrown into the rebel columns which attacked us closely massed, over 200 rounds of double-shotted 10-pounder canister, at a range varying from 70 to 350 yards, and at the same time kept up a constant fire with our repeating rifles, causing a most fearful destruction in the rebel ranks. After this we were not again that day attacked. [*O.R.*, XXX, Part I, pp. 447–448.]

Return to your car.
Before continuing to Stop 11, you might want to take an excursion to Lee and Gordon's Mills (See Instructions below). If you decide not to visit the mills, skip these instructions and resume your tour with the Directions to Stop 11.

TO LEE AND GORDON'S MILLS

Resume driving south for 1.5 miles to the stop light. TURN LEFT onto LEE-GORDON ROAD. Drive 0.2 mile and make a hard RIGHT TURN at the STOP sign. Drive 0.1 mile to CHICKAMAUGA CREEK. Lee and Gordon's Mill is the wooden structure on your left.

This is the location of the Union left flank on September 18. Had not the Confederate army been delayed at Reed's Bridge and Alexander Bridge and Thomas' XIV Corps shifted north to Kelly Field, this is the likely area where *Bragg's* main attack would have fallen on the Union left flank. By mid-afternoon on September 19th, however, the Union army had been shifted to the north and this now became the right flank of Rosecrans' army. Cavalry of both armies covered the crossing here.

Cross the bridge. Within 0.5 mile there are several adequate places to turn around. Retrace your route to the bridge and then follow the road STRAIGHT for 0.3 mile back to the LA FAYETTE ROAD. TURN RIGHT onto this road and drive 1.2 miles to the GLENN-VINIARD ROAD. TURN LEFT onto this road and pick up the directions to Stop 11 starting with the second sentence (below).

TO STOP 11

Drive south 0.1 mile and TURN RIGHT onto the GLENN-VINIARD ROAD. Drive 0.8 mile to the Wilder Monument Tower, which you may wish to climb for an elevated view of the southern part of the battlefield.

Here the name of the road changes to GLENN-KELLY ROAD. After driving about 0.7 mile beyond the tower, you pass a sign on your left marking the site of the old tanyard — the farthest penetration by *Clayton's* brigade of *Stewart's* division, forced back by lack of support and the arrival of Negley's Union division between this area and Dry Valley Road to the west.

Drive about 0.2 mile beyond the old tanyard to the intersection with the DYER ROAD. Cross that road and drive another 0.7 mile to a fork in the road. BEAR RIGHT and drive 0.7 mile farther to the junction with the LA FAYETTE ROAD. Cross that road to the ALEXANDER BRIDGE ROAD and continue for an additional 0.3 mile. TURN RIGHT onto BATTLE LINE ROAD and park.

This would be an appropriate place to read the following pages on preparations for the second day.

PREPARATIONS FOR THE SECOND DAY
The View from Union Headquarters
September 19, 1863

Charles A. Dana, Assistant Secretary of War, was with Rosecrans' headquarters throughout the battle. His frequent reports to Secretary of War Edwin M. Stanton throughout the first day of battle doubtless reflect the perceptions of the moment among Union commanders.

Dispatches of C. A. Dana to Hon. E. M. Stanton, U.S. Secretary of War

Widow Glenn's, September 19, 1863 – 2:30 p.m. Fight continues to rage. Enemy, repulsed on left by Thomas, has suddenly fallen on right of our line of battle, held by Van Cleve; musketry and artillery there fierce and obstinate. Crittenden with remainder of his corps is just going in. Negley's and Sheridan's divisions and cavalry alone remain unengaged and Sheridan is ordered here, leaving Negley to hold the fords beyond Crawfish Spring. The mass of cavalry guards the gaps beyond it. Thomas loses pretty heavily in men; also lost one battery of Brannan. Decisive victory seems assured to us.

3 p.m.

Enemy forced back by Crittenden on right, has just massed his artillery against Davis on center. His attack there is the most furious of the day. He seems giving way.

3:20 p.m.

Thomas reports that he is driving rebels, and will force them into Chickamauga tonight. It is evident here their line is falling back. The battle is fought altogether in a thick forest, and is invisible to outsiders. Line is 2 miles long.

4 p.m.

Negley being nearer than Sheridan has come up in his stead. Negley's first brigade is just going in. Everything is prosperous. Sheridan is coming up. Cavalry has been brought to Crawfish Spring ready for use.

4:30 p.m.

I do not yet dare to say our victory is complete, but it seems certain. Enemy silenced on nearly whole line. *Longstreet* is here. *Governor Brown* has taken part in battle.

5:20 p.m.

Firing has ceased. Reports are coming in. Enemy holds his ground in many places. We have suffered severely. Reynolds reported killed. Now appears to be undecided contest, but later reports will enable us to understand more clearly.

7:30 p.m.

Immediately after my last dispatch Negley opened on enemy with two fresh brigades and drove him back half a mile. The firing did not cease till an hour after dark, the feeble light of the moon favoring the combatants. This gives us decidedly the advantage in respect of ground. The result of the battle is that the enemy is defeated in attempt to turn and crush our left flank and regain possession of Chattanooga. His attempt was furious and obstinate, his repulse was bloody, and maintained till the end. If he does not retreat Rosecrans will renew the fight at daylight. His dispositions are now being made. There are here two brigades and one regiment which have not been engaged at all, and two brigades which have been engaged but little. At Rossville are 8,000 men of Reserve Corps not engaged at all. We have lost no prominent officer. Reynolds safe. Weather cool; favorable to wounded.

11 p.m.

Dr. Perin, medical director of this department, estimates the number of our wounded as not exceeding 2,000. . . . [*O.R.*, XXX, Part I, pp. 190–192.]

Report of Maj. Gen. William S. Rosecrans, USA, Commanding the Army of the Cumberland

The roar of battle hushed in the darkness of night, and our troops, weary with a night of marching and a day of fighting, rested on their arms, having everywhere maintained their positions, developed the enemy, and gained thorough command of the Rossville and

Dry Valley roads to Chattanooga, the great object of the battle of the 19th. . . .

The battle had secured us these objects. Our flanks covered the Dry Valley and Rossville roads, while our cavalry covered the Missionary Ridge and the Valley of Chattanooga Creek, into which latter place our spare trains had been sent on . . . the 18th.

We also had indubitable evidence of the presence of *Longstreet's* corps and *Johnston's* forces, by the capture of prisoners from each, and the fact that at the close of the day we had present but two brigades which had not been opportunely and squarely in action, opposed to superior numbers of the enemy, assured us that we were greatly outnumbered, and that the battle the next day must be for the safety of the army and the possession of Chattanooga.

During the evening of the 19th the corps commanders were assembled at headquarters at Widow Glenn's house, the reports of the positions and condition of their commands heard, and orders given for the disposition of the troops for the following day.

Thomas' corps, with the troops which had re-enforced him, was to maintain substantially his present line, with Brannan in reserve.

McCook, maintaining his picket line till it was driven in, was to close on Thomas, his right refused, and covering the position at Widow Glenn's, and Crittenden to have two divisions in reserve near the junction of McCook's and Thomas' lines to be able to succor either.

Plans having been explained, written orders given to each and read in the presence of all, the wearied corps commanders returned about midnight to their commands.

No firing took place during the night. The troops had assumed position when the day dawned. The sky was red and sultry, the atmosphere and all the woods enveloped in fog and smoke. As soon as it was sufficiently light I proceeded, accompanied by General [James A.] Garfield and some aides, to inspect the lines.

I found General McCook's right too far up on the crest, and General Davis in reserve on a wooded hill-side west of and parallel to the Dry Valley road. I mentioned these defects to the general, desiring Davis' division to be brought down at once, moved more to the left and placed in close column by division, doubled on the center, in a sheltered position.

I found General Crittenden's two divisions massed at the foot of the same hill in the valley and called his attention to it, desiring them to be moved farther to the left.

General Thomas' troops were in the position indicated, except Palmer's line was to be closed more compactly.

Satisfied that the enemy's first attempt would be on our left, orders were dispatched to General Negley to join General Thomas and to General McCook to relieve Negley. [*O.R.*, XXX, Part I, pp. 57–58.] [Garfield, the twentieth President of the United States, served at Chickamauga as Rosecrans' chief of staff.]

Report of Maj. Gen. George H. Thomas, USA, Commanding Fourteenth Army Corps, Army of the Cumberland (Continued)

About 5 p.m., [September 19] my lines being at that time very much extended in pursuing the enemy, I determined to concentrate them on more commanding ground, as I felt confident that we should have a renewal of the battle in the morning. I rode forward to General Johnson's position and designated to him where to place his division; also to General Baird, who was present with Johnson.

I then rode back to the cross-roads to locate Palmer and Reynolds on Johnson's right and on the crest of the ridge about 500 yards east of the State road. Soon after Palmer and Reynolds got their positions, and while Brannan was getting his on the ridge to the west of the State road, near Dyer's house, and to the rear and right of Reynolds, where I had ordered him as a reserve, the enemy assaulted first Johnson and then Baird in a most furious manner, producing some confusion, but order was soon restored, and the enemy repulsed in fine style; after which these two divisions took up the positions assigned them for the night.

Before adjusting the line satisfactorily, I received an order to report to department headquarters immediately, and was absent from my command until near midnight. After my return . . . about 2 a.m. on the 20th, I received a report from General Baird that the left of his division did not rest on the Reed's Bridge road, as I had intended, and that he could not reach it without weakening his line too much. I immediately addressed a note to the general commanding requesting that General Negley be sent me to take position on Baird's left and rear, and thus secure our left from assault. During the night the troops threw up temporary breastworks of logs, and prepared for the encounter which all anticipated would come off the next day. [*O.R.*, XXX, Part I, pp. 250–251.]

BRAGG PLANS TO RENEW THE ASSAULT
September 20, 1863

Report of General Braxton Bragg, CSA, Commanding
Army of Tennessee (Continued)

Night found us masters of the ground, after a series of very obstinate contests with largely superior numbers. From captured prisoners and others we learned with certainty that we had encountered the enemy's whole force, which had been moving day and night since they first ascertained the direction of our march. Orders had been given for the rapid march to the field of all re-enforcements arriving by railroad, and three additional brigades from this source joined us early next morning. The remaining forces on our extreme left, east of the Chickamauga, had been ordered up early in the afternoon, but reached the field too late to participate in the engagement of that day. They were ordered into line on their arrival, and disposed for a renewal of the action early the next morning.

Information was received from *Lieutenant-General Longstreet* of his arrival at Ringgold and departure for the field. Five small brigades of his corps (about 5,000 effective infantry, no artillery) reached us in time to participate in the action, three of them on the 19th and two more on the 20th.

Upon the close of the engagement on the evening of the 19th, the proper commanders were summoned to my camp fire, and there received specific information and instructions touching the dispositions of the troops and for the operations of the next morning. The whole force was divided for the next morning into two commands and assigned to the two senior lieutenant-generals, *Longstreet* and *Polk* – the former to the left, where all his own troops were stationed, the latter continuing his command of the right. *Lieutenant-General Longstreet* reached my headquarters about 11 p.m., and immediately received his instructions. After a few hours' rest at my camp fire he moved at daylight to his line, just in front of my position.

Lieutenant-General Polk was ordered to assail the enemy on our extreme right at day-dawn on the 20th, and to take up the attack in succession rapidly to the left. The left wing was to await the attack by the right, take it up promptly when made, and the whole line was then to be pushed vigorously and persistently against the enemy throughout its extent.

Before . . . dawn . . . myself and staff were ready for the saddle, occupying a position immediately in rear of and accessible to all parts of the line. With increasing anxiety and disappointment I waited until after sunrise without hearing a gun, and at length dispatched a staff officer to *Lieutenant-General Polk* to ascertain the cause of the delay and urge him to a prompt and speedy movement. This officer, not finding the general with his troops, and learning where he had spent the night, proceeded across Alexander's Bridge to the east side of the Chickamauga and there delivered my message.

Proceeding in person to the right wing, I found the troops not even prepared for the movement. Messengers were immediately dispatched for *Lieutenant-General Polk*, and he shortly after joined me. My orders were renewed, and the general was urged to their prompt execution, the more important as the ear was saluted throughout the night with the sounds of the ax and falling timber as the enemy industriously labored to strengthen his position by hastily constructed barricades and breastworks. A reconnaissance made in the front of our extreme right during this delay crossed the main road to Chattanooga and proved the important fact that this greatly desired position was open to our possession.

The reasons assigned for this unfortunate delay by the wing commander . . . . are entirely unsatisfactory. It also appears from . . . reports that when the action was opened on the right about 10 a.m. the troops were moved to the assault in detail, and by detachments, unsupported, until nearly all parts of the right wing were in turn repulsed with heavy losses. [*O.R.*, XXX, Part II, pp. 32–33.]

Lieut. Gen. L. Polk, CSA, to Lieut. Col. George
William Brent, CSA, Assistant Adjutant-General,
Army of Tennessee, September 28, 1863

After leaving army headquarters on the night of the 19th, where I received a verbal order to attack the enemy at daylight, I rode immediately to my headquarters, beyond Alexander's Bridge, where I arrived 11 p.m.

On the way, accompanied by *General Breckenridge*, I met with a staff officer of *Lieutenant-General Hill*, to whom I communicated my orders, and from whom I learned that *General Hill's* headquarters were at Thedford's Ford. I asked him to say to *General Hill* that my headquarters were beyond and near to Alexander's Bridge, and that I desired to see him there. On arriving at my headquarters, I issued orders, dated 11:30 [o'clock], to *Lieutenant-General Hill* and *Major-General Cheatham* to attack the enemy simultaneously at daylight, *General Walker's* division being held in reserve.

I also posted two couriers at the bridge to keep up fires and inform persons where my headquarters were. My orders were sent by couriers to the headquarters of the respective generals—*General Hill's* to Thedford's Ford. The couriers to *Generals Cheatham* and *Walker* returned promptly. The courier sent to *General Hill,* after searching for the general through the night, returned about daylight, saying that he could not find him. *General Hill* did not make his appearance at my headquarters.

Hearing nothing of the attack, and not knowing where to find *General Hill,* I sent staff officers in haste directly to *Generals Breckinridge* and *Cleburne,* with information that *General Hill* could not be found, and with orders to make the attack at once, and rode myself to the front. Shortly afterward I received, in reply to these orders, a communication from *General Hill* stating that his divisions were getting their rations and would not be ready to move for an hour or more, and also reporting that *Breckinridge's* wagons had been lost between Thedford's Ford and the battle-field.

On reaching *General Hill's* line, I saw *General Cleburne,* of *General Hill's* corps, and asked if he had received my order to attack. He said he had received it in the presence of *General Hill.* I found also that *General Hill* had delayed his attack in consequence of a misapprehension on his part as to the relation between his line and that of *General Cheatham,* he supposing that *Cheatham's* line was formed . . . on his left at nearly a right angle to his own. In this he was mistaken. . . . *General Hill* mistook the line of one of *Cheatham's* reserve brigades *(Jackson's)* for that of his front line.

The order to attack was then repeated and executed. [*O.R.*, XXX, Part II, p. 47.]

STOP 11, POSITION A—BRECKINRIDGE BEGINS THE ATTACK

Walk back across **ALEXANDER BRIDGE ROAD** to the woodline just beyond. Turn to face the parking area. The night action mentioned in the following reports took place in the woods some distance to the left of this position. *Breckinridge's* attack the next morning hit the Union line here.

Report of Lieut. Gen. Daniel H. Hill, CSA, Commanding Corps, Army of Tennessee

In the afternoon [of September 19] I received an order to report in person to the commanding general at Thedford's Ford, and to hurry forward *Cleburne's* division to the same point. . . . I found upon reporting . . . that while our troops had been moving up the Chickamauga, the Yankees had been moving down, and thus outflanked us and had driven back our right wing. *Cleburne* was ordered to take position on the extreme right and begin an attack. We did not get into position until after sundown, but then advanced in magnificent style, driving the Yankees back some three-fourths of a mile. . . . The action closed between 9 and 10 at night. Farther pursuit in the darkness was not thought advisable.

After readjusting our line (considerably deranged by the fight), and conferring with *General Cleburne,* and each of the brigade commanders individually, I left at 11 o'clock to find *General Bragg* at Thedford's Ford, where the orders for the day stated that his headquarters would be. It was near 5 miles to the ford, but as I had no orders for the next day, I deemed it necessary to find the commanding general. . . . About midnight *Lieutenant-Colonel Anderson,* adjutant-general, reported that my corps had been placed under command of *Lieutenant-General Polk* as wing commander, and that the general wished to see me that night at Alexander's Bridge, 3 miles distant. I was much exhausted, having been in the saddle from dawn till midnight, and therefore resolved to rest until 3 o'clock. . . .

At 7:25 a.m. an order was shown me (just received) from *Lieutenant-General Polk* and addressed to my division commanders, and directing them to advance at once upon the enemy. . . . At 8 o'clock *General Bragg* himself came on the field, and I then learned for the first time that an attack had been ordered at daylight. However, the essential preparations for battle had not been made up to this hour. . . . The position of the Yankees had not been reconnoitered. Our own line of battle had not been adjusted, and part of it was at right angles to the rest. There was no cavalry on our flanks, and no orders had fixed the strength or position of the reserves. . . .

About 8:30 a.m. a report came from the extreme right that a line of the Yankees was extending across the Reed's Bridge road, and

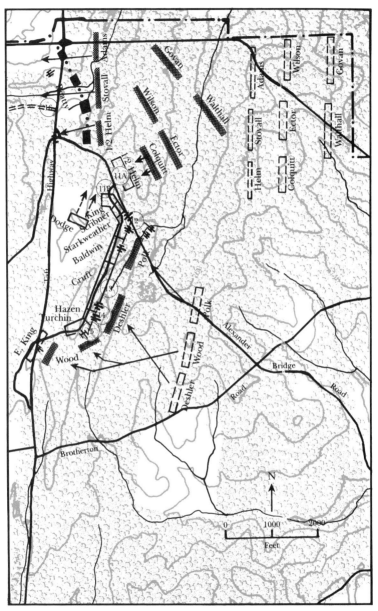

Stops 11A, 11B, 12, 13, 14, 15, & 16
Situation Morning
September 20, 1863

nearly at right angles to our line. *General Adams* was directed to push back their line of skirmishers. This was handsomely done, and a personal reconnaissance made with *Generals Forrest* and *Adams* proved that our line extended beyond that of the Yankees, and that their flank was covered for a great distance by infantry skirmishers, and that no cavalry was visible. During the fight of the night before I had discovered the practicability of outflanking the Yankees, and had placed *Breckinridge* on the right of *Cleburne*, so that he might turn the log breastworks which the Yankees could be heard working at from the close of the action until after daylight.

My corps was now the extreme right of our infantry force. *General Forrest* had brought up his cavalry to guard our flank, and had dismounted a portion of it to act as sharpshooters. A general advance was ordered. As the right was to begin the action, *Cleburne* was directed to dress by *Breckinridge*.

As soon as the movement began, a staff officer was sent to *Lieutenant-General Polk*, with a note reminding him that the corps was in single line without reserves, and if broken at one point was broken at all points.

Breckinridge advanced at 9:30 a.m., with *Adams'* brigade on the right, *Stovall's* in the center; and *Helm's* on the left. The Yankee skirmishers were driven rapidly, and within about 700 yards the left portion of the breastworks were encountered by *General Helm*. [O.R., XXX, Part II, pp. 140–142.]

Report of Maj. Gen. John C. Breckinridge, CSA, Commanding Division, Hill's Corps, Army of Tennessee

During the night *General Polk* informed me that I was to prolong the line of battle upon the right of *Major-General Cleburne*. . . . My division reached *Cleburne's* right a little after daybreak. Upon the readjustment of his line, I formed on his right and became the extreme right of the general line of battle. *Helm* was on the left of my line, *Stovall* in the center, and *Adams* on the right . . . extending across a country road leading from Reed's Bridge and striking the Chattanooga road at . . . Glenn's farm [site of the modern Visitor Center]. The country was wooded with small openings, and the ground unknown to me. Our skirmishers, a few hundred yards in advance, confronted those of the enemy. . . .

Soon after sunrise I received a note from *Lieutenant-General Polk* directing me to advance, and about the same time *Major-General*

Cleburne, who happened to be with me, received one of the same tenor. *Lieutenant-General Hill* having arrived, the notes were placed in his hands. By his order the movement was delayed for the troops to get their rations, and on other accounts. . . .

At 9:30 a.m., by order of *Lieutenant-General Hill,* I moved my division forward in search of the enemy. At the distance of 700 yards we came upon him in force, and the battle was opened by *Helm's* brigade with great fury. The Second and Ninth Kentucky, with three companies of the Forty-first Alabama, encountered the left of a line of breastworks before reaching the Chattanooga road and, though assailing them with great courage, were compelled to pause. . . .

The line on my left had not advanced simultaneously with my division, and in consequence, from the form of the enemy's works, these brave troops were, in addition to the fire in front, subjected to a severe enfilading fire from the left. Twice they renewed the assault with the utmost resolution, but were too weak to storm the position.

The rest of *Helm's* brigade, in whose front there were no works, after a short but sharp engagement, routed a line of the enemy, pursued it across the Chattanooga road, and captured a section of artillery posted in the center of the road. This portion of the brigade was now brought under a heavy front and enfilading fire, and being separated from its left and without support, I ordered *Col. Joseph H. Lewis,* of the Sixth Kentucky, who succeeded to the command upon the fall of *General Helm,* to withdraw the troops some 200 yards to the rear, reunite the brigade, and change his front slightly to meet the new order of things by throwing forward his right and retiring his left. The movement was made without panic or confusion.

This was one of the bloodiest encounters of the day. Here *General Helm,* ever ready for action, and endeared to his command by his many virtues, received a mortal wound. . . . In the meantime . . . *Adams* and *Stovall* [farther to the right] advanced steadily, driving back two lines of skirmishers. *Stovall* halted at the Chattanooga road. *Adams,* after dispersing a regiment and capturing a battery, crossed the road at Glenn's farm and halted a short distance beyond in an open field. [*O.R.,* XXX, Part II, pp. 198–199.]

You are in the center of *Helm's* battle line. The left flank was about 200 yards to your left, the right flank a similar distance on your right. You will find low stone monuments to the Kentucky regiments just inside the woods along this 400 yard trace.

*Report of Col. Joseph H. Lewis, CSA, Sixth Kentucky
Infantry, Commanding Helm's Brigade, Breckinridge's
Division, Army of Tennessee*

Between 9 and 10 a.m. the brigade advanced in the following order, viz, the Sixth Kentucky . . . and the Second Kentucky, on the extreme right and left respectively; the Fourth Kentucky . . . and Ninth Kentucky . . . on the right and left center, respectively, and the Forty-first Alabama . . . in the center.

The enemy's fortifications did not extend the entire length of the brigade front; but the Sixth, Fourth, and seven companies of the Forty-first in advancing passed to the right and clear of them, consequently fighting the foe on something like equal terms. This portion of the command, with but a momentary halt and no hesitation, steadily drove the enemy back to within 100 yards of the Chattanooga road, where I discovered a battery of two Napoleon guns 50 yards beyond the road. Here I also discovered for the first time what the thicker growth of timber had prevented me from before observing, that the left of the brigade was considerably in rear. Neither a halt nor retreat at this juncture was, in my judgment, proper or allowable; so the command was given to take the battery, and it was done.

Soon after crossing the road, *Captain McCawley*, of *Brigadier-General Helm's* staff, informed me that the general had been mortally wounded near the position occupied by the left of the brigade.

The right not then being under fire, I left it in command of *Lieutenant-Colonel Cofer*, and started on *Captain McCawley's* horse to where the other portion of the brigade was. I encountered considerable difficulty in reuniting the brigade on account of the distance apart and the want of staff aid. . . .

After advancing about 400 yards [the left of the brigade] . . . encountered a heavy musketry and artillery fire in front, and also an enfilading fire from the left, which the failure of the command on their left to advance stimultaneously with *Breckinridge's* division enabled the enemy to pour into their ranks. Besides, I am satisfied they were subjected to a fire on their right from the two pieces subsequently captured by the right of the brigade; yet three several times this devoted little band charged the enemy, securely fortified and in a favorable position. Though necessarily repulsed, their frightful loss shows their constancy and bravery. . . .

As soon as I ascertained the exact position of the left, I caused it to be moved by the right flank to the right and in advance of where it then was till the right of the brigade . . . was met . . . when I formed the brigade in line of battle nearly perpendicular to the road and to the enemy's works. About this time I received orders from *Lieutenant-General Hill*, through one of his staff, not to advance, but to await the arrival of fresh troops.

In a short time *Gist's* brigade attacked the enemy, passing through my lines for that purpose, but was driven back. *Ector's* brigade then advanced, but being unable to drive the enemy from his works, finally fell back, leaving this brigade again to confront the enemy. My men, though at this time nearly exhausted by several hours' fighting, and suffering greatly for water, remained firm, no one leaving his place. After the repulse of the other two brigades, I was ordered to retire several hundred yards to the rear for the purpose of resting the men, which was done in good order and without confusion.

Late in the afternoon *Walker's* division advanced against the enemy, a portion of it attacking the same point the left of his brigade did in the morning. Being with my command about 400 yards in rear at that time, and out of sight of the combatants, I could not see with what result the attack was made, though a short time thereafter *Cheatham's* division moved to the attack over the same ground, *Wright's* brigade, of that division, passing through the lines of this brigade.

After some time had elapsed . . . this brigade was moved forward, being on the left of the division. In advancing it was discovered that the center brigade of the division lapped on mine, making it necessary for me to oblique to the left at least 200 yards. It was also necessary to advance the left more rapidly than the right wing, in order to get on a line parallel with the enemy. Both these difficult movements were executed while marching through the woods without any material derangement of the line. . . .

Upon arriving in sight of the enemy's fortifications, the brigade rapidly charged upon them, driving them from their stronghold in confusion toward the Chattanooga road. The pursuit was continued across an open field till the road was reached, when, it being dark, I judged it prudent to halt, which met the approval of *Lieutenant-General Hill*, who, close after us, immediately came up. In passing through the fortifications a considerable number of prisoners were captured. . . . We also captured 2 pieces of artillery in the road. . . . [*O.R.*, XXX, Part II, pp. 203–205.] [*Brig. Gen. Helm*, who met his death in this action, was President Abraham Lincoln's brother-in-law.]

Major General William H. T. Walker's Corps, which had been held in reserve by *Polk* until mid-morning, was now sent forward to support *Hill*. The manner in which this corps was committed is a classic example of how combat power can be frittered away when a reserve is committed piece-meal.

Report of Brig. Gen. States Rights Gist, CSA, Commanding Walker's Division, Walker's Corps, Army of Tennessee

I was ordered by a staff officer of the general commanding to move forward, reporting to *Lieutenant-General Polk*, and join *Major-General Walker's* corps. . . . Upon reporting my command (at this time numbering only 980 . . .) I was ordered by *Major-General Walker* to at once assume command of the division, consisting of *Brigadier-General Ector's, Colonel Wilson's*, and my own brigade, the brigades of *Ector* and *Wilson*, numbering about 500 each, having suffered heavy losses in the engagement on the previous day.

Lieutenant General D. H. Hill was present when I reported to *Generals Polk* and *Walker*, and as I was turning off to assume command of the division [he] requested *Major-General Walker* to send a brigade to the support of *Major-General Breckinridge's* division, which was hotly engaged in our front and upon our left. *Major-General Walker* indicated one of *General Liddell's* brigades, near by. *General Hill* asked for *Gist's* brigade. . . . *General Walker* remarked that "*Gist's* brigade is just coming up," and directed me to report to *General Hill*. I did so. The brigade being now under the command of *Col. P. H. Colquitt*, of the Forty-sixth Georgia Volunteers, he at once reported and received his instructions from *General Hill*.

General Walker then directed me to report the other two brigades also to *General Hill*, which was promptly done. *Colonel Colquitt*, having his instructions from *General Hill*, advanced his command in the direction indicated, being cautioned that he was to support *General Breckinridge*, two of whose brigades were reported in his immediate front. I was afterward directed by *General Hill* to follow up and support the advance of the First Brigade with the brigades of *Ector* and *Wilson*.

Colonel Colquitt, upon advancing a few hundred yards in the woods before him, found himself in the presence of the enemy, strongly posted and massed behind a breastwork of logs, the troops reported in his front having retired before the galling fire of the enemy. The direction taken by *Colonel Colquitt* was too far to the right, and the left regiment (Twenty-fourth South Carolina Volunteers) only came directly upon the enemy's lines, which were so disposed by a salient as to rake the entire front of the brigade as it came forward with a severe and destructive enfilading fire.

The brigade could not have changed direction, as the position of the enemy was not discovered by *Colonial Colquitt* until the left was within a short distance of the breastworks. The right, however, changed front sufficiently to become directly engaged. *Colonel Colquitt* did not reconnoiter the position, as he was instructed that our troops were in his front.

The enemy now poured forth a most destructive and well-aimed fire upon the entire line, and though it wavered and recoiled under the shock, yet, by the exertions of the gallant *Colquitt* . . . order was promptly restored, and for some twenty-five minutes the terrific fire was withstood and returned with marked effect by the gallant little band.

It was here that the lamented *Colquitt* fell mortally wounded while cheering on his command. . . . One-third of the gallant command was either killed or wounded. Reeling under the storm of bullets, having lost all but 2 of their field officers, the brigade fell back fighting to the position from which they advanced. [*O.R.*, XXX, Part II, pp. 245–246.]

Report of Brig. Gen. St. John R. Liddell, CSA, Commanding Division, Walker's Corps, Army of Tennessee (Continued)

About 6 o'clock [a.m.], in obedience to orders . . . I moved my command, with *General Ector's* brigade, about 1½ miles to the right on the prolongation and in support of *General Breckinridge's* right. After arriving there I was ordered to move forward to the attack in place of *General Breckinridge's* division, which had been repulsed in its attack on the enemy's left flank and rear. Here, at the order of *Lieutenant-General Polk*, *General Walthall's* brigade was detached from me and moved to the left of *General Gist's* brigade, which was then making a direct attack on the left of the enemy's line near his breastworks. At the same time an order was given me by *General Hill* to take *Colonel Govan's* brigade and move on the Chattanooga road and engage the enemy in his rear. This was about 11 o'clock.

After moving forward a short distance I ordered *Colonel Govan* to change direction to the left, which he did, finding the enemy in some woods after passing a small field, and pushing him back to the open ground in rear of the left of his fortifications. This was about half a mile in advance of *Gist's* brigade, and on the Chattanooga road, cut off from all connection with any of our forces. [*O.R.*, XXX, Part II, pp. 252–253.]

Major General Walker understood the consequences of dispersion. His division commanders "received their orders direct from *General Hill,*" while his own Reserve Corps, "being thus disposed of, brigades being sent in to take the places of divisions," was frittered away. "My only occupation," he commented in his official *Report*, "was to help form the detached portions of my command as they came out from a position I felt certain they would have to leave when they were sent in." [*O.R.*, XXX, Part II, p. 241.]

Return to your car and then face back toward the wood line at Position A.

POSITION B – THE UNION LEFT HOLDS

You are standing at the northern point of Thomas' defensive position where Brig. Gen. John H. King's brigade refused its left continuing the Union line a short distance west toward the La Fayette Road.

From your location the battle line ran generally south for approximately 1100 yards, turned southwest for 300 yards, crossed the La Fayette Road, and then continued south, about 100 yards west of the La Fayette Road, for another 1700 yards. Here the line again turned southwest for another 1100 yards (passing the Wilder Tower) to the position of the right flank Union unit – Wilder's brigade.

Report of Brig. Gen. Absalom Baird, USA, Commanding First division, XIV Corps, Army of the Cumberland (Continued)

At 3 o'clock on the morning of the 20th, I put my men in position, ready to meet the enemy. We were posted upon a wooded ridge running parallel to the State road, and about one-fourth of a mile to the east of it. An open field extending along the east side of the road, from near one-fourth of a mile south of McDonald's to a point beyond Kelly's, lay a short distance in our rear. The rest of the country as far as the Chickamauga, in all directions, was thickly wooded.

My division was posted around the northeast corner of the field, but about 150 yards in advance of it, in the woods. General Johnson's division was on my right, and beyond him, I think, General Palmer's. My Second Brigade, Brigadier-General Starkweather, was placed next to Johnson, facing to the east, with four guns in position, so as to enfilade our front, besides having a direct fire. The First Brigade, Colonel Scribner, was upon the turn, a portion of his force facing in the same direction as Starkweather, and the rest sloping to the rear, so as to face partially to the north. The Third Brigade, Brigadier-General [John] King, was upon the left of Scribner. When the line was established there was no force whatever upon King's left, and no natural obstruction, and I was compelled thus to refuse or *en échelon* that flank in order to cover it.

I formed my men generally in two lines; King's brigade was even more concentrated, and I used only the four pieces of artillery of General Starkweather; the rest, much of it disabled, indeed, was held in reserve in rear.

About 7 o'clock General Beatty's brigade, four regiments, of Negley's division, came up and formed line on the north side of the field, and then passed into the woods, where I had his right joined on to King's left; but subsequent orders caused him to move farther to the left, and, as he informs me, he posted one of his regiments on the west of the State road, looking toward McDonald's, and the other three on the east in line with it, and all looking toward the north. This arrangement gave General Beatty a long, thin line, easily brushed away, and at the same time left an important gap between him and King. To fill this gap I had no troops, but finally I induced a regiment—perhaps the Seventy-ninth Indiana—coming to this quarter with only general instructions, to move into it. . . . During the interval between daylight and the first attack our men worked vigorously and covered themselves with a hastily constructed breastwork of logs and rails, which proved of vast service to them during the day. [*O.R.*, XXX, Part I, p. 277.]

According to William F. G. Shanks, war correspondent of the *New York Herald*, "General Thomas had wisely taken the precaution to make rude works about breast-high along his whole front, using rails and logs for the purpose. The logs and rails ran at right angles to each other, the logs keeping parallel to the proposed line of battle and lying upon the rails until the proper height was reached. The spaces between these logs were filled with rails, which served to add to their security and strength. The spade had not been used." [Robert Underwood Johnson and Clarence Clough Buel, *Battles and Leaders of the Civil War* (4 vols., New York: *The Century Magazine*, 1888), Vol. IV, p. 654.]

Report of Brig. Gen. Absalom Baird (Continued)

The battle began upon my front at about 8:30 a.m. Previous to this there had been some sharp skirmishing along the front, and our skirmishers were at times compelled to fall back, but as often returned to their original position, and continued throughout the day to reform their first line whenever the assaults of the enemy were repulsed. It was also reported to me that distinct words of command were heard by our advanced pickets, as in the formation of bodies of rebel troops, both upon our front and flank, and we awaited their attack, quietly working upon our defenses.

At about 9 o'clock the enemy, in force, advanced upon us through the woods, and attempted, by throwing strong bodies of infantry upon King and Scribner on the left, while they likewise assailed Starkweather furiously in front, to crush that portion of our line. . . . This attack continued about an hour, during which repeated efforts were made to dislodge us from our position, but in vain. The battle-flags of the rebel generals, borne with the lines of troops, approached quite close to our position, but each time those lines exposed themselves they were broken and driven back. When they withdrew, our skirmishers were thrown to the front and took many prisoners, by whom we were informed that it was the division of *Breckinridge* which we had been fighting, together with troops from Virginia.

An interval of about an hour now elapsed, during which there was but little fighting upon our portion of the line. Warned, however, by the previous attack, of the vulnerability of my left, I strove to obtain forces to secure it. There were regiments lying in reserve in rear of General Johnson's division . . . which I thought might be of more service on the left. I went to their commanders, and explaining to them the danger of an attack from that quarter . . . I asked them to keep a lookout in that direction, and, should the regiments on the left seem to waver, to rush to their assistance. As all had different orders, I received no satisfactory reply. I then went to General Johnson and got him to visit with me the left of his own line, where I . . . asked him to take his left regiment of the second line and place it in column in rear, so as to be ready to move to whatever point should require it the most.

While speaking of this matter the attack came . . . and was made with large force and great impetuosity. General Beatty's line was cut in two in the middle. . . . My own left was also forced back, and our line seemed ready to crumble away on this flank. The rebels were already in the field behind us, and the column which had forced Beatty's center was pushing down the road toward Kelly's house. I immediately caused the second line to rise and face about, and then to wheel forward toward the right. . . . The unexpected direction of the attack, the facing to the rear, and the crowd of our retiring troops coming upon them caused some disorder in their line, but, riding to their front with a cheer, two regiments took it up, formed a good line, and advanced gallantly. The rest followed, and the rebels were driven back into the woods. . . .

My line was re-established as it had been in the morning, and was not for some four hours again attacked in force. [*O.R.*, XXX, Part I, pp. 277-278.]

Report of Brig. Gen. John H. King, USA, Commanding Third Brigade, First Division, XIV Corps, Army of the Cumberland (Continued)

At daylight on the 20th my brigade went into position on the left of the First Brigade, First Division, Colonel Scribner commanding. I formed my command in four lines, the First Battalion Eighteenth Infantry, Capt. G. W. Smith commanding, in front, and behind a breastwork of logs 2 feet in height, connecting with Colonel Scribner's. My brigade was thus again on the extreme left.

Between 7 and 8 a.m. I moved Capt. Smith's command forward about 50 paces across an open piece of ground to a ridge skirted by timber; he took the logs forming the breastwork in his front forward, and placed them in front of his new position. The Second Battalion, Eighteenth Infantry, commanded by Capt. Henry Haymond, moved to the ground vacated by the First Battalion. The Fifteenth . . . [and] Nineteenth Infantry . . . were ordered to support the front line, or to wheel to the left in case of an attack on the flank.

About 9 a.m. the enemy drove in my line of skirmishers, and advancing in force, attacked my front and flank. Capt. Haymond was sent forward to support Capt. [G. W.] Smith, and the Fifteenth and

Nineteenth Infantry wheeled to the left; after a contest of about an hour the enemy withdrew. I then relieved the First Battalion Eighteenth Infantry by the Fifteenth Infantry; the Nineteenth Infantry was relieved by a regiment belonging to Colonel Dodge's brigade, this regiment connecting with the left of the Fifteenth Infantry, the remnants of the Eighteenth and Nineteenth Infantry constituting a reserve.

These dispositions were scarcely completed when the enemy again renewed his attack, pouring in a destructive direct and enfilade fire. This attack lasted an hour; the enemy was again repulsed, my command still retaining its original position. [*O.R.*, XXX, Part I, p. 310.]

Report of Capt. Albert B. Dod, USA, Commanding
Fifteenth U.S. Infantry, Third Brigade, First Division,
XIV Corps, Army of the Cumberland

At about half past 8 o'clock, . . . as my battalion was in line of battle, I received orders from Brigadier-General King to change front forward on the left company, and move forward to the support of the Eighteenth U.S. Infantry, who were sorely pressed. This was done while under fire, but before we could engage the enemy they were repulsed. We were left in this position (the extreme left of the division) for about an hour, the Eighteenth having moved to our right and occupied the outermost breastworks. I was then ordered to relieve the Eighteenth in these breastworks, which were only a few logs raised about a foot and a half above the ground, and which were about 100 yards beyond the woods, and while occupying it my left flank was entirely exposed.

I had only occupied this position a few moments when I perceived two regiments of the enemy marching in double-quick time to my left. I waited until they commenced fire and were pouring an enfilading fire down my ranks—which it was impossible for me to return—when I gave the order to rise up, and the battalion marched across the open field to the woods under a terrific fire as steadily and in as good order as if on drill or parade.

Upon arriving in the woods I was met by Captain Forsyth [of General King's staff], who informed me that General Baird ordered those works held at all hazards, and promising that my left should be protected. Again I marched across that field, my left this time supported by a regiment sent out for that purpose by Colonel Dodge.

The enemy made four efforts to take these works, but were each time repulsed with terrible slaughter, the ground in front being literally strewn with their dead and wounded. [*O.R.*, XXX, Part I, p. 316.]

Drive along **BATTLE LINE ROAD** for about 0.1 mile to the monument to the **Fourth Indiana Battery.**

STOP 12 – STARKWEATHER PROVIDES ENFILADING FIRE

Report of Brig. Gen. John C. Starkweather, USA,
Commanding Second Brigade, First Division, XIV Corps,
Army of the Cumberland

The command was moved by order of the general commanding, at 3 a.m. on the 20th, taking position on a ridge; formed in two lines, with two guns in the center of the two lines and two guns upon the left, my right resting upon General Johnson's division and my left upon the right of the First Brigade. I immediately commenced felling trees, and formed two barricades, one to the front of my first line and one to the front of my second line. This first line so formed was supported by a second line, and to my right and rear was the Fifth Indiana Battery, covering with their fire to the front the point where my right rested on General Johnson's left. Skirmishers from my lines were kept continually to the front, retaking again and again their positions when driven to the breastworks, holding their positions faithfully and well until the whole line retired at night. This position was held and retained during the whole day under repeated attacks from the enemy in heavy columns supported with batteries, repulsing and driving the enemy back from time to time; driving the enemy also back from the extreme left with my artillery, thus supporting the left with my battery and portions of my command thrown into position for that purpose, until peremptory orders were received through Captain Cary, one of the general's staff, that I should fall back as well as possible from my position.

While holding this position the ammunition of my first line was expended, and most of that of the second line, together with all the ammunition of the battery except 3 rounds of canister. While working the battery at this point my guns, caissons, and limbers from time to time were made unserviceable from the shot and shell of the enemy's batteries, and from the fire of his infantry; so that I retired guns, limbers, and caissons when necessary, refitting and replacing those portions thereof damaged from the two guns left unused, so keeping four guns in continuous operation.

When ordered to retire, I instructed the two rear regiments to fall back upon the second line together with the battery; and when such was accomplished, for the first line to retire upon the second, which had been retired, not knowing that the Fifth Indiana Battery, together with the second line, was also being retired. When the movement was made, the enemy opened upon my position three batteries with grape and canister. On reaching the second line, and finding the troops retiring and retired, with the battery gone, the enemy charging my front line with the bayonet, supported by their batteries, the troops gave way and a portion only rallied at the point where General Willich's command rested near sunset. . . . [*O.R.*, XXX, Part I, p. 301.]

If you look back toward Stop 12 you will gain an appreciation of the ability of the artillery and the regiments composing the left of Starkweather's brigade to provide enfilading fire into the ranks of any force attacking the other two brigades of the division. Note, too, that the right of this position was able to enfilade any force attacking units located to the south.

Continue to drive south along Battle Line Road for 0.3 mile and park in the vicinity of the monument to Battery B, First Ohio Artillery.

STOP 13 – CLEBURNE JOINS THE ATTACK

You are now in the center of the position occupied by Major General John M. Palmer's Second Division, XXI Corps. Palmer's division had been attached to XIV Corps to assist in the defense of this area. Two brigades were deployed on line. Colonel William Grose's Third Brigade was being held in Kelly field.

To the north of your location was Brigadier General Charles Cruft's First Brigade, and to Cruft's left was the Third Brigade of Brigadier General Richard W. Johnson's Second Division, XX Corps, which was also attached to XIV Corps. This brigade joined with the right of Starkweather's brigade in the salient.

To your south was the Second Brigade of Palmer's division. Southeast of this location was the Confederate division of *Major General Patrick R. Cleburne,* which had fought the night action the previous evening described in *D. H. Hill's* report and now was ordered to assault this position in support of *Breckinridge's* attack. Because night actions were rare during the Civil War, Cleburne's report begins on the evening of the 19th.

Report of Maj. Gen. Patrick R. Cleburne, CSA, Commanding Division, Hill's Corps, Army of Tennessee

During the afternoon of . . . the 19th . . . I moved my division in a westerly direction across the Chickamauga River . . . and was directed . . . to form a second line in rear of the right of the line already in position. Accordingly, soon after sunset my division was formed partially *en échelon* about 300 yards in rear of the right of the first line. My right rested in front of a steam saw-mill, known as Jay's Mill, situated on a small stream running between the Chickamauga and the road leading from Chattanooga to La Fayette. My line extended from the saw-mill almost due south for nearly a mile, fronting to the west. *Polk's* brigade, with *Calvert's* battery . . . composed my right wing; *Wood's* brigade, with *Semple's* battery, my center, and *Deshler's* brigade, with *Douglas'* battery, my left wing.

I now received orders from *Lieutenant-General Hill* to advance (passing over the line which had been repulsed) and drive back the enemy's left wing. In my front were open woods, with the exception of a clearing (fenced in) in front of my center, the ground sloping upward as we advanced. Ordering the brigades to direct themselves by *Wood's* (the center) brigade and preserve brigade distance, I moved forward, passing over the first line, and was in a few moments heavily engaged along my right and center. The enemy, posted behind hastily constructed breastworks, opened a heavy fire of both small-arms and artillery.

For half an hour the firing was the heaviest I had ever heard. It was dark, however, and accurate shooting was impossible. Each party was aiming at the flashes of the other guns, and few of the shot from either side took effect. *Major Hotchkiss,* my chief of artillery, placed *Polk's* and *Wood's* artillery in position in the cleared field in front of my center. Availing themselves of the noise and the darkness, *Captain Semple* and *Lieutenant Key* ran their batteries forward within 60 yards of the enemy's line and opened a rapid fire. *Polk* pressed forward at the same moment on the right, when the enemy ceased firing and quickly disappeared from my front. There was some confusion at the time, necessarily inseparable, however, from a night attack. This, and the difficulty of moving my artillery through the woods in the dark, rendered a farther advance inexpedient for the night. I consequently halted, and, after readjusting my lines, threw out skirmishers a quarter of a mile in advance and bivouacked. In this conflict the enemy was driven back about a mile and a half. . . .

At about 10 o'clock next morning, I received orders from *Lieutenant-General Hill* to advance and dress on the line of *General Breckinridge*, who had been placed on my right. Accordingly, directing each brigade to dress upon the right and preserve its distance, I moved forward. *Breckinridge* was already in motion. The effort to overtake and dress upon him caused hurry and some confusion in my line, which was necessarily a long one. Before the effects of this could be rectified, *Polk's* brigade and the right of *Wood's* encountered the heaviest artillery fire I have ever experienced.

I was now within short canister range of a line of log breastworks, and a hurricane of shot and shell swept the woods from the unseen enemy in my front. This deadly fire was direct, and came from that part of the enemy's breastworks opposite to my right and right center. The rest of my line, stretching off to the left, received an oblique fire from the line of breastworks, which, at a point opposite my center, formed a retiring angle running off toward the Chattanooga and La Fayette road behind. . . .

Opposite to my right and right center the enemy's works ran about half a mile north and south, and nearly parallel to the Chattanooga and La Fayette road, which was about 300 yards behind . . . at a point opposite my center, his works formed . . . a retiring angle running in a westerly and somewhat oblique direction to the Chattanooga and La Fayette road, and that at a point nearly opposite my right his works formed another retiring angle running back also to the road. My right and right center, consisting of *Polk's* brigade and *Lowrey's* regiment, of *Wood's* brigade, were checked within 175 yards of the advanced part of this portion of the enemy's works, and the rest of the line were halted in compliance with the order previously given to dress upon the right.

Passing toward the left at this time, I found that the line of advance of my division, which was the left of the right wing of the army, converged with the line of advance of the left wing of the army. The flanks of the two wings had already come into collision. Part of *Wood's* brigade had passed over *Bate's* brigade, of *Stewart's* division, which was the right of the left wing, and *Deshler's* brigade, which formed my left, had been thrown out entirely and was in rear of the left wing of the army.

I ordered *Wood* to move forward the remainder of his brigade, opening at the same time in the direction of the enemy's fire with *Semple's* battery. That part of *Wood's* brigade to the left of *Lowrey's* regiment and to the left of the southern angle of the breastworks in its advance at this time entered an old field bordering the (Chattanooga and La Fayette) road and attempted to cross it in the face of heavy fire from works in its front. It had almost reached the road, its left wing being at Poe's house (known as the burning house), when it was driven back by a heavy oblique fire of small-arms and artillery which was opened upon both its flanks, the fire from the right coming from the south face of the breastworks, which was hid from view by the thick growth of scrub-oak bordering the field. Five hundred men were killed and wounded by this fire in a few minutes. Upon this repulse . . . I ordered the brigade still farther back to reform. *Semple's* battery, which had no position, I also ordered back.

I now moved *Deshler's* brigade by the right flank, with the intention of connecting it with *Polk's* left, so filling the gap left in my center by the withdrawal of *Wood.* This connection, however, I could not establish, as *Polk's* left had in its turn been also driven back. Finding it a useless sacrifice of life for *Polk* to retain his position, I ordered him to fall back with the rest of his line, and with his and *Wood's* brigades I took up a strong defensive position some 300 or 400 yards in rear of the point from which they had been repulsed.

Dreshler's brigade had moved forward toward the right of the enemy's advanced works, but could not go beyond the crest of a low ridge from which *Lowrey* had been repulsed. I therefore ordered him to cover himself behind the ridge and hold his position as long as possible. . . . In effecting this last disposition of his command, *General Deshler* fell, a shell passing fairly through his chest. [*O.R.*, XXX, Part II, pp. 153–156.]

Report of Brig. Gen. Lucius E. Polk, CSA, Commanding Brigade, Cleburne's Division, Army of Tennessee

My brigade was . . . ordered forward, commencing to move about 9 o'clock, *General Breckinridge* having placed his line upon the prolongation of my right, with two batteries of artillery between the right of my brigade and the left of his division. Owing to some mistake, I did not receive the order to advance until a few moments after *General Breckinridge's* division had been put in motion.

Immediately upon the order being received, I moved my brigade

forward, obliquing slightly to the right, so as to keep my right connected with *General Breckinridge's* left. The enemy's fortifications running off at right angles to the rear of their lines opposite the right of
my brigade, I was not able to recover my immediate connection with
his left before I encountered the enemy strongly posted in a strong
line of fortifications on the crest of a hill.

My line from right to left soon became furiously engaged, the
enemy pouring a most destructive fire of canister and musketry into
my advancing line—so terrible, indeed, that my line could not advance in the face of it, but lying down, partially protected by the crest
of a hill, we continued the fight some hour and a half. *Wood's* brigade
not promptly supporting me upon the left, it was impossible to
charge their breastworks. My ammunition becoming exhausted, by
orders I fell back some 400 yards, leaving a line of skirmishers in my
front to oppose the advance of the enemy until my ammunition
could be replenished. . . . I remained in this position some hours.

In this engagement my loss was very great, amounting to some
350. [*O.R.*, XXX, Part II, pp. 176–177.]

Report of Col. J. A. Smith, CSA, Commanding Third and Fifth Confederate Infantry, Polk's Brigade, Cleburne's Division, Army of Tennessee

When the attack was renewed we met the enemy at his works,
which were located on the crest of a rise that commanded the space
in front of it. The strife at this point was fearful. Such showers of
grape, canister, and small-arms I have never before witnessed. We
remained here until our supply of ammunition was exhausted without losing or gaining ground. Through the misapprehension of an
order, or from some other cause unknown to me, the right of my
regiment gave way, and it was with some difficulty that order was
restored and the line re-established. Failing as we did to drive the
enemy from his position, and our ammunition being exhausted,
we were ordered by *Brigadier-General Polk* to fall back. [*O.R.*, XXX,
Part II, p. 180.]

Report of Maj. Gen. John M. Palmer, USA, Commanding
Second Division, XXI Corps, Army of the Cumberland
(Continued)

About 8 o'clock [on the evening of the 19th] I visited department and corps headquarters, and learned that from the difficulties of changing the positions of troops, it was expected, in the anticipated battle of the next day, my command would be subject to the immediate orders of Major-General Thomas. . . .

Early on the 20th, I was directed by Major-General Thomas to form along a ridge running from northeast to southwest and terminating near the Rossville road, closing on the left upon Johnson's division. Intending to avoid what seemed to me the common error of the day before (too extensive lines), Hazen and Cruft were put in positions in two lines, and Grose in double column in reserve. The men hastily constructed barricades of logs, rails, and other materials, and awaited the attack.

The engagement commenced by a furious assault upon the position of Baird on the extreme left, and soon extended along the whole front. This was repulsed with great slaughter.

Then a more persistent attack was made, the chief weight of which fell upon the extreme left; some troops posted there fell back. By order of General Thomas my reserve brigade was moved in that direction, and took part in the obstinate contest there. The enemy were repulsed, but Grose suffered very severely. . . . in that bloody affair.

The positions held by the divisions of Reynolds, Johnson, Baird and my own were frequently assailed during the day, but were maintained firmly by the willing men behind the barricades. A glance at the field along the front proved what these efforts were costing the enemy.

At 2 o'clock unusually heavy firing was heard on the right of our position, which seemed like a determined effort on the part of the enemy to force the center of our line. Hazen was ordered by me to go in that direction. He moved off rapidly in obedience to the order. I heard his volley when he went in, and saw him no more that day. . . .

The remains of Grose's brigade had by this time returned, and now took Hazen's position in the line, but no formidable attempt was made upon us afterward. The enemy's sharpshooters were busy, and killed and wounded several officers, and some of our adventurous men tumbled—some of them from the trees upon which they were perched. [*O.R.*, XXX, Part I, pp. 714–715.]

Report of Brig. Gen. Charles Cruft, USA, Commanding
First Brigade, Second Division, XXI Corps, Army of the
Cumberland (Continued)

By daylight of the morning of 20th, the various regiments of the brigade had constructed rough log breastworks along the front. There were but few tools in the hands of the men, but they worked cheerfully and industriously with what they had, and availed themselves of every device to provide some protection. The ground was favorable for a line. It lay along a crest which fell off gradually to the front for the distance of about good musket range, and then rose up to a corresponding ridge, lower, however, than that which we occupied. A narrow road ran along the crest. . . .

The attack commenced on our front at 7:40 a.m. It was very sharp and determined, and consisted of a series of persistent assaults with musketry and occasional artillery, continuing until about 12 m. Musketry and artillery were required almost constantly along the brigade line, during these four hours, to repel the enemy.

At the commencement of the fight the brigade was disposed in two lines. The Second Kentucky and Thirty-first Indiana comprised the first line, the Ninetieth Ohio and battalion of First Kentucky, the reserve line. . . . The battery was on the right flank. The lines were passed at 11 a.m., and the Ninetieth Ohio and battalion of the First Kentucky became the front line.

This position was held firmly against every attack, and with but few casualties on our side, and apparently with considerable losses on the part of the enemy. So complete was the protection afforded by the rude breastworks which had been constructed, that not an enlisted man was killed while the brigade occupied this position, and but very few wounded. The enemy's sharpshooters constantly fired from trees at long rifle range at officers, and it was exceedingly hazardous for them to move about. One officer was killed and several wounded here during the morning.

At 11:30 a.m. a very severe attack was made on the troops upon our left. Their line curved around toward the Rossville road. The attack seemed to be made at a point about midway between the road and the front of my line. The musketry indicated a heavy engagement, and our lines seemed to give way under it to such a degree as seriously to threaten my left flank and rear. The reserve line of the brigade was faced to the rear, and marched a short distance with change of direction so as to be opposite the line of the enemy's fire, and the battery placed in position to be speedily withdrawn in case we should be flanked. The arrival of re-enforcements, however, soon repelled the attack.

At 12 m. another and apparently more determined attack was made in the same quarter. About 12:30 p.m. the sound indicated heavy work upon the extreme right of our lines. Occasional attacks were made of the skirmish lines in my front from 12 to 2 p.m., but the lines, having been strengthened, were sufficient to resist them successfully.

About 2 p.m. the fighting to the right of our position again became severe. At 2:40 p.m., General Hazen's brigade having been withdrawn from my right, orders were received to occupy the breastworks which had been held by his line. The Thirty-first Indiana and Second Kentucky were taken from my reserve line and thrown into them. At this time the enemy commenced using artillery freely on the position held by the brigade from three directions. Their range, however, was imperfect, and their shells generally passed over the men. [*O.R.*, XXX, Part I, pp. 731–732.]

Drive south about 100 yards to the location of Battery F, First Ohio Artillery. Battery F's position is marked by two cannons and is the approximate center of Hazen's brigade.

STOP 14 – HAZEN DRAWS SOME CONCLUSIONS

Report of Brig. Gen. William B. Hazen, USA, Commanding Second Brigade, Second Division, XXI Corps, Army of the Tennessee (Continued)

On the morning of the 20th, the men were roused at 3 a.m. and directed to make coffee where they had water, and at daybreak a breastwork of logs and rails was commenced. . . . Wherever this work was done, the line remained the entire day with firmness and with little loss.

At about 8 o'clock the attack commenced upon the left of this line and swept along toward the right, arriving at my position about fifteen minutes afterward, passing on but producing no effect until it had passed General Reynolds. This assault was kept up without intermission till about 11 o'clock with a fury never witnessed upon the field either of Shiloh or Stone's River. The repulse was equally terrific and finally complete. A few light attacks upon this front were made from time to time up to 1 p.m., after which everything was comparatively quiet.

The value of this simple breastwork will be understood since my loss behind it this day was only about 13 men during a period of more stubborn fighting than at Shiloh or Stone's River, when the same brigade at each place lost over 400 men. Our left flank was twice turned and partially driven this day, but the enemy was easily checked and our lines speedily restored.

At about 10 a.m. our couriers for ammunition, previously prompt to return, failed to come back, and it soon came to be believed that our trains had been captured. I at once cautioned my colonels, who fired only by volley, not to waste a single round of ammunition, and my battery was similarly cautioned.

During the quiet that afterward settled upon us, several officers were struck by sharpshooters from distant trees. Ascertaining the proper direction, I caused volleys to be fired into the tops of the trees, and thus brought several of them from their hiding places, checking for a time this species of warfare. Skirmishers sent out along this front reported the execution of our arms during this engagement to have been terrible beyond anything seen in this war, as I believe the fighting from 8 to 11 o'clock to have been. . . .

There are several lessons to be learned from this fight, and to me none more plainly than that the iron hand that strikes justly, yet firmly, can alone make the soldiers that can be relied upon in the hour of trial. The effect of firing by volleys upon the enemy has invariably been to check and break him. It further gives a careful colonel complete control of his fire. The effect of sending in fractions to battle with an entire army is to waste our own strength without perceptibly weakening the enemy. [*O.R.*, XXX, Part I, pp. 763–764.]

Continue to the turnout on the left for the Alabama Monument. Stop and dismount.

STOP 15 – TURCHIN'S DEFENSE

You are now in the approximate center of the position occupied by Brigadier General John B. Turchin's Third Brigade of Major General Joseph J. Reynold's Fourth Division, XIV Corps. The left of Turchin's brigade was joined with Hazen's right; from there the position traced generally south to your location, then turned west toward the La Fayette Road. This deployment allowed the right of the brigade to bring flanking fire into the battle line of any unit attacking to the west across Poe Field. There was a small break in the battle line on Turchin's right that was covered by fire. Just across the La Fayette Road Brigadier General Edward King's Second Brigade of Reynold's division assumed responsibility for the defense. East of Battle Line Road is the Alabama Monument. *Brigadier General James Deshler's* brigade and the right regiments of *Brigadier General S. A. M. Wood's* brigade were attacking this sector of the defense.

Report of Brig. Gen. John B. Turchin, USA, Commanding Third Brigade, Fourth Division, XIV Corps, Army of the Cumberland

On the morning of the 20th I was ordered to shift my brigade to the left and move to the front to take the place of General Hazen's brigade, which moved to the left, the Second Brigade taking my place. I had the Thirty-sixth Ohio, Ninety-second Ohio, and a portion of the Eleventh Ohio in the first line, several companies of the latter and the Eighteenth Kentucky Regiment being in the reserve. At about 10 o'clock we were attacked by the enemy, and for about one hour the infantry and the battery kept up a continual fire. The breastworks of rails and timbers protected our men. The enemy suffered severely. At noon and after until 2 o'clock there was a comparative lull in our front, while the battle raged on the right and left of the position of the army.

Receiving orders to change front and to abandon a portion of the fortifications, to complete the line with the Second Brigade [King's], I directed my battery to move back and take place on the left of Captain Harris' battery, of the Second Brigade, and the Thirty-sixth Ohio Regiment to support it, and was preparing to move other regiments when an order came from General Thomas to hold the position. I moved the Thirty-sixth and battery to their original positions, driving the enemy's sharpshooters back. [*O.R.*, XXX, Part I, p. 474.]

Report of Col. Roger Q. Mills, CSA, Tenth Texas Infantry, Commanding Deshler's Brigade, Cleburne's Division, Army of Tennessee

About 9:30 o'clock on the morning of the 20th, we moved off a short distance by the left flank and then advanced to the front, passing through a portion of *Major-General Cheatham's* division. Having gained an open ground several hundred yards in our front, the enemy began, from one or two long-range guns, to shell our line, and as we approached nearer gave us several shots of canister, killing and wounding some 15 or 20 men.

We finally arrived, about 10 a.m., on the ground we were ordered to occupy. We found it being hastily abandoned by the troops who were occupying it before we came. We advanced to the crest of the hill, some 200 yards in front of the enemy's barricades and breastworks, when he opened a destructive fire upon us. We were ordered to lie down and commence firing.

We now began the engagement in earnest, but at great disadvantage. The enemy was behind his defenses and we without cover. He had two batteries of artillery; we had none, our own battery not being able to get a position to give us aid. *Captain Semple's* splendid battery was on the hill with us and on the extreme left of the brigade when we moved up and occupied the hill. It fired a few shots, and was moved to some other portion of the field. The enemy poured on our heads from 10 a.m. to 1:30 or 2 p.m. a constant and terrible fire of artillery and musketry, which we returned with our rifles with the same constancy and stubbornness.

About 12 m. our supply of ammunition began to give out, and I sent a courier to *Brigadier-General Deshler* to inform him of the fact, and to ask where we could get more. A few minutes after I saw him coming toward my right, some 40 paces from me, when he was struck by a shell in the chest and his heart literally torn from his bosom. . . .

A messenger from *Colonel Wilkes'* regiment informed me . . . that *Colonel Wilkes* was wounded and not with the regiment. Just at this critical juncture our ammunition was exhausted, and no one knew where to get more. I assumed command, and supposing that the enemy would advance as soon as the firing ceased, I ordered bayonets fixed and the cartridge boxes of the wounded and dead to be gathered, and one round from them to be given to each man to load his gun with, and hold his fire in reserve to repel an assault.

While this order was being executed *Lieutenant-Colonel Anderson*, who was on the left of my regiment, sent *Lieutenant Graham* to inform me that the four left companies had not been firing. Being at too great a distance from the enemy, he had the good sense to prevent them from wasting their ammunition unnecessarily. I immediately ordered those four companies to the front on the hill, where the fire was hottest, and ordered *Lieutenant-Colonel Anderson* to take command of them, and hold the hill at every hazard till I could get ammunition and have it distributed. I soon procured the ammunition and refilled my cartridge boxes.

At this time one of the major-general's staff came to me and informed me that I was ordered to hold the hill on which the brigade was formed; that I was not permitted to advance, and must not retire if it were possible to hold my position. I therefore moved my command at once some 20 or 30 paces to the rear of the crest and on the side of the hill, for cover, leaving a body of sharpshooters behind trees on the top of the hill to keep up a fire with the enemy. The enemy's fire soon slackened down to a contest between the skirmishers. At the same time he advanced a line of skirmishers toward the open space between my command and *Brigadier-General Polk*, on my right. I soon received information . . . that the enemy was moving around my right flank in force. . . . I immediately ordered *Lieutenant-Colonel Hutchinson* to re-enforce the skirmishers with one company from his regiment, which was promptly done. Still hearing of this flank movement, I ordered *Captain Kennard*, of *Lieutenant-Colonel Anderson's* regiment, to re-enforce the other two companies with his, take command himself of those companies, put his men under good cover, and hold the enemy in check at all hazards. He very promptly moved with his company to the ground, assumed command of the three companies, repulsed the enemy's skirmishers, and held his position without a serious struggle. A straggling fire was kept up between the enemy and my sharpshooters till late in the evening, when the advance of our left wing caused him to abandon his works and take to his heels. . . . I lost in the fight 52 killed and 366 wounded. [*O.R.*, XXX, Part II, pp. 188–191.]

The official reports from both armies give a clear impression of the strength of the Union defensive position on this part of the battlefield. The study of the action here provides a good example of what disciplined troops in a well-constructed position could do. Ultimately the Confederates seized these lines because of successful attacks farther to the south.

Return to your car for the drive to Stop 16.

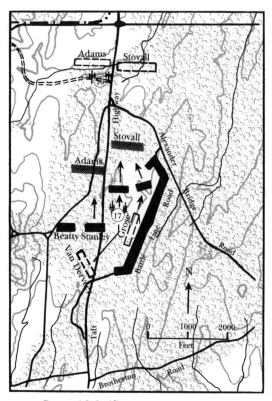

Stops 16 & 17
Situation Late Morning
September 20, 1863

ATTACK AND COUNTERATTACK
IN KELLY FIELD
September 20, 1863

Continue for 0.3 mile to the **LA FAYETTE ROAD** intersection. **TURN RIGHT** and drive 0.9 mile. Just beyond the **ALEXANDER BRIDGE ROAD** intersection, **TURN LEFT** into a small parking lot. Dismount, position yourself among the guns representing *Slocomb's* Louisiana Battery, and face the La Fayette Road.

This road was the Savannah Church Road in 1863. You can still walk along its westward trace.

STOP 16 – BRECKINRIDGE FLANKS THE UNION LEFT

As you drove along the La Fayette Road and by Kelly Field you passed behind the positions of the Union brigades that were defending along what is today called Battle Line Road. King's brigade was initially the left-most Union unit on this position. Eventually Dodge's brigade was deployed to King's left. Both brigades were located in the trees southeast of your present location.

An extension of this line was made at 7 a.m. when Brigadier General John Beatty's First Brigade, Second Division, XIV Corps, formed on the extreme left of the Union position. Beatty's brigade was positioned astride the road facing north near the guns to your right. At 7:30 a.m. Beatty was ordered to move his brigade forward to the vicinity of the McDonald house.

When this move was complete, the four regiments of this brigade were facing generally northeast along an over-extended line that ran from the field across the road, left to the McDonald house, which was approximately where the Visitor Center is today. The monument to the Eighty-eighth Indiana, which was Beatty's left-most regiment, is visible about one-fourth of a mile to your left.

Report of Brig. Gen. John Beatty, USA, Commanding
First Brigade, Second Division, XIV Corps, Army of the
Cumberland

Sunday, September 20, at an early hour in the morning, I was ordered to move northward on the Chattanooga road and report to Major-General Thomas, who, when I reached him, directed me to move to the extreme left of our line, form perpendicularly to the rear of General Baird's division, connecting with his left, and be in readiness to meet any force of the enemy attempting to turn General Baird's left. I disposed my brigade as ordered. General Baird's line appeared to run parallel with the road; mine, running to the rear, crossed the road.

On this road and near it I posted my artillery, and advanced my skirmishers to the open fields in front of the left and center of my line. This was a good position, and my brigade and the one on General Baird's left could have co-operated and assisted each other in maintaining it. Fifteen minutes after this line was formed Captain Gaw, of General Thomas' staff, brought an order to advance my line to a ridge or low hill (McDonald's house) fully one-quarter of a mile distant. I represented to him that my line was long; that in advancing it I would necessarily leave a long interval between my right and General Baird's left, and also that I was already in the position indicated to me by General Thomas. He replied that the order to advance was imperative; that I would be supported by General Negley. I could not urge objections further, and advanced my line as rapidly as possible toward the point indicated.

The Eighty-eighth Indiana . . . on the left moved into position without difficulty. The Forty-second Indiana, . . . on its right, met with considerable opposition in advancing through the woods, but finally reached the ridge. The One hundred and fourth Illinois . . . and the Fifteenth Kentucky . . . on the right, became engaged almost immediately, and being obstinately opposed, advanced slowly. The enemy, in strong force, pressed them heavily in front and on the right flank, preventing them from connecting with the regiments on their left.

At this time I sent an aide to request General Baird or General King to throw in a force to cover the interval between their left and my right, and dispatched Captain Wilson, my assistant adjutant-general, to the rear to hasten forward General Negley to my support. The two regiments forming the right of my brigade were confronted by so large a force that they were compelled to halt, and ultimately to fall back, which they did in good order, contesting the ground stoutly as they retired.

About this time a column of the enemy pressed into the interval between the One hundred and fourth Illinois and Forty-second Indiana and turned, with the evident design of capturing the latter, which was at the time busily engaged with the enemy in front. Immediately on discovering the object of this movement, I got my artillery in position and opened on them with grape and canister. The column . . . broke and fell back under shelter of the woods, in the direction from whence it came. Colonel McIntire [Forty-second Indiana], but a moment before almost surrounded, was thus enabled to fight his way to the left, which he did, uniting at the same time with Colonel Humphrey, Eighty-eighth Indiana.

Soon after the enemy, pressing back the One hundred and fourth Illinois and Fifteenth Kentucky, advanced through the woods to within 100 yards of my battery and poured into it a heavy fire, killing Lieutenant Bishop, and killing or wounding all the men and horses belonging to his section, [located 150 yards to your right, where you see the guns] which, consequently, fell into the hands of the enemy. Captain Bridges and his officers, by the exercise of great coolness and courage under a terrible fire, succeeded in saving the remainder of the battery.

The enemy having gained the woods south of the open fields and west of the road, I opposed his farther advance as well as I could with the Fifteenth Kentucky and One hundred and fourth Illinois, and soon after checked him entirely by directing a battery stationed on the road some distance in the rear to change front and open fire on him.

The Eighty-eighth Indiana and Forty-second Indiana, compelled to make a *détour* round the hills on the left and rear, became separated from me . . . [*O.R.*, XXX, Part I, pp. 367–369.]

Stovall's and *Adams'* brigades, having reached the La Fayette Road, wheeled to their left and commenced an attack south. This attack, supported by the battery where you are, began on a line generally east to west and on line with the supporting artillery. The La Fayette Road was a natural boundary between the two attacking brigades. *Stovall's* brigade was deployed east of the road, while *Adams'* brigade was on the west side. This attack moved from your present position south towards Kelly Field and the left rear of the Union army. You can see the northwest part of Kelly Field in the distance.

Report of Major General John C. Breckinridge, CSA, Commanding Division, Hill's Corps, Army of Tennessee (Continued)

When *Helm's* brigade was checked, and I had given *Colonel Lewis* orders in reference to his new position, I rode to the commands of *Adams* and *Stovall*, on the right. It was now evident, from the comparatively slight resistance they had encountered and the fact that they were not threateneed in front, that our line had extended beyond the enemy's left. I at once ordered these brigades to change front perpendicular to the original line of battle, and with the left of *Adams* and the right of *Stovall* resting on the Chattanooga road to advance upon the flank of the enemy. *Slocomb's* battery, which had previously done good service, was posted on favorable ground on the west of the road to support the movement. [Your present location.]

The brigades advanced in fine order over a field and entered the woods beyond. *Stovall* soon encountered the extreme left of the enemy's works, which, retiring from the general north and south direction of his intrenchments, extended westwardly nearly to the Chattanooga road. After a severe and well-contested conflict, he was checked and forced to retire.

Adams, on the west of the road, met two lines of the enemy, who had improved the short time to bring up re-enforcements and reform nearly at a right angle to the troops in his main line of works. The first line was routed, but it was found impossible to break the second, aided as it was by artillery, and after a sanguinary contest which reflected high honor on the brigade, it was forced back in some confusion. Here *General Adams* . . . was severely wounded and fell into the hands of the enemy. . . .

Stovall had gained a point beyond the angle of the enemy's main line of works. *Adams* had advanced still farther, being actually in rear of his intrenchments. A good supporting line to my division at this moment would probably have produced decisive results. [*O.R.*, XXX, Part II, pp. 199–200.]

Report of Capt. C. H. Slocomb, CSA, Commanding
Fifth Company (Louisiana) Washington Artillery,
Breckinridge's Division, Army of Tennessee

We . . . took position beyond the ravine. The enemy here opened a heavy artillery fire upon us, which was returned, *Adams'* brigade charging them as their fire was silenced. It was in this position that *Major Graves* received a mortal wound.

Adams' brigade charged most nobly, but, unsupported, was met by superior numbers; was compelled to fall back, the enemy charging them in turn with infantry and artillery. Having placed my battery in front of the Glenn [McDonald] orchard to receive the enemy's charge, I waited until the brigade had gained the ravine in my immediate front, when I opened upon the advancing lines and drove them back in fine style, the brigade in the meantime rallying upon my battery. I was soon subjected to a terrific fire from the enemy's batteries in front, right, and left. My position being far in advance of the whole line, I received orders from *Colonel Gibson*, commanding *Adams'* brigade, to withdraw my battery, our lines having been reestablished under its fire. [*O.R.*, XXX, Part II, pp. 229–230.]

Stovall's brigade was east of the road and initially attacked on line with *Adams*. *Captain Joseph Cone* describes the attack west to the La Fayette Road and then south towards Kelly Field.

Report of Capt. Joseph S. Cone, CSA, Commanding
Forty-seventh Georgia Infantry, Stovall's Brigade,
Breckinridge's Division, Army of Tennessee

On Sunday morning, about 9 o'clock, our lines being formed and our position assigned us near the right, we were ordered to advance. After advancing in line of battle for a few hundred yards through a piece of woods we emerged . . . into an open glade, or meadow-like piece of ground, almost entirely free from all undergrowth.

Here we encountered the enemy's line of skirmishers. . . . They commenced a brisk and rapid fire on us as we crossed the open space. . . . Here the regiment was much exposed to their fire. . . . Upon emerging from the woods we discovered that we had obliqued too much to the left, thus leaving quite a space between us and the regiment on our right. As the guide was right, and as we were ordered to dress to that point and conform ourselves to the movements of the regiment on our right, we proceeded to dress and align ourselves while in this open space as directed, thus keeping the regiment for some length of time exposed to the fire coming from the enemy's line of sharpshooters stationed in our front along the piece of woods skirting the open space. While thus engaged we lost 1 man killed and several others wounded.

Having obtained our proper distance and dress, all the while advancing, we soon entered the woods. . . . The enemy's line of sharpshooters now gave way, fleeing precipitately through the woods. In a few minutes after, we came to a large, open field, seemingly a corn field. Here there appears to have been another line of the enemy's sharpshooters, as quite a number appeared in the field running in every direction. Several came running up to us and surrendered themselves. Among the number a captain. . . .

We proceeded across the fields and were halted on the opposite side, where we remained about ten or fifteen minutes. We then recrossed the field in nearly the direction from which we had first marched. While recrossing the field two shells from the enemy's battery passed through our ranks between the files without doing any injury. . . .

We were now ordered to cross a wood, the undergrowth of which was quite thin and sparse. Beyond this wood in an open old field [Kelly] on quite an elevated piece of ground was stationed a battery of the enemy, which occasionally sent a shell crashing through the piece of wood through which we were now advancing. On nearing the edge of this field, we were halted and skirmishers deployed in our front. Company F, our left-flank company, armed with rifles, having been sent out the night before on picket, and being still behind, Company E, our right-flank company, armed with rifles, and Company D, muskets, were thrown out as skirmishers. After a few shots exchanged the enemy's line retired. . . .

We again advanced. Their battery now commenced a regular fire with grape, at the same time continuing to throw shells around and above us, cutting down tops of trees, limbs, etc. among us. We advanced steadily, gained the [Kelly] field, and continued on 75 or 100 paces in the field. Seeing that the regiments of our brigade on our left did not advance into the field, we halted and. . . . remained . . . until . . . we had fired . . . a dozen or more rounds, when *Captain Phillips*, seeing that our line did not advance, and deeming it prudent to fall back into the edge of the woods and align our regiment on the other regiments of the brigade, gave the order to that effect. [*O.R.*, XXX, Part II, pp. 236–237.]

TURN RIGHT onto the **LA FAYETTE ROAD** and drive 0.6 mile to the Kelly cabin. Park in the turnout on the right. Dismount, cross the **LA FAYETTE ROAD**, and walk to the artillery pieces on your left. Face north.

STOP 17 – CONFEDERATE ATTACK INTO KELLY FIELD

You have driven over part of the ground covered by the right of *Stovall's* brigade and the left of *Adams'* brigade in their attack into Kelly Field. *Adams'* brigade was able to penetrate to a position on the other side of the road about 250 yards to your left front. The woods on the west side of the road had less undergrowth in 1863 than today. *Stovall's* brigade pushed south as far as the tree line on the northern edge of the field, but reports from subordinate commanders give little detail beyond that con-

Kelly Cabin and field as seen from the main road looking to the east. Union defenses were located in the far tree line facing east. (Commissioners for the Chickamauga and Chattanooga National Military Park, *Indiana at Chickamauga* [Indianapolis: Sentinel Publishing Co., 1900]).

tained in *Captain Cone's Report.* The Sixtieth North Carolina, which had advanced into the field on the left of *Cone's* Forty-seventh Georgia, fell back soon after the regiment on its left was forced back by a threat to its left flank "after a sharp engagement for twenty minutes." The two stone monuments next to the tree line are to the Forty-seventh Georgia and Sixtieth North Carolina. [*O.R.*, XXX, Part II, p. 238.]

You are standing on the elevated piece of ground that *Captain Cone* of the Forty-seventh Georgia mentioned in his report. From here you can gain a perspective of the ground as the Union troops saw it on September 20th, when the two Confederate brigades attacked south into this area. The Union's main defensive line was located to the east, just through the tree line to your right, on Battle Line Road. The Union brigade of Brigadier General John Beatty had made the initial contact with the Confederate attack in the open area around McDonald's farm. (See Stop 16.) The two left regiments of that brigade were forced to fall back in a westerly direction and, therefore, lost contact with the two right regiments that retreated to a position just across the La Fayette Road from your location.

Report of Brigadier General John Beatty, USA, Commanding First Brigade, Second Division, XIV Corps, Army of the Cumberland (Continued)

Firing having ceased in my front, and being the only mounted officer present, I left the Fifteenth Kentucky and One hundred and fourth Illinois temporarily in charge of Colonel Taylor, of the former regiment, and hurried back to see General Thomas or General Negley and report the necessity for more troops; on the way I met the Second Brigade of our division, Col. T. R. Stanley commanding, advancing to my support. Had it reached me an hour earlier I would have been enabled to maintain the position which I had just been compelled to abandon, but its detention was doubtless unavoidable. I directed Colonel Stanley to form immediately at right angles with and on the left of the road, facing north, and returning to Colonel Taylor ordered him to fall back with the Fifteenth Kentucky and One hundred and fourth Illinois, and form in rear of the left of Colonel Stanley's line. [*O.R.*, XXX, Part I, p. 369.]

Report of Col. Timothy R. Stanley, USA, Commanding Second Brigade, Second Division, XIV Corps, Army of the Cumberland

I . . . formed my line of battle at right angles with the road. The line was hardly formed before the enemy advanced upon us in heavy force. The Eighteenth Ohio and the Eleventh Michigan, forming the first line, opened a rapid and effective fire, which checked the enemy. Observing this, I ordered the Nineteenth Illinois forward, and upon their closing up I ordered the line forward, which all responded to with cheers of triumph, and the enemy fled in disorder. . . . We thus drove them for half a mile or more, strewing the ground with killed and wounded, and taking a large number of prisoners. Among the latter were *Brigadier-General Adams* and one or two of his staff, who surrendered to officers of this brigade. . . . I myself talked with *General Adams*. . . . He was wounded and asked me to send him a stretcher, which I was unable to do. Quite a number of other officers were near him, dead and wounded, and one of my officers who observed closely thinks there was another brigadier-general among the number.

Our volleys were destructive to them, and I attribute their utter rout to the skillful fire and impetuosity of my brigade.

Having followed up the enemy a considerable distance, and finding myself wholly unsupported, I slowly fell back a few paces under heavy fire from the *Washington* Battery (which had opened on my line) for the purpose of closing up my ranks and securing some support.

General Beatty had in the mean time brought up a brigade to my rear, which he had "borrowed," and I halted my command in their front, informing them that I would check the enemy and, if the fire became too hot, would fall back on them . . . but was only allowed a few minutes' rest before the enemy in strong force again attacked me. Being hard pressed I gave the order, after firing a number of rounds, to fall back fighting to the support. Upon looking around, however, I found the support had disappeared and we were left to our own resources.

I would be glad to state what brigade this was that so shamefully deserted us without firing a gun, but . . . I am not sufficiently certain to express my opinion. My brigade continued to fall back slowly, halting and firing at intervals, presenting a good front to the enemy, until I withdrew my command and took position next to some log buildings on the brow of the hill, near the Rossville road. [*O.R.*, XXX, Part I, p. 379.]

The thin finger of raised ground pointing into Kelly's Field, where you now stand, provided an excellent firing position for artillery shooting north. The batteries of Lieutenants Cushing and Russell—which played so important a role in Poe's Field the previous day—now provided a sustained volume of fire against the attacking regiments of *Adams'* and *Stovall's* brigades.

Colonel Ferdinand Van Derveer's Union brigade was also instrumental in halting the Confederate flank attack. Earlier in the morning this brigade was located a mile to the southwest, in the vicinity of the Dyer and Glenn-Kelly Roads. Around 10 o'clock Van Derveer was ordered to move to his left front to support the Union defense on the left, which brought him here at a very critical time. In this action he maneuvered his command under tight discipline and—in the absence of instructions—did not hesitate to take the initiative.

Report of Col. Ferdinand Van Derveer, USA, Commanding Third Brigade, Third Division, XIV Corps, Army of the Cumberland (Continued)

I received an order to move quickly over to the left and support General Baird, who . . . was being hard pressed by the enemy. I wheeled my battalions to the left, deployed both lines, and moved through the woods parallel to the Chattanooga road, gradually swinging round my left until when, in the rear of Reynolds' position, I struck the road perpendicularly at a point just north of Kelly's house, near and back of his lines.

On approaching the road, riding in advance of the brigade, my attention was called to a large force of the enemy moving southward in four lines, just then emerging from the woods at a run, evidently intending to attack Reynolds and Baird, who were both hotly engaged, in the rear, and apparently unseen by these officers. I immediately wheeled my lines to the left, facing the approaching force, and ordered them to lie down. This movement was not executed until we received a galling fire delivered from a distance of 200 yards. At the same time a rebel battery, placed in the road about 500 or 600 yards in our front, opened upon us with two guns.

My command continued to lie down until the enemy approached within 75 yards, when the whole arose to their feet, and the front line, composed of the Second Minnesota and the Eighty-seventh Indiana, delivered a murderous fire almost in their faces, and the Thirty-fifth and Ninth Ohio, passing lines quickly to the front, the whole brigade charged and drove the enemy at full run over the open ground for over a quarter of a mile, and several hundred yards into the woods, my men keeping in good order and delivering their fire as they advanced. . . . We took position in the woods, and maintained a determined combat for more than an hour. At this time I greatly needed my battery, which had been taken from the brigade early in the day by command of Major-General Negley.

Finding a force moving on my right to support us, and the enemy being almost silenced, I ordered a return to the open ground south of the woods; this movement was executed by passing lines to the rear, each line firing as it retired. . . .

I thence moved to a position on the road by the house near General Reynolds' center, and there remained resting my men and caring for my wounded for an hour or more. Although I had not reported to either General Reynolds or Baird, as ordered in the morning, I believe I rendered them very substantial assistance, and at a time when it was greatly needed. [*O.R.*, XXX, Part I, pp. 429–430.]

East of this position Colonel William Grose's brigade and several regiments of Brigadier General August Willich's brigade were participating in this violent struggle to protect the rear of the Union main battle line. Grose's brigade probably conducted a flanking movement against the left of *Stovall's* brigade.

***Report of Colonel William Grose, USA, Commanding
Third Brigade, Second Division, XXI Corps, Army of the
Tennessee (Continued)***

Early I was ordered to take position on the right of General Hazen's brigade on the right of our division . . . and each regiment quickly threw before it barricades of logs and such materials as could readily be obtained, but before the action on our part of the line commenced, one of my regiments, the Twenty-third Kentucky, had been loaned to General Hazen to fill out his lines. . . .

With the other four, about 9 o'clock, I was ordered to the left of General Baird's division . . . to strengthen his left. Before we arrived at the intended position . . . the enemy came upon Baird's division, and consequently upon my command, in fearful numbers. I formed the four regiments under a destructive fire from the enemy in a woodland covered with a heavy underbrush, fronting nearly north and at right angles with the main line of battle, the Thirty-sixth Indiana and Eighty-fourth Illinois in the front line, the Sixth and Twenty-fourth Ohio in the second line.

Thus formed we met the enemy, and had a desperate struggle with fearful loss on both sides. The brigade advanced and was repulsed, advanced a second time and was again repulsed, and, with some forces that now came to our assistance, advanced the third time and held the woodland.

In this contest . . . fell many of my best and bravest officers and men. The dead and dying of both armies mingled together over this bloody field. Here I parted with many of my comrades forever, particularly old mess-mates of the Thirty-sixth Indiana . . . whose remains I was unable to remove from the field. In this conflict and amid the shifting scenes of battle, Colonel Waters, of the Eighty-fourth Illinois, with a part of his regiment became detached from the brigade to the west of the road and became mingled with the division of General Negley, who, it seems, shortly after ordered . . . Colonel Waters' regiment . . . toward Chattanooga . . . as train guard. . . .

After the fighting had ceased, and with seeming success to our arms on this portion of the line, now about 1 or 2 p.m., I withdrew . . . to near the position we had taken in the forenoon near the right of General Hazen's brigade, and put my men in position to rest and to await further developments. [*O.R.*, XXX, Part I, pp. 781–782.]

The Confederate flank attack into this field was re-enforced by *Govan's* brigade, who advanced into the same area as *Adams'* brigade before being repulsed. The attackers were not able to generate the combat power necessary to exploit the initial advantage gained when they reached the La Fayette Road north of the Union left. No other major attempts were made to flank the Union left. Confederate forces did not gain Kelly Field until late afternoon, when the Union forces along Battle Line Road were ordered out of position due to events farther south and west.

THE BATTLE FOR POE FIELD
Late Morning, September 20, 1863

Return to your car.

Continue on the LA FAYETTE ROAD for 0.3 mile. TURN RIGHT onto POE ROAD and park immediately by the monument to the Seventy-fifth Indiana Infantry. Dismount, cross the La Fayette Road, and walk to the stone monument to the Thirty-seventh Georgia Infantry in POE FIELD. Face the La Fayette Road. The road on your right is Battle Line Road.

STOP 18, POSITION A – THE FIRST ASSAULT

You are now looking at the Union defense in the area of Poe Field as viewed by Confederate troops around 11:00 a.m. on September 20, 1863. To your right, in the tree line across Battle Line Road, was the right of Brigadier General John B. Turchin's Third Brigade of Reynolds' Fourth Division, XIV Corps. This was the extreme right of the Union defensive position covered at Stops 11–15.

Disregard the guns just on the other side of Battle Line Road, which mark a position taken on the previous day. Here there was a short break in the Union line, which was picked up by Colonel Edward King's brigade, Reynolds' division, just right of where you parked. King's brigade was posted at an angle to the road, which enabled his brigade and Turchin's right regiments to support each other by fire and also place a cross fire on the northern end of Poe Field.

To King's right (your left) were the brigades of Col. John T. Croxton and Col. John M. Connell, of Brig. Gen. John M. Brannan's Third Division, Connell's right flank being near the southern edge of Poe Field. Both brigades faced east, paralleling the La Fayette Road. The guns that you see in the southern portion of Poe Field were not there at this time, but came into action in mid-afternoon.

The attack into this area was made by *Wood's* brigade of *Cleburne's* division and the three brigades of *Stewart's* division. The starting position for this attack was two small ridges about 400 yards east of the field.

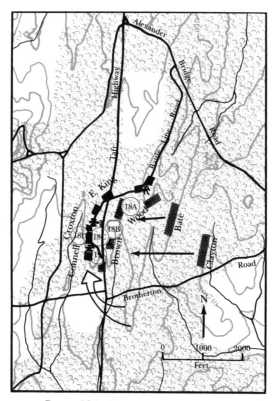

Stops 18A, 18B, 18C, 18D, & 19
Situation Late Morning
September 20, 1863

Report of Maj. Gen. Alexander P. Stewart, CSA,
Commanding Division, Buckner's Corps, Army of Tennessee

Early the next morning (20th), *Lieutenant-General Longstreet*, who
had arrived during the night, came to see me and informed me that I
would receive my orders on that day directly from him; that the
attack was to commence on our extreme right at daylight, was to be
followed on the left and gradually, or, rather, successively, to extend
to the center, and that I should move after the division on my right or
the one on my left had moved, according to circumstances. Apprising
him of the fact that there were no troops to the right, at least within a
half mile, he directed me to move something more than a quarter of a
mile in that direction. This was done, *Brown's* brigade forming in the
front line on the crest of a slight ridge and constructing a breastwork
of logs, *Clayton's* a few hundred yards in rear on a parallel ridge, and

Bate with his left resting on *Brown's* right, his line extending obliquely to the right and rear to prevent the enemy from turning our position. . . . My division was the right of the Left Wing, commanded by *Lieutenant General Longstreet*, and *McNair's* brigade was on the left of *Brown's*. Subsequently *Wood's* brigade, of *Cleburne's* division, was formed on the right and in prolongation of *Brown's*, and about 9 a.m. *Deshler's* was formed on the right of *Bate's*.

In the meantime, a heavy fire was opened upon us from the enemy's batteries in our immediate front and but a few hundred yards distant, by which some losses were occasioned.

At length, about 11 a.m., *Major Lee*, of *General Bragg's* staff, came to me with an order to advance at once and attack the enemy. I informed him what orders had previously been received, and that no attack had been made on my right. He replied that *General Bragg* had directed him to pass along the lines and give the order to every division commander to move upon the enemy immediately.

Accordingly, I arranged with *General Wood* that he should advance with *Brown*, which was done without delay; *Clayton* was moved up immediately to *Brown's* position, and *Bate's* right thrown forward to bring him on line with *Clayton*, when they also advanced to be within supporting distance of *Brown* and *Wood*.

For several hundred yards both lines pressed on under the most terrible fire it has ever been my fortune to witness. The enemy retired, and our men, though mowed down at every step, rushed on at double-quick until at length the brigade on the right of *Brown* broke in confusion, exposing him to an enfilade fire. He continued on, however, some 50 to 75 yards farther, when his two right regiments gave way in disorder and retired to their original position. His center and left, however, followed by the gallant *Clayton* and indomitable *Bate*, pressed on, passing the corn-field in front of the burnt house and to a distance of 200 to 300 yards beyond the Chattanooga road, driving the enemy within his line of intrenchments and passing a battery of four guns, which were afterward taken possession of by a regiment from another division. Here new batteries being opened by the enemy on our front and flank, heavily supported by infantry, it became necessary to retire, the command reforming on the ground occupied before the advance.

During this charge, which was truly heroic, our loss was severe. [*O.R.*, XXX, Part II, pp. 363–364.]

The center regiment of *Wood's* brigade reached the area where you are now standing.

Report of Brig. Gen. S. A. M. Wood, CSA, Commanding Brigade, Cleburne's Division, Army of Tennessee

On the morning of the 20th, the troops were aroused at early dawn, the line rectified, the skirmishers in front relieved, and everything made ready to engage the enemy. Ammunition had been replenished during the night. Shortly after daylight a day's rations of cooked provisions were brought up and distributed. The morning was cold, and the men were allowed to have small fires and eat their breakfast.

At 10 o'clock I was notified the line was about to move on the enemy, and that the movement would commence on my right. I had already heard that it was probable that my brigade overlapped troops to my left not of this division, and that some irregularity existed in the lines as formed.

At a few minutes past 10 the brigade on my right moved forward and I moved with it. Its left soon crowded on my right, when I obliqued to the left to give room. In a few minutes it made a rapid movement obliquely to the right, leaving a gap. The brigade was at once ordered to follow this movement, and every exertion was made to do so; but we were now under fire of artillery, and had advanced but a short distance when my right was within short range of the enemy's rifles. They were hidden behind logs covered with bushes.

The whole line to the right was now at a halt and firing. This was followed by the right of my brigade—*Hawkins'* sharpshooters and *Colonel Lowrey's* regiment. The major general passed me at this moment and I informed him that my left had passed over some of our troops lying down and were in front of them. The whole front of the brigade to my left was covered by other troops. He directed me to see to the left of my command, and said that *Deshler's* brigade would be taken to the right. The Sixteenth and Thirty-third Alabama Regiments were ordered to lie down on a line with the troops in the front line to my left, who were also lying down.

I found *Brigadier General Brown* at the right of his line and told him that the batteries now firing on us would enfilade me if I advanced without a corresponding advance to my left. He said he had no orders to advance but would send to *Major-General Stewart* for orders. *Major-General Stewart* came to that position, and having ordered his division forward, I immediately ordered the Forty-fifth Alabama Regiment, supporting my battery, up into line with the Sixteenth and Thirty-third Alabama Regiments and ordered them all forward.

About this time the line to the right had fallen back, and the position occupied by *Colonel Lowery* and *Major Hawkins* was taken by *Deshler's* brigade. [Because of] the peculiar character of the enemy's works . . . while the right of my command was very near them, an angle was formed in its front and the enemy's line was thrown back, so as to give them the cover of woods and compel us to advance through a wide field.

My brigade advanced into this field. The Thirty-third Alabama . . . under the lead of its gallant colonel, crossed the field and the Chattanooga road. The fire of the enemy at this point was most destructive, and . . . it was not long before all had to retire, and were again assembled and formed at the position from which they last advanced. My command, being the right of the line advancing against this retired line of the enemy, was subjected to a cross and enfilading fire which was very severe on all, but especially on the Forty-fifth Alabama Regiment, which was forced back earlier than the Sixteenth and Thirty-third Alabama and reformed. . . . During this movement *Semple's* battery . . . followed the brigade and opened effectively on the enemy. In the second advance it was not deemed desirable that the battery should advance with the brigade, the batteries of other brigades on our left being allowed to remain in position. . . .

No command conducted itself with more spirit or determination. By subsequent examination of the field, it was observed that at no point was the enemy's works so strong as in our front. And the peculiar formation of his lines, which, owing to the heavy timber and undergrowth, could not be ascertained by any effort but an assault, subjected the command to a very destructive cross and enfilading fire. . . . The loss . . . in the brigade was 96 killed on the field and 680 wounded. [*O.R.*, XXX, Part II, pp. 161–162.]

The Forty-fifth Alabama, which crossed the ground just to your right, was unable to maintain position because of the fire into its right flank. To your left were the Sixteenth and the Thirty-third Alabama. The Thirty-third managed to advance and cross the La Fayette Road before being stopped by the Union fire. This may have been possible because the small dip in the ground in Poe Field would have provided partial protection from the flanking fire until the road was reached.

Report of Col. Samuel Adams, CSA, Commanding
Thirty-third Alabama Infantry, Wood's Brigade,
Cleburne's Division, Army of Tennessee

About 10 a.m. I received an order from *Brigadier-General Wood* to move my regiment forward and keep it in line with the Sixteenth Alabama Regiment. After advancing about a half mile obliquely, most of the time to the right . . . the Sixteenth Alabama Regiment, under a heavy fire of grape and canister and shell, halted. Ten or 15 paces in advance of this position was a ravine, to which position I moved my regiment before halting it. During most of the time that I remained in this position my regiment was under a very heavy fire of grape, canister, and shell. . . .

After I had remained here an hour or an hour and a half, I received an order from *Brigadier-General Wood* to move forward and keep in line with Sixteenth Alabama Regiment. Previous to this time *Deshler's* brigade had moved to the right. *Brown's* brigade was near me on the left. After moving forward about 200 yards I received a general volley of small-arms from the enemy's line. At this point the Sixteenth Alabama regiment halted. On a line with it halted my regiment. Here my company of skirmishers that had covered my front in the whole advance came in, having driven the enemy's line of skirmishers back to the main line.

Near my line in front was a fence covering my whole regiment except the right company. The enemy's line of battle was distant about 275 yards behind barricades. In this position I was subjected to a very severe enfilading fire from the right. In front a low hill protected me. Shortly after I halted, *Brown's* Brigade came up on my left, and supporting it and very near in its rear was *Clayton's* brigade, the right regiment of which lapped my whole regiment.

I moved forward my regiment with these two brigades about 100 yards to the crest of the hill in my front. At this point most of both brigades fell back, carrying with them many of my men. I continued to advance until I reached a house on the western side of the Chattanooga road, about 75 yards from the enemy's line. This house caught fire about the close of the engagement and burned down. At this point I found myself with but 60 or 70 of my own men, and but very few, if any, of the other two brigades. With this squad of men and my colors I fell back to the ravine where I had previously halted. After I had remained here half an hour engaged in collecting my stragglers, I received an order from *Brigadier-General Wood* to rejoin the brigade, which was 700 or 800 yards farther in the rear. In this engagement I lost 16 killed and 133 wounded. [*O.R.*, XXX, Part II, pp. 166–167.]

Walk south about 125 yards to the small stone monuments near the road that commemorate the Eighteenth and Forty-fifth Tennessee Regiments.

POSITION B—ASSAULT TO THE ROAD

The monuments where you now stand represent the right regiments of *Brown's* brigade. The three remaining regiments were deployed on line to your left.

Report of Brig. Gen. John C. Brown, CSA, Commanding Brigade, Stewart's Division, Army of Tennessee

At about 11 o'clock, when ordered to advance, I moved in line to the front, preceded by my skirmishers, who, soon driving in the enemy's skirmishers, rallied upon the command. We moved at double-quick nearly 300 yards through an open woods, the enemy retiring before us, when the brigade on my right broke in confusion. My line still advanced 50 or 75 yards farther, and to within 50 yards of the enemy's battery and line of defenses, when the right, wholly unsupported and receiving a terrible cross-fire of musketry and artillery upon its flanks, broke and retired in disorder to our temporary defenses. I found all efforts to rally the Eighteenth and Forty-fifth Tennessee short of the defenses in vain, and, indeed impracticable, under the storm of grape and canister which prevailed upon every part of the field over which these two regiments passed.

The center and left continued steadily to advance until they crossed the Chattanooga road 200 or 300 yards, and passed the battery in our front, but on the right flank of the Thirty-second Tennessee Regiment; but being unsupported on the right in consequence of the retreat of the Eighteenth and Forty-fifth Tennessee Regiments, it became necessary to retire the remainder of the line, because to have advanced farther would have exposed it to the hazard of being cut off, while to have remained stationary without shelter and under fire from a protected foe would have sacrificed the men without obtaining any compensating advantage.

I therefore ordered it to retire, which it accomplished in comparatively good order, to the original line. [*O.R.*, XXX, Part II, p. 372.]

Report of Col. Edmund C. Cook, CSA, Commanding
Thirty-second Tennessee, Brown's Brigade, Stewart's
Division, Army of Tennessee

About 11 a.m. we were moved forward to engage the enemy. . . .
The line moved rapidly forward, driving before it a heavy line of the
enemy's skirmishers and soon engaged his line of battle. . . . Driving
him from a log breastwork in our advance, we crossed the Chattanooga road, encountering at this point an enfilading fire from the
enemy's battery on our right and situated on the Chattanooga road,
pressing him to a second line of breastworks. Here we lost 4 men
killed and many wounded, being exposed now to a fire almost immediately in our rear, having in our advance passed on the right of the
battery on the road and several hundred yards to its rear. This was
caused by that portion of the brigade to the right of my regiment
falling back before it reached the battery.

The regiment being thus exposed to a murderous fire, fell back in
somewhat of disorder, and was partially formed in the Chattanooga
road, but being still exposed to the enfilading fire, we were ordered by
General Brown to fall back to the breastworks. [*O.R.*, XXX, Part II,
pp. 378–379.]

Neither *Wood's* nor *Brown's* brigades could force the Union defense or
hold their positions under heavy defensive fire. Both fell back, and the
attack was taken up by the two supporting brigades of *Brigadier General
William B. Bate* and *Brigadier General Henry D. Clayton*, which moved
forward, conducted a passage of lines, and assaulted the Union position.

The two right regiments—Twentieth Tennessee and Thirty-seventh
Georgia—of *Bate's* brigade advanced to approximately Position A. The
next regiment to their left, the Fifty-eighth Alabama, halted at the tree
line. The extreme left regiment, the Fifteenth and Thirty-seventh Tennessee (Combined) advanced to the low stone monument to your right front
just on the other side of the La Fayette Road back toward your car. This
is also the same position reached by the Thirty-third Alabama of *Wood's*
brigade.

Report of Brig. Gen. William B. Bate, CSA, Commanding
Brigade, Stewart's Division, Army of Tennessee
(Continued)

Under the order of *Major-General Stewart*, I moved my command by the right flank 500 or 600 yards and took position forward

and on the right of *General Brown's* brigade; but in forming the line was compelled to retire the right to an angle of about 45 degrees on account of the proximity of the enemy located to my right oblique. . . . Having assumed this line of battle, I had a temporary barricade of logs hastily constructed, which gave partial protection against the shower of grape, canister, and shell which continuously and most angrily saluted us. . . .

At about 9 a.m. the brigade of *General Deshler* was placed upon my right, prolonging the line and observing the same inclination to the rear. Soon thereafter I received notice that *General Wood's* brigade was in my front, and that the general movement would be a successive one, by brigade, commencing on the right, and was ordered by *Major-General Stewart* to follow up the movement of *General Deshler*. After waiting, under a severe and incessant fire of artillery, until about 11 a.m., I communicated to *General Stewart* that no movement on my right had taken place; that *General Deshler* had been killed, and desired to know if I should longer remain inactive. About this time there was firing in my front, and soon thereafter *General Wood's* command came back, passing over my line.

I was then ordered by *Major-General Stewart* to advance and attack. My command received the order with a shout and moved upon the foe at a rapid gait. The battalion of sharpshooters was ordered to maintain its position at right angles to the line and check, if possible (if not, to delay), any movement in that direction, giving the earliest notice of the same.

My right . . . became hotly engaged almost the instant it assumed the offensive. It was subject to a most galling fire of grape and musketry from my right oblique and front, cutting down with great fatality the Twentieth Tennessee and Thirty-seventh Georgia at every step, until they drove the enemy behind his defenses, from which, without support either of artillery or infantry, they were unable to dislodge him.

General Deshler's brigade not having advanced, I called on *Major-General Cleburne*, who was near my right and rear, for assistance; but he having none at his disposal which could be spared, I was compelled to retire that wing of my brigade or sacrifice it in uselessly fighting thrice its numbers, with the advantage of the hill and breastworks against it. I did so in good order and without indecent haste, and aligned it first in front and then placed it in rear of our flimsy defenses. My left (the Fifty-eighth Alabama and Fifteenth and Thirty-seventh Tennessee . . .), being farther from the enemy's line than my right, did not so soon become engaged, neither at this time subject to so severe a cross-fire, proceeded steadily on and drove the enemy behind his works, which had been constructed the night previous . . . and maintained their position with a dogged tenacity until the Twentieth Tennessee and Thirty-seventh Georgia were put in position [after falling back] behind the barricade and the battalion of sharpshooters drawn in. . . .

I am unable to give as accurate an account of my left as of my right, for the reason that the right became first engaged, and the commanders of the three right battalions having been wounded the evening previous, devolving the commands upon junior officers, I felt that my personal services were most needed there. . . . I found, however, their dead in the breastworks of the enemy, which is the highest evidence that can be afforded of what they did. In this fight my command lost 30 per cent killed and wounded. [*O.R.*, XXX, Part II, pp. 385–386.]

Report of Colonel Bushrod Jones, CSA, Commanding Fifty-eighth Alabama, Bate's Brigade, Stewart's Division, Army of Tennessee (Continued)

At 11:30 a.m. the brigade was again ordered forward . . . . the men and officers obeying the command with promptness and enthusiasm. The regiment advanced, cheering, on a run, amid a shower of grape from twelve pieces of artillery 400 yards distant, and a terrific storm of Minie balls that made dreadful havoc in the ranks, the fire increasing as we approached the enemy. Advancing the first 200 yards up a hill the men were partially protected, but after passing the crest we descended a gentle slope about the same distance, over which the combined fire of grape and Minie balls was terrific, but not a man faltered in his duty or shrank from the danger.

On arriving at the edge of the woods, we were within 100 yards of the enemy's batteries and long lines of infantry support, still thinning our ranks with increasing fury. An open field alone separated us. If the brigade had been on a line with me and in good order, the batteries, I believe, could have been captured by a charge, but when I arrived at the edge of the woods with every man of my command who had not been disabled, there was little or no support on my right. Consequently a charge . . . would have been the extreme of rashness, and would probably have caused the sacrifice of every man in the regiment in a vain attempt.

I therefore ordered a halt just at the edge of the woods. Under cover of trees, logs, and such irregularities of the ground as furnished any protection, my command held this advanced position, pouring repeated volleys of musketry into the ranks of the enemy until 12:30. I noted the time by my watch. I looked anxiously, but in vain, for re-enforcements . . . but thinking I had held the position as long as practicable, after conference with *Lieutenant-Colonel Inzer*, I resolved to retire as soon as a slackening of the enemy's fire would permit. . . . Not a man fell back until I ordered it and fell back in person. . . . I acted on my own judgment, and retired only after half of my men were killed and wounded. [*O.R.*, XXX, Part II, p. 390.]

Recross the road and walk north to the small stone monument to the Fifteenth and Thirty-seventh Tennessee Regiments (Combined).

POSITION C – THE FARTHEST ADVANCE

Report of Lieut. Col. R. Dudley Frayser, CSA, Commanding Thirty-seventh Tennessee Infantry, Bate's Brigade, Stewart's Division, Army of Tennessee

The Fifteenth and Thirty-seventh Tennessee Volunteers at this time were on the left of the brigade, its left being some 400 yards or more from the main Chattanooga road. Immediately on my right, between my command and the Fifty-eighth Alabama, were in position two pieces of the Eufaula Light Artillery. . . . This battery did not fire a shot while here, [and] was removed soon afterward to a more favorable position.

In about fifteen minutes after I took command, the regiments still being shielded by rudely constructed breastworks of logs and bushes hastily thrown up, an order came to forward from the briga-dier-general commanding. I repeated the command, and my boys moved with alacrity over our works.

Having gained some 60 or 70 yards, I ordered double-quick with the yell, which was obeyed to a man, the men almost assuming the run, still keeping an unbroken line. Firing from the enemy's sharp-shooters and batteries was constant in our front, but more injury was inflicted upon us from the left flank, there seeming to be no support on the left of *Bate's* brigade. On emerging from the woods in an open, shrubby field we could see our stubborn foe defiantly resisting our march across this field. Grape, canister, and musket-shot here greatly decimated my command, but swerving not it bore steadily onward. Near the center of this field I was disabled and fell from a wound received just below the knee, which for many minutes paralyzed my left leg. I observed as I fell that both colors were steadily moving forward through this dreadful ordeal of shell, shot and fire.

I lay here many minutes entirely conscious, but unable to rise. Many of my companions lay wounded and dead around me. Upon seeing some of my command returning through this same field and reporting orders having been issued to fall back, I, with their assistance, reached the position the regiment formerly held before this murderous charge. On my way I was handed the colors of the Thirty-seventh Tennessee Volunteers by *Mullins*, Company A, the color-bearer, brave boy, having been shot dead. . . . After some little time I sent forward a party . . . to assist in bringing the wounded from the field. I feared they would burn, as the grass and bushes were on fire. [*O.R.*, XXX, Part II, p. 397.]

To the left of *Bate's* was *Clayton's* three-regiment brigade, which kept pace with *Bate* as the attack moved into Poe Field. *Clayton*, however, could not capture the Union defenses in his front nor maintain his position in the field and, like the other brigades, he fell back to the low ridges to the east.

Walk west to the cannons and monument to Battery C, First Ohio Artillery on the POE ROAD. Face the La Fayette Road.

POSITION D–THE UNION DEFENSE

You are now in the center of the defensive position occupied by Croxton's Second Brigade, Third Division, XIV Corps. Connell's First Brigade of the same division was deployed to the right. Beyond Connell's brigade was the division commanded by Brigadier General Thomas J. Wood. To the left of Croxton was Colonel Edward A. King's Second Brigade, Fourth Division (Reynolds), XIV Corps.

Today the heavy growth of vines and brush on the east side of Poe Field limits your view. However, in September 1863 the open woods east of Poe Field allowed observation several hundred yards farther than is possible today. At that distance the defender could easily see the closer of the two ridges from which *Stewart's* brigades launched their attacks.

One must remember, when studying Union reports, that the defenders did not see the Confederates as coming in two separate assaults, but rather as one sustained attack. This was probably because the two supporting Confederate brigades were following the lead brigades so closely that the repulse of the first attack and the beginning of the second was one continuous action.

Report of Lieut. Col. Myron Baker, USA, Commanding Seventy-fourth Indiana Infantry, Second Brigade, Third Division, XIV Corps, Army of the Cumberland (Continued)

About 8 a.m. the Seventy-fourth Indiana, with the Tenth Indiana on its immediate right, moved to the left and joined on the Seventy-fifth Indiana, the right regiment of Reynolds' division. The skirmishers moved to the left at the same time covering our front. The Seventy-fourth . . . occupied a low ridge of ground with an open field in front . . . on the extreme left of the Second Brigade. On the brow of this ridge I caused the men to construct a rude breastwork of logs and rails behind which they could take shelter from the enemy's musketry, and which proved to be of very great advantage in the subsequent fight.

At about 10:30 a.m. the firing, which had been very heavy to my left and along the line of Reynolds' division, struck my line of battle. I ordered the men to kneel down behind their works and hold their fire until the enemy were within 60 or 70 yards of our line. The companies of skirmishers were soon driven in, but not a shot was fired by us until the rebels who were charging on us with a yell had come within 70 yards of us, when I ordered the men to rise up and commence firing.

The men mostly aimed deliberately and fought with a spirit and determination which could not well be surpassed, for the comparative security and strength of their position gave them increased confidence. The Seventy-fourth Indiana and Tenth Indiana held their position, keeping up an incessant and untiring fire, until their ammunition was nearly exhausted, when they were ordered to cease firing, fix bayonets, and await the nearer approach of the foe. Twice during this engagement the enemy was thrown into confusion and driven back from before our position.

About this time the line to the right of the Tenth Indiana gave way, and the rebels made their appearance in an open field on the right flank of the Tenth Indiana. Lieutenant-Colonel Taylor, commanding that veteran regiment, changed his front almost perpendicularly to the rear, and the Seventy-fourth Indiana protected the original line until he had completed that movement, when I faced the regiment by the rear rank and formed line of battle on his right at an acute angle with the original line and in rear of a fence and some old log buildings. Here the regiment fought until its ammunition was completely exhausted, and the rebels were driven back from the open field over which they were advancing.

At this time the Tenth and Seventy-fourth Indiana were separated from the rest of the brigade, which had been sent to the right to fill a breach in the line, and Lieutenant-Colonel Taylor, being the ranking officer, took command of both regiments. The regiment now moved through the woods toward the left and awaited the arrival of ammunition in an open ground where Hazen's brigade was lying behind some log fortifications. [*O.R.*, XXX, Part I, pp. 420–421.]

At Position B the commander of the Thirty-second Tennessee mentioned "encountering an enfilading fire from the enemy's battery on our right" as the regiment stormed across the road. This was Battery C, First Ohio Artillery. You stand now in the center of the position occupied by that battery.

Report of Lieut. Marco B. Gary, USA, Commanding Battery C, First Ohio Light Artillery, Third Division, XIV Corps, Army of the Cumberland

At 7 o'clock, by order of Colonel Croxton, I took position on the rear line of the brigade, and as the enemy attacked . . . I received orders from Colonel Croxton to send two 12-pounder pieces to the front. I accordingly ordered Lieutenant Turner forward, who took position in easy range and opened on the enemy with shell and spherical case with fine effect.

Thirty minutes later I received orders from Colonel Croxton to move forward on the front line with the balance of the battery, take position on the left of Lieutenant Turner, and open fire on the enemy as soon as he appeared in force. I immediately moved by piece into position leaving my caissons 50 yards in rear, partially covered by a ridge in front, and in charge of First Sergeant Shaw, by whom they were handled . . . in a very efficient manner.

A heavy column of the enemy immediately appeared marching by the flank directly across my front, and at a distance of 600 yards from my pieces. I opened fire upon him with shell and spherical case. Changing direction to the right, he attacked in great force the line on which I was posted, and about 200 yards to my right, and after capturing nearly all of the Fourth Michigan Battery and driving away the infantry, he pushed to within 100 yards of my right piece. Changing the direction of my fire to the right oblique, I threw canister into his solid masses with great rapidity and . . . with fine effect, my guns some portion of the time being double shotted with canister.

The enemy soon fell back so far as to allow the infantry on my right to regain their position on the front line. Fifteen minutes later the support on my right again fell back, and the enemy again advanced on a line nearly perpendicular to my original front and to within 100 yards of the battery.

Ten to fifteen minutes later, having no support on my right, with a loss of 13 men killed and wounded, and 25 horses killed, and believing it impossible to save the battery, after further resistance, I moved the battery without orders to the left and rear, where I fell in, and, by order of General Brannan, moved with the troops of Major-General Negley's command. [*O.R.*, XXX, Part I, pp. 426–427.]

Return to your car. Drive 0.2 mile along the Union line to the monument to Battery D, First Michigan Artillery (also called Fourth Michigan Battery) on your left.

STOP 19 – COLLAPSE OF THE UNION RIGHT FLANK

You are now in the center of Connell's Union brigade. The Confederate frontal attack into this area was successful in closing with and in some cases temporarily pushing back the defenders. However, shortly before noon a strong Confederate force penetrated the Union defensive line further south. As the assault pushed west, follow-on units fell upon the right flank of Connell's brigade, just beyond the curve in the road.

Report of Col. John M. Connell, USA, Commanding First Brigade, Third Division, XIV Corps, Army of the Cumberland

Heavy fighting was going on for hours on my left during the continued movement by the flank to the left, but nothing but slight skirmishing occurred for some time on my front. About 9 o'clock Stanley's brigade left our right flank, which was wholly exposed. I at once dispatched an aide to inform the commander of the division that the enemy were forming on our right and front about 300 yards distant, and received answer that my right would be supported, and in a short time a division moved down on to my right—I believe Van Cleve's.

About this time Captain Church got effective range upon the enemy then engaged to my left, and opened a continuous, rapid, and deadly fire, which was kept up, notwithstanding our continued movement to the left, for more than an hour.

The battle now steadily approached us from the left. . . . The division on my right moved away, passing in my rear rapidly, and again uncovering and exposing my right flank. I was at this time left without support either in my rear or upon my right flank. I dispatched Lieutenant Davis, acting assistant adjutant-general, at once to inform the commander of the division of my critical position; threw out flankers to my right under command of Major Slocum, of the Eighty-second Indiana, to watch the enemy's approach there, where I knew it would be sure to come, and gave orders to the commanders of regiments to change front by the right flank as soon as the enemy appeared on that flank. These orders had scarcely been delivered before the enemy, making an oblique advance, following almost the retiring division on my right, most furiously and in tremendous force, attacked my front and flank.

The Seventeeth Ohio, forming the right of my front, attempted to change front, but could not, and after vigorously resisting for a few moments, and when the enemy had approached on its front and flank to within 75 yards of its line, was completely broken on its right wing, which retired in confusion, soon followed in confusion by its left wing. The Eighty-second Indiana, forming the right of the rear line, very gallantly moved forward through the flying ranks of the Seventeeth Ohio and attacked the advancing enemy, then nearly inside of our breastworks, but was unable to stay, and fell back in confusion, at which time the whole brigade, together with the Second Brigade, broke in confusion and fled to the rear. In the meantime a portion of the Seventeenth Ohio had rallied and again moved forward upon the enemy, only, however, at great sacrifice, to be driven quickly back.

Before my brigade gave way, a large portion of the division which had passed to my rear, without firing a gun or making an effort to assist me, and without being under direct fire, fled panic stricken from the field, hurrying away over, and running down the fleeing men of my command, whom I was vainly endeavoring to rally in the road and in the corn-field in rear of our position.

All efforts after this to rally my command seemed fruitless, but pushing after the fleeing men, and with scores of other officers engaged in the same apparently vain and painful task, we succeeded in occasionally collecting squads of men from different commands, and finally halted on the second range of hills to the rear of the road. [*O.R.*, XXX, Part I, pp. 409–410.]

Return to your car for the drive to Stop 20.

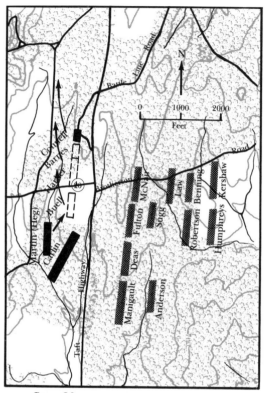

Stop 20
Situation 11:15 A.M.
September 20, 1863

BREAKING THE UNION RIGHT
Midday, September 20, 1863

Drive to the STOP sign. Turn right onto the LA FAYETTE ROAD and drive 0.1 mile to the DYER ROAD. TURN RIGHT and drive about 100 yards. Pull off on the right side of the road and park. You should stay with your car since there is no improved turnout for parking. Look back toward the Brotherton cabin.

STOP 20 – LONGSTREET'S ATTACK

You are now in the area where Confederate forces under the command of *Lieutenant General James Longstreet* broke through the Union defensive position just before noon on September 20.

Longstreet's attack forces involved elements of three divisions, totaling eight brigades, whose lead regiments were only a little over a quarter of a mile east of this location. *Johnson's* division was in the lead, followed by three brigades of *Hood's* division commanded by *Brigadier General E. McIver Law*, who in turn was followed by two brigades of *McLaw's* division under *Brigadier General Joseph B. Kershaw*. These three divisions formed a corps commanded by *Major General John B. Hood*.

South of this assault column was the division of *Major General Thomas C. Hindman*, which crossed the La Fayette Road and attacked across the southern half of Brotherton Field and through the woods to the south. To *Hindman's* left and back from the La Fayette Road *Brigadier General William Preston's* division was held as the reserve for *Longstreet's* Left Wing.

The Union defensive position was along the tree line west of Brotherton Field. Directly west of your location was Col. George P. Buell's brigade, comprising the right of Brigadier General Thomas J. Wood's First Division, XXI Corps. On Buell's left, Col. Charles G. Harker's brigade stretched northward from the Dyer Road to join Colonel Sidney Barnes' brigade of the Third Division, XXI Corps, which had been left behind and attached to Wood when the rest of the Third Division was pulled out of line and sent north.

Brig. Gen. Jefferson C. Davis' First Division, XX Corps, was deployed along the west edge of Brotherton Field and in the woods to the south. To the southwest of these units and moving to close on Davis' right was Maj. Gen. Philip H. Sheridan's division. Col. John T. Wilder's mounted infantry remained still farther to the southwest.

There has been a continuing controversy over what happened with Wood's division prior to *Longstreet's* attack. The facts indicate that sometime around 10:00 a.m. Captain Kellogg of Major General Thomas' staff was proceeding from Thomas' location to Rosecrans' headquarters. As he passed behind that part of the line next to Reynolds' division, which was occupied by Brannan, he could see no troops in position—probably because of the woods. When Kellogg reached army headquarters he reported that Brannan was out of position and Reynolds' flank was exposed. Rosecrans, thinking he had an opening in the line between Reynolds and Wood, sent Wood the order to "close up on Reynolds as fast as possible and support him." This reached Wood about 10:45 a.m. He promptly issued march instructions to his brigade commanders and in a very short time the division began to move north.

The order to Wood created the very condition it was designed to fix.

Report of Lieut. Gen. James Longstreet, CSA, Army of Northern Virginia, Commanding Left Wing of the Army of Tennessee

Our train reached Catoosa Platform, near Ringgold, about 2 o'clock in the afternoon of September 19. As soon as our horses came up (about 4 o'clock), I started with *Colonels Sorrel* and *Manning*, of my staff, to find the headquarters of the commanding general. We missed our way and did not report till near 11 o'clock at night.

Upon my arrival, I was informed that the troops had been engaged during the day in severe skirmishing while endeavoring to get in line for battle. The commanding general gave me a map showing the roads and streams between Lookout Mountain and the Chickamauga River, and a general description of our position, and informed me that the battle was ordered at daylight the next morning, the action to be brought on upon our right and to be taken up successively to the left, the general movement to be a wheel upon my extreme left as a pivot. I was assigned to the command of the Left Wing, composed of *Hood's* and *Hindman's* divisions, an improvised division under *Brig. Gen. B. R. Johnson*, and *Buckner's* corps, consisting of *Stewart's* and *Preston's* divisions. The artillery consisted of the battalions of *Majors*

Williams, Robertson, and *Leyden,* together with some other batteries attached to brigades.

As soon as the day of the 20th had dawned, I rode to the front to find my troops. The line was arranged from right to left as follows: *Stewart's, Johnson's, Hindman's,* and *Preston's* divisions. *Hood's* division (of which only three brigades were up) was somewhat in the rear of *Johnson's. Kershaw's* and *Humphreys'* brigades, of *McLaws'* division, were ordered forward from Ringgold the night before, but were not yet up. *General McLaws* had not arrived from Richmond [Va].

I set to work to have the line adjusted by closing to the right, in order to occupy some vacant ground between the two wings and to make room for *Hood* in the front line. The divisions were ordered to form with two brigades in the front line, and one supporting, where there were but three brigades, and two supporting where there were more than three. *General Hood* was ordered to take the brigades of *Kershaw* and *Humphreys* and use them as supports for his division, thus making his division the main column of attack.

Before these arrangements were completed the attack was made by our right wing about 10 o'clock. The battle seemed to rage with considerable fury, but did not progress as had been anticipated. As soon as I was prepared I sent to the commanding general to suggest that I had probably better make my attack. Before the messenger returned I heard that the commanding general had sent orders for the division commanders to move forward and attack. I had no time to find the officer who brought the order, as some troops were in motion when I heard of it. Upon this information I at once issued orders to attack to the troops not already in motion, holding one of *Buckner's* divisions (*Preston's*) in reserve. As the battle upon our right was not so successful as had been expected . . . I was obliged to reverse the order of battle by retaining my right somewhere near the left of the Right Wing. [*O.R.*, XXX, Part II, pp. 287–288.]

Report of Brig. Gen. Bushrod R. Johnson, CSA, Commanding Provisional Division, Army of Tennessee, Attached to Longstreet's Corps, Army of Northern Virginia (Continued)

My line was formed by 7 a.m., with *McNair's* brigade on the right, *Johnson's* brigade in center, and two regiments . . . on the left. The rest of *Gregg's* brigade, commanded by *Colonel Sugg,* formed a second line. *Culpeper's* battery was placed in position on the right of

McNair's brigade; *Everett's* on the right of *Johnson's* brigade and *Bledsoe's* on the right of the two regiments in the front line from *Gregg's* brigade. *Hindman's* division formed on my left and *Stewart's* on my right. *Hood's* division, commanded by *Brigadier-General Law*, formed in rear of my division, giving us a depth of three lines.

About 10 a.m. our skirmishers fell back under the advance of the enemy. My line promptly opened a steady fire with artillery and small-arms, which soon repulsed the attack. Ten minutes after 11 a.m. a general advance was ordered, which, commencing somewhere on the right, included *Hindman's* division on the left. The enemy occupied the ground in our front along the road leading from Chattanooga to Lee and Gordon's Mills. Their line was formed along the fence at Brotherton's house, and they had a battery in the open field south of the house where *Johnson's* brigade had captured a battery on Saturday. The enemy also occupied two lines of breastworks made of rails and timber extending along my front and to the left of it in the woods west of Brotherton's farm.

By order of *Major-General Hood*, I moved my division forward and at once engaged the enemy. We advanced about 600 yards through the woods under a heavy fire of artillery and infantry, which swept our ranks with terrific effect, and crossed the road to Lee and Gordon's Mills, the left brigades of my division passing on either side of Brotherton's house. Our charge was irresistible, and the Yankees who did not flee were killed and captured at the fences and outhouses. . . .

Everett's battery now took position in a field south of Brotherton's house and opened to the front and left, firing about 6 rounds to the piece, and my line again moved forward under a heavy fire from the enemy's breastworks. The fire was so heavy that my right brigade faltered for a moment, and some of the men commenced falling back, but it was soon rallied and moving forward again. My whole line, *Gregg's* brigade in rear, supported by *Hood's* division, under *Law*, in a third line, swept forward with great force and rapidity and carried the breastworks, from which the foe precipitately retreated under a heavy fire, particularly directed to the left from my left brigade. [*O.R.*, XXX, Part II, pp. 456–457.]

The center brigade of *Johnson's* division crossed the La Fayette Road near the cabin.

Report of Col. John S. Fulton, CSA, Commanding
Johnson's Brigade, Provisional Division, Army of
Tennessee (Continued)

About 10 a.m. a general advance was ordered. The left of the brigade had advanced but a short distance before it became engaged with the enemy, the battle having commenced some three hours earlier on the right. The Seventeenth Tennessee recrossed the Chattanooga and La Fayette road, where it engaged the enemy. The whole line crossing the fence, the engagement became general. Here we passed a house and garden and through an open field. . . .

On entering the house, cribs, etc., many prisoners, both officers and men, were captured, and here some fine swords were taken from the enemy. . . . The enemy's breastworks, which had been built at intervals along his line, offered but a poor assistance to the enemy to resist our advance, which was not only vigorous and spirited, but irresistible. We found he had a second line of breastworks, about 80 yards in rear of the first, made of logs and rocks, behind which they scarcely halted. [*O.R.*, XXX, Part II, p. 474.]

Now direct your attention to the point about 50 yards north of the Dyer Road where the tree line turns.

That is the vicinity of the center of Wood's defensive position. Starting from this position and moving south it is possible to look at the breakthrough from the Union perspective.

Report of Brig. Gen. Thomas J. Wood, USA, Commanding
First Division, XXI Corps, Army of the Cumberland

In the early morning I was directed to move my division eastward from the slope of Missionary Ridge and take the position hitherto occupied by Negley's division, keeping my left in constant communication with General Brannan's right. Colonel Barnes' brigade, of Van Cleve's division, was ordered to report to me for service during the day.

Placing his brigade on the left, Harker's in the center, and Buell's on the right (the whole formed in two lines, the front one deployed, the second one in double column closed *en masse*, with their batteries following and supporting), I advanced my command and occupied the position assigned. In doing so I met with no opposition from the enemy. I was instructed not to invite an attack, but to be prepared to repel any effort of the enemy. In throwing out skirmishers to cover my front I aroused the enemy, and had quite a sharp affair with him. . . .

The position my command then occupied closed the gap in our lines between Sheridan's left and Brannan's right. Although I had not been at all seriously engaged at any time during the morning, I was well satisfied the enemy was in considerable force in my immediate front. Consequently I was extremely vigilant. Such was the status of the battle in my immediate vicinity when I received the following order:

HEADQUARTERS DEPARTMENT OF THE CUMBERLAND

September 20 — 10:45 a.m.

Brigadier-General Wood
Commanding Division, &c.:

The general commanding directs that you close up on Reynolds as fast as possible, and support him.
Respectfully, &c.,

FRANK S. BOND
Major, and Aide-de-Camp

I received the order about 11 o'clock . . . a short distance in rear of the center of my command. General McCook was with me. . . . I informed him that I would immediately carry it into execution, and suggested that he should close up his command rapidly on my right to prevent the occurrence of a gap in our lines. He said he would do so, and immediately rode away. I immediately dispatched my staff officers to the brigade commanders with the necessary orders, and the movement was at once begun. Reynolds' division was posted on the left of Brannan's division, which, in turn, was on the left of the position I was just quitting. I had consequently to pass my command in rear of Brannan's division to close up on and go to the support of Reynolds.

So soon as I had got the command well in motion, I rode forward to find General Reynolds and learn where and how it was desired to bring my command into action. I did not find General Reynolds, but in my search . . . I met General Thomas, to whom I communicated the order I had received . . . and desired to know where I should move my command to support General Reynolds. General Thomas replied that General Reynolds did not need support, but that I had better move to the support of **General Baird**, posted on our extreme left, who needed assistance. I exhibited my order to him, and asked whether he would take the responsibility of changing it. He replied he would. . . . I requested General Thomas to furnish me a staff officer who could conduct me to General Baird, which he did. Taking this staff officer with me, I rode at once to Barnes' brigade and directed the staff officer to conduct it to and report it to General Baird. I then rode to the other two brigades for the purpose of following with them in the rear of Barnes' brigade to the assistance of General Baird. When I rejoined them I found the valley south of them swarming with the enemy. [*O.R.*, XXX, Part I, pp. 634–635.]

Harker's brigade occupied the area near this position.

Report of Col. Charles G. Harker, USA, Commanding Third Brigade, First Division, XXI Corps, Army of the Cumberland

The morning of the 20th . . . at 8 a.m. we were . . . ordered forward to an eminence about one-fourth mile in our immediate front, and, as I understood, the rear of a position occupied by General Negley's command. We soon took up the position indicated, the Third Kentucky and Sixty-fourth Ohio Regiments occupying the front in line of battle, with a strong line of skirmishers in front, the One hundred and twenty-fifth and Sixty-fifth Ohio Regiments in double column at half distance on the second line about 200 yards in rear, the battery having a very commanding position near the front line. My brigade was then on the left of the First Brigade, commanded by Colonel Buell.

We had been in this position but a short time when we received orders to move forward and relieve General Negley's division. . . . We marched in battle array . . . . the First Brigade . . . on the right and my own in the center and Colonel Barnes' brigade of General Van Cleve's division on my left . . . . and relieved General Negley's division, which was posted immediately on the left of General Brannan's division, and was a continuation of the main . . . line of battle. We were advised that General Brannan had marched obliquely to the left and front, and that we must bear well to the left and "keep well closed up on Brannan." I kept well closed up on the right of Colonel Barnes.

The position to be occupied was pointed out to me by Major Lowrie, of General Negley's staff. The line of battle on my front was in a wooded valley east of a by-road leading to the Rossville road and nearly parallel to it. Temporary breastworks of wood, rocks, &c., had been erected by our troops, affording fair protection against infantry. Immediately on my front there was an open field about 400 yards wide, bounded by timber on the south and east. My skirmishers were thrown out in this field, and at once an exchange of shots with those of the enemy occurred. We got well into position about 10 a.m.

For some time previous, light firing of artillery and infantry was heard on our left, which continually grew heavier and appeared to extend toward the right. I had previously directed Captain Bradley to keep well to the rear with his battery. I kept well apprised of movements, and told him to conform his own to mine, moving to the right or left as he might be directed, but not to bring it into the woods where it could not be used to advantage.

About 10:15 a.m., a section of the enemy's battery opened upon my front. I ordered up a section of Bradley's battery, which silenced the enemy's. I again ordered his section to the rear, as it was but a useless expenditure of ammunition to continue the fire longer. About 11 a.m., I received orders, through General Wood, to move to the left and support General Reynolds. . . . I immediately got my command in readiness, and sent word to Captain Bradley to conform himself to my movements. Though we knew that the enemy was immediately in our front ready to take advantage of any false step that we might make, yet as a part of General McCook's corps was immediately on our right, and, as I understood, ready to fill the gap which our removal would make, we at once moved to the left and rear in search of General Reynolds' division.

Having passed General Brannan's division, we were halted, as I understood that General Wood was not advised as to the exact position of General Reynolds. I was soon directed by General Wood to move to the right again, as General Brannan was being pressed. While executing this move, Lieutenant Germaine, of General Brannan's staff, came up, laboring under great excitement, and requested me to hasten to General Brannan's relief. He stated that Brannan's right had been turned, that Van Cleve's division, which had come to their relief, had broken. I had moved but a short distance . . . before I was fired upon from the right. I immediately formed line of battle, facing to the right and nearly perpendicular to the general line of battle . . . all of my regiments on the same line. [*O.R.*, XXX, Part I, pp. 693–694.]

Now note the markers and plaques along the tree line south of the Dyer Road.

About 100 yards south of the road is the center of the position occupied by Buell's brigade, which formed the right of Wood's division. The One hundredth Illinois, with its left touching Dyer Road, was positioned on the left of Buell's line and the Twenty-sixth Ohio was located on the right. These two regiments were backed up by the Fifty-eighth Indiana and Thirteenth Michigan. Notice that the rise in ground in Brotherton Field protected this part of the Union line from Confederate long range rifle and artillery fire. In order to prevent surprise a skirmish line was deployed on the rise.

Report of Col. George P. Buell, USA, Commanding First Brigade, First Division, XXI Corps, Army of the Cumberland

About 9 a.m., . . . by order of General Wood, my brigade was moved forward and put in position behind some temporary works of rails and logs . . . on the immediate right of Colonel Harker. About this time I was informed that General McCook's corps would join me on my right. My brigade at this time was formed in two lines of battle with skirmishers about 75 yards to the front.

I soon learned that the enemy was massing immediately in my front and perhaps on my right. Staff officers were immediately sent . . . with a heavy line of skirmishers for the purpose of learning if there were yet any of our own troops on my immediate right. Soon the report came there were none as yet. My two reserve regiments, Fifty-eighth Indiana and Thirteenth Michigan, were immediately deployed on my right with a heavy line of skirmishers, so that my right might not be turned without timely knowledge of the fact. My battery . . . was placed so as to sweep the crest of a low ridge in my front.

Very soon after this, perhaps 10:30 a.m., one brigade of General Davis' division reported to join me on the right. I immediately drew in two regiments from the right, so that my brigade would have but two regimental fronts, allowing General Davis' left to rest against the right of the Twenty-sixth Ohio, which was my right front battalion, the One hundredth Illinois the left front, the Fifty-eighth Indiana left rear, and Thirteenth Michigan right rear battalions. . . . The enemy was making bold demonstrations in my front, so much so that whenever one of my skirmishers moved or rose to his feet he was shot at.

Now that my right flank was protected I felt confident that we could hold our position.

About this time I received notice from a staff officer that the One hundredth Illinois . . . had charged to the front, and that the colonel asked to be supported. Thinking perhaps a general charge had been ordered by General Wood and that the left of my brigade was moving to the front with Colonel Harker's, and that the officer bearing me the order might have fallen (I then being at the extreme right of my brigade), I ordered the Twenty-sixth Ohio to charge as far as the crest of the low ridge . . . in front, but to go no farther without further orders until I could investigate the cause of the One hundredth Illinois being in front of the position assigned it by me. The Twenty-sixth Ohio had hardly gotten to the front as ordered when the One hundredth Illinois came back without its colonel and resumed its former position. Colonel Bartleson leading his regiment had run into a masked battery and heavy line of the enemy, and is supposed . . . wounded and captured. . . .

About half past II a.m. . . . I received orders to move my brigade by the left flank at the double quick, following Colonel Harker's brigade, for the purpose of supporting some portion of the line to our left. The orders . . . were immediately issued; before moving the brigade, however, orders were issued for the skirmishers to remain and hold their position until relieved by the command still on my right, and to be certain that this would be done . . . I sent two staff officers to attend personally to it. Orders were also issued to my battery commander, Captain Estep, to move his battery around on my left flank, which would be in my rear when facing the enemy. I was fearful of making the movement, with the enemy not over 200 yards distant, closely watching every maneuver.

Two brigades on my left had already moved off, and of course my command must move by the gap left by them. Having my line of skirmishers secure, and, as I thought, my battery safe, the movement was commenced, myself leading the direction.

We had scarcely moved one brigade front when the shock came like an avalanche on my right flank. The attack seemed to have been simultaneous throughout the enemy's lines, for the entire right and part of the center gave way before the overpowering numbers of the foe. My own little brigade seemed as if it were swept from the field. Captain Estep with all speed moved his battery about 400 yards to the rear, on the crest of a hill, where he opened on the enemy with great effect. The greater portion of my brigade was cut off from me and driven to the rear. My staff, who were executing orders at this time, were also cut off; the orderly carrying my headquarters flag, who was in the rear at the time, was captured. That portion of my command that was near me, the Fifty-eighth Indiana and some stragglers of other regiments that were rallied, remained on the field, and while we were still in front of and to the left of the battery the enemy came around my right flank and shot down 35 horses of my battery, thus capturing the same.

I retreated with a portion of my command to the left oblique, fighting at the crest of every hill for a distance of at least three-fourths of a mile. At one point we advanced again from one hill to the next in front, and fought the left flank of a long line of battle (all of which was in full view) until we were almost surrounded and flanked on our right. . . .

About this time I discovered General Wood with Colonel Harker's brigade, several hundred yards to my left, also on the retreat. I continued to retreat with the remnant of my brigade until we came up to the right flank of General Brannan's division, which was in position on the top of a high hill [Snodgrass Hill]. Here I reported to General Brannan. . . . [*O.R.*, XXX, Part I, pp. 655–657.]

Report of Lieut. Col. William H. Young, USA, Commanding Twenty-sixth Ohio Infantry, First Brigade, First Division, XXI Corps, Army of the Cumberland (Continued)

I received an order from one of the brigade staff . . . to move my command off by the left flank, and to follow the One hundredth Illinois. As my skirmishers (four companies) were then engaged, I asked if they were to be called in, and was told they were. I hesitated a moment lest there might be some mistake, but was told the order was imperative and the movement to be executed promptly. . . . I at once ordered my skirmishers in.

The movement I since learned was made by the whole division. My skirmishers were scarcely drawn in until their line was occupied by the enemy's, and before I had marched a regimental front stray shots came whistling through the trees. I was marching in very quick time to keep in sight of the One hundredth. The battery marching in a parallel line on my left found much difficulty in making its way over the rocks and through the timber, and the enemy's fire was rapidly approaching nearer and increasing in rapidity.

At this time we received orders to double-quick, which tended much to increase the excitement of the moment, the artillery dashing along against trees and over stones at a headlong rate. The One hundredth rapidly gaining the rear, first by a left oblique, and then by the rear rank, and the growing unsteadiness of my own men made me extremely anxious for the issue. I immediately fell back from the head of the column to gain a position on its left flank, as it was now very sensibly inclining to the rear, but at the same moment a mass of fugitives from the front struck my command on its right flank, and, becoming completely mingled with it, carried the whole to the rear about 50 or 75 paces into a corn-field before we could extricate ourselves and rally. This . . . was soon effected under fire. . . . [O.R., XXX, Part I, pp. 672–673.]

Having been swept from the defensive line and separated from its brigade, the Twenty-sixth Ohio attempted to rally in Dyer's cornfield, about 700 yards northwest of this location. We shall rejoin the regiment in a later stop, but first it is instructive to review the action of the brigade originally on Buell's right.

Look yet another 100 yards south. The small monument to the Eighth Kansas Infantry just inside the woods or the Fifteenth Wisconsin monument outside the tree line may be visible.

This is the left part of the position occupied by Heg's (Martin's) brigade of Davis' division. The brigade line extended to the south almost to the southern edge of Brotherton Field. To the right of this brigade was Carlin's brigade, whose line extended through the woods almost to the next field. When Wood's division moved north, the left flank of Davis' division was uncovered. Before Davis could move units north to fill in the gap, the Confederates had attacked.

Report of Col. John A. Martin, USA, Commanding Third Brigade, First Division, XX Corps, Army of the Cumberland (Continued)

At noon we received an order to support General Sheridan on the right. We advanced across the road again and formed in line of battle, and then advanced to near a small barricade in the woods, fronting an open field. Finding the barricade already occupied by our troops, the brigade was moved by the right flank to the rear of General Carlin's brigade, and was ordered to lie down in a small ravine.

This order had hardly been executed when I received an order to move back by the left flank and take position on the left of General Carlin's brigade, the troops that had occupied the ground having been moved away to the left. I directed the movement, passing General Carlin and moving by the right flank forward to the barricade. The three regiments on the right of the brigade reached their position, but . . . the regiment on the left of the line had not reached its position, when the enemy rose up from the tall weeds in front and advanced on us four columns deep, pouring in a destructive fire. The left flank of the brigade was entirely exposed, as the troops that had occupied that position had moved so far to the left as to be out of sight, and we were soon flanked and exposed to a destructive enfilading fire.

The enemy in front was terribly punished as he came up. Our men fired coolly from behind the barricade and with terrible effect, the closed ranks and heavy columns of the enemy making their loss very heavy. The brigade held the position until the enemy had mounted the barricade, when, flanked on the left and overpowered by numbers in front, the men fell back in confusion, partially rallying about 200 yards in rear, but, finding all support gone and the line on the left in disorder, breaking again.

On the brow of the hill in the woods across the road they were again rallied, formed in line, and left the field by order in the rear of Sheridan's division, which had rallied at the same point. . . . The loss [was] . . . fully 60 per cent of those engaged, and amply attests the courage, stubbornness, and determination with which the troops fought. [*O.R.*, XXX, Part I, p. 530.]

The Confederate force attacking directly into Martin's position was *Deas'* brigade, the right brigade of *Hindman's* division. The report of one of *Deas'* regiments reveals the violence of the battle as the Confederates crossed Brotherton Field.

Report of Col. Samuel K. McSpadden, CSA, Commanding Nineteenth Alabama Infantry, Deas' Brigade, Hindman's Division, Army of Tennessee

Early on . . . the 20th, we were ordered forward, and about 8 a.m. took position behind some temporary breastworks of logs, chunks, &c. My skirmishers were hotly engaged with those of the enemy at this point, while I lost several men killed and wounded by shell and canister along my line. Those works were in open woods of heavy timber, with like timber and thick undergrowth in front for some 200 yards to an open field.

About 11 a.m. we were ordered forward. Scaling our breast-works, we advanced in good order, driving the enemy from the woods and across the field, but upon rising a hill in the field some 50 to 75 yards from its farther boundary, we were met by a volley of musketry from the enemy, who had been securely placed behind breastworks in the edge of another woods. At the first fire of the enemy, so unexpected and near, my regiment exhibited a momentary hesitancy and wavering, but upon my ordering "charge," it moved at double-quick, and, with a shout, scaled the enemy's works, and pursued their panic-stricken and shattered ranks through the woods and undergrowth until, reaching the borders of another open field, the enemy were discovered behind some houses, potash-works, and rail breastworks.

At this point there was not even a momentary hesitancy, but with an increased shout and rapidity of step, we drove the enemy from these works with great slaughter, and pursued them through the open field some 250 yards to an elevated skirt of heavy open woods. . . . [O.R., XXX, Part II, pp. 333–334.]

Continue on the DYER ROAD to the STOP sign. Cross the GLENN-KELLY ROAD and drive an additional 0.2 mile and park in the parking area on the right. This is the site of the old Dyer house. Dismount and face the direction in which you were traveling.

The railroad near Union Mills, Tennessee. This is an extension of the tracks that carried Longstreet's Corps north from Atlanta. (Benson Lossing, *A History of the Civil War, 1861–65* [New York: War Memorial Association, 1912]).

STOP 21, POSITION A – JOHNSON LEADS THE BREAKTHROUGH

About 400 yards to your left front, a small stack of cannon balls on the hillside marks the spot where Major General William S. Rosecrans, commanding the Army of the Cumberland, was located when the Union lines were penetrated at Brotherton Farm.

The Dyer Road continues west for approximately 0.3 mile, where it intersects the Dry Valley Road. This north-south road and the La Fayette Road are the only two major routes to Chattanooga.

The rising ground you see starting just north of the Dyer Road continues to ascend to the north and northeast, forming a commanding position overlooking the Dyer's field north of the farm house, and increases in height for another 600 yards, through the trees, to form Snodgrass and Horseshoe Ridges. These connecting ridges became the final Union line of defense.

After *Johnson's* division punctured the Union lines in Brotherton Field it inclined slightly to the right. By the time it reached the vicinity of the intersection of Dyer and Glenn-Kelly Roads, the entire division was north of the Dyer Road and attacking in a westerly and northwesterly direction.

Report of Brig. Gen. Bushrod R. Johnson, CSA, Commanding Provisional Division, Army of Tennessee, attached to Longstreet's Corps, Army of Northern Virginia (Continued)

Having advanced some distance in the woods west of Brotherton's farm to the foot of a small ascent, covered with a thick growth of young pines, my right brigade [*McNair's*] halted under the effect of a heavy fire, which was also severely damaging my second line. *Colonel Sugg* now pressed to the front the three regiments of *Gregg's* brigade which had formed my second line, *Johnson's* brigade moving to the left at the same time, and again my line advanced rapidly on the enemy, driving them from the woods east of Dyer's house, *McNair's* brigade bearing to the right.

Our lines now emerged from the forest into open ground on the border of long, open fields, over which the enemy were retreating under cover of several batteries, which were arranged along the crest of a ridge on our right and front, running up to the corner of a stubble-field, and of one battery on our left and front posted on an

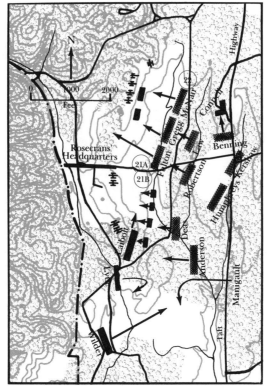

Stops 21A, 21B, & 22
Situation Noon
September 20, 1863

elevation in the edge of the woods, just at the corner of a field near a peach orchard and southwest of Dyer's house.

The scene now presented was unspeakably grand. The resolute and impetuous charge, the rush of our heavy columns sweeping out from the shadow and gloom of the forest into the open fields flooded with sunlight, the glitter of arms, the onward dash of artillery and mounted men, the retreat of the foe, the shouts of the hosts of our army, the dust, the smoke, the noise of fire-arms—of whistling balls and grape-shot and of bursting shell—made up a battle scene of unsurpassed grandeur. Here *General Hood* gave me the last order I received from him on the field, "Go ahead, and keep ahead of everything." . . .

The unusual depth of our columns of attack in this part of the field, and the force and power with which it was thrown upon the enemy's line, had now completely broken and routed their center and cast the shattered fragments to the right and left. *Everett's* battery was here ordered into action on the right of *Johnson's* brigade and opened upon the retreating foe, while my line continued to advance.

There was now an interval of about 800 yards between *Hindman's* division, on my left, and my command. *Johnson's* brigade, on the left, bore but slightly to the right, its left regiment stretching across the road from Dyer's house to Crawfish (Spring) road [the Dry Valley Road] and passing on both sides of the house. *Gregg's* brigade, in the center, moved a little to the right, so as to flank and capture 9 pieces of artillery on its right, posted on the ascent to the eminence in the corner of the field north of Dyer's house. *McNair's* brigade, now somewhat in rear of the two left brigades, moved obliquely to the right and directly upon this eminence. My line was here uncovered by *Hood's* division, which must have changed its direction to the right.

In this advance *Brig. Gen. E. McNair*, commanding the right brigade . . . [was] wounded . . . and the command of *McNair's* brigade devolved upon *Colonel Coleman*, of the Thirty-ninth North Carolina. . . . *Colonel Coleman* reports that *McNair's* brigade charged and carried the eminence in the corner of the field to our right, capturing the 10 guns, 8 of which were immediately carried off, and 2 were subsequently removed; and that the brigade fell back for the want of ammunition and support and formed on the left of *Robertson's* brigade, of *Hood's* division. . . .

In the meantime, I discovered what I conceived to be an important position directly in our front — an elevated ridge of open ground running nearly north and south beyond the narrow strip of woods on the western borders of open fields in our front, and about 600 yards west of the elevation on which the . . . artillery had been captured — and I hastened to press forward *Gregg's* brigade, which had halted for a moment on the flank of the guns that were being removed while *Johnson's* brigade approached the same position from the left.

From the crest of this ridge the ground descends abruptly into a corn-field and cove lying south of Vidito's house. West of the cove is a range of the Missionary Ridge, while north of it a spur of that ridge spreads out to the east. Through a gap at the angle between this spur on the north and the ridge on the west of the cove, and about 1,000 yards from the ridge on the east where my division was now taking position, passed the Crawfish (Spring) road, which continues south along the base of the ridge on the western side of the cove. Along this road a line of telegraph wires extended from Chattanooga to General Rosecrans' headquarters, and at the gorge of the gap a train of wagons filled the road, while a number of caissons and a battery of artillery for defense of the train occupied the grounds near Vidito's house. The ridge on the east of the cove was taken without resistance, though the enemy had there constructed a breastwork of rails and had piled up a large number of their knapsacks, secure, as they doubtless thought, from the danger of the battle-field.

As soon as this ridge was occupied, which was a few minutes before 12 m., our advance position, commanded by adjacent hills and separated on the right and left as far as I could see from our troops, induced me to send my aide-de-camp, *Captain Blakemore*, to report our position to *Lieutenant-General Longstreet*, commanding our wing, and to bring up artillery and infantry to our support, while I disposed of my command for defense. *Gregg's* brigade was at once posted, partly facing to the north, at the edge of the woods at the north end of the field and partly facing to the west along a portion of the adjacent ridge. *Johnson's* brigade was posted, facing to the west, on the crest of the ridge about 100 yards to the left of *Gregg's* brigade. Both brigades immediately advanced their skirmishers to the front.

When I discovered the train of wagons at the gorge of the Crawfish (Spring) road the enemy were making every effort to get them away. I promptly posted *Everett's* battery on the ridge between *Johnson's* and *Gregg's* brigades, where it opened fire on the train. The fire of the artillery and some shots from our advancing skirmishers created the utmost consternation among the drivers and teams, causing some of the wagons to be upset and others to be run against trees and up the precipitous acclivities adjacent. . . . Our skirmishers now advanced and took possession of the wagons, caissons, and guns. [*O.R.*, XXX, Part II, pp. 457–459.]

Cross the DYER ROAD and walk about 30 yards into the field.

POSITION B—HINDMAN JOINS THE BREAKTHROUGH

Beyond the thin wood line to your left and left front is the western edge of the woods marking the west side of Brotherton Field. The right of Wood's division and Davis' division were on the far side of these woods. Southeast of your location, at a distance of 700 yards, these tree lines join and then intersect with another to form a right angle. This marks the southeast corner of the field where the Confederate division of *Major General Thomas C. Hindman* charged, opposed initially by Davis' division.

Report of Maj. Gen. Thomas C. Hindman, CSA, Commanding Division, Army of Tennessee

About 11 a.m. on . . . September 20, under orders from *Lieutenant-General Longstreet*, commanding the Left Wing, my command moved forward simultaneously with the troops on my right. At the distance of 300 yards skirmishing commenced, and immediately my whole line was engaged. Rushing on at the double-quick through a storm of bullets, shot, and shell, *Deas'* brave Alabamians and *Manigault's* Alabamians and South Carolinians, equally brave, drove the enemy from his breastworks, then pushed him beyond the La Fayette road, and charged his second line of breastworks, 300 yards farther on. The troops on *Manigault's* left not advancing with him, he was enfiladed on that flank by infantry and artillery, checked, and at length forced to retire. . . .

Deas swept like a whirlwind over the breastworks. *Anderson's* fearless Mississippians, carrying the breastworks in their front, moved up rapidly on his left to *Manigault's* place. Without halting, these two brigades then drove the enemy across the Crawfish Spring road [actually the Glenn-Kelly Road] and up the broken spurs of Missionary Ridge to its first elevation, 100 yards west. Hiding behind this, the enemy opened a tremendous fire of musketry and cannon upon our line as it advanced, and at the same time enfiladed it from an eminence in a field on the right; but, without faltering, he was charged, driven from his strong position, and pursued upward of three-quarters of a mile, when he ceased resisting and disappeared, going north completely routed. A body of Federal cavalry, covering the retreat of the infantry, made a demonstration against my right, but retired hastily when about to be attacked. [*O.R.*, XXX, Part II, p. 303.]

The only major attempt to stop *Hindman's* division was the action against *Manigault's* brigade, a counter attack by Wilder's mounted infantry brigade, launched with such violence that *Manigault's* command was disorganized and forced to retreat back across the La Fayette Road. Here it was reorganized and later reentered the action on Horseshoe Ridge.

The Union division of Major General Philip H. Sheridan had spent most of the morning in a position southwest of this field. Just prior to the movement of Wood's division, Sheridan had also received orders to move northward. At the time *Longstreet* attacked, most of Sheridan's division was in motion and his right flank was hit by *Hindman's* assault. Futile attempts were made to turn Sheridan's brigades and counterattack the Confederates, but the force and surprise of *Hindman's* assault drove his units across the Dry Valley Road, where they were able to retreat north.

Report of Maj. Gen. William S. Rosecrans, USA, Commanding the Army of the Cumberland (Continued)

Thus Davis' two brigades, one of Van Cleve's, and Sheridan's entire division were driven from the field, and the remainder, consisting of the divisions of Baird, Johnson, Palmer, Reynolds, Brannan, and Wood, two of Negley's brigades and one of Van Cleve's, were left to sustain the conflict against the whole power of the rebel army, which, desisting from pursuit on the right, concentrated their whole efforts to destroy them.

At the moment of the repulse of Davis' division, I was standing in rear of his right, waiting the completion of the closing of McCook's corps to the left. Seeing confusion among Van Cleve's troops, and the distance Davis' men were falling back, and the tide of battle surging toward us, the urgency for Sheridan's troops to intervene became imminent, and I hastened in person to the extreme right, to direct Sheridan's movement on the flank of the advancing rebels. It was too late. The crowd of returning troops rolled back, and the enemy advanced. Giving the troops directions to rally behind the ridge west of the Dry Valley road, I passed down it accompanied by General Garfield, Major McMichael, Major Bond, and Captain Young of my staff, and a few of the escort, under a shower of grape, canister, and musketry, for 200 or 300 yards, and attempted to rejoin General Thomas and the troops sent to his support, by passing to the rear of the broken portion of our lines, but found the routed troops far toward the left, and hearing the enemy's advancing musketry and cheers, I became doubtful whether the left had held its ground, and started for Rossville. On consultation and further reflection, however, I determined to send General Garfield there, while I went to Chattanooga, to give orders for the security of the pontoon bridges at Battle Creek and Bridgeport, and to make preliminary dispositions either to forward ammunition and supplies, should we hold our ground, or to withdraw the troops into good position. [*O.R.*, XXX, Part I, pp. 59–60.]

Upon leaving this position you will proceed to a point where you can look directly west at the artillery position to the north and west of Dyer's Field. Before departing, however, it may be beneficial to visualize how the Union artillery was deployed in this phase of the battle.

To the north, near the cluster of monuments, were four Union batteries and two supporting infantry regiments, three batteries of Van Cleve's division and the battery from Buell's brigade that had retreated to that position.

Approximately 200 yards to the west of your position and just south of the Dyer Road was the Sixth Battery, Ohio Light Artillery from Wood's division. Directly south, along the tree line on the hill at a distance of 400 yards stood Battery C, First Illinois Artillery of Sheridan's division. The commanders of the Union regiments and brigades falling back from the Confederate assault attempted to rally their units along the general line of these batteries. The openness of this area and the commanding positions where the guns were located offered the potential to develop a line of resistance with interlocking fire, but the ferocity and momentum of the Confederate assault routed the infantry and either captured the artillery or forced it to fall back.

Return to your car. Retrace your route on the DYER ROAD. At the STOP sign TURN LEFT onto the GLENN-KELLY Road. Drive 0.2 mile to the field on your left. Park on the right side of the road. Dismount and face the field.

STOP 22 – FIGHTING FOR TIME

The sloping field between the near and far tree lines is the northern part of Dyer's Field. The monuments on the ridge in front of the far tree line are those that you saw from Stop 21.

Four batteries of artillery had taken position on that ridge. From your right to left they were: Seventh Indiana Battery, Twenty-sixth Pennsylvania Battery, Third Wisconsin Battery – all from Van Cleve's division – and the Eighth Indiana Battery of Buell's brigade. In position forward of the artillery and half way down the ridge were the Twenty-sixth Ohio Infantry and Thirteenth Michigan Infantry Regiments of Buell's brigade, which had retreated from the northern part of Brotherton Field. On the high ground farther to the right, beyond the point of woods, was part of Battery D, First Michigan Artillery, which had withdrawn from the south end of Poe Field.

Johnson reported that his division crossed the road in the area between this location and the intersection of the Dyer and Glenn-Kelly Roads. His right brigade—*McNair's*—moved obliquely and attacked the artillery from the front. The other two brigades—*Gregg's* and *Johnson's* (*Fulton's*) attacked the position from the flank or cut it off from retreat to the Dry Valley Road by passing in rear of the artillery.

You can walk directly to the artillery position or remain where you are. If you choose the former, drive forward to the point where the tree line meets the road on the west side, where you will find a turn-out. You can safely park there.

There are several reports that provide a vivid description of the fight in and around these guns. The Twenty-sixth Ohio, of Buell's brigade, rallied in a cornfield, faced to the front, and attempted to defend the artillery.

Report of Lieut. Col. William H. Young, USA, Commanding Twenty-sixth Ohio Infantry, First Brigade, First Division, XXI Corps, Army of the Cumberland (Continued)

An extended rebel line [was] rapidly approaching and already considerably advanced on my right. I immediately retired my regiment to the low ground in the corn about 200 paces from the edge of the timber from which we had just emerged and just at the foot of the hill in our rear, but finding myself supported neither on the right nor left, and the position being untenable by reason of timber 150 yards to the right from which the enemy was already firing upon me . . . I retired half way up the hill to a fence now parallel to my line.

Rallying behind this, I hoped, with the support of several batteries posted on the crest of the hill several hundred yards above and another regiment rallied under cover of the same fence row with mine 100 yards to my left, to hold the position. Captain Baldwin, of Colonel Buell's staff, here joined me and assisted in rallying the men of various commands who were falling back from the woods below.

He could give me no information of Colonel Buell's whereabouts. I remained at this fence about fifteen minutes, maintaining and receiving a steady fire. The enemy in front was held in the timber below, but meeting no opposition he advanced on the right under a cover of a tongue of timber stretching part way up the hillside, and being entirely hidden from view by the weeds and bushes along a fence row perpendicular to my line and at the edge of the timber, had almost turned my right flank before he became visible. At the same time I discovered the regiment on the left had fallen back before a heavy line advancing on its left, and that the guns above were being retired.

I promptly fell back rapidly, but in tolerable order, halting for a moment in rear of the Eighth Indiana battery; but the enemy had already gained the timber crowning the prolongation of the ridge to the right, and scarcely 150 yards distant, from which position he had forced back a portion of the Thirteenth Michigan; he was also coming up in heavy lines on the left.

There was no support anywhere in sight; every man in the command saw and felt the hopelessness of attempting a stand at this point, and as the batteries were already moving off, finding it impossible to rally my command in any force, I fell back into the woods, assisting one of the batteries as we retired. The woods here were filled with fugitives from various commands (utterly disordered, and, in spite of [the efforts of] my own and other officers of Colonel Buell's brigade . . .), making their way to the rear. [*O.R.*, XXX, Part I, pp. 673–674.]

Captain Estep's battery was initially on the western edge of Brotherton Field in support of Buell's brigade, but when the brigade began moving north, Estep moved his guns with the infantry.

Report of Capt. George Estep, USA, Commanding Eighth Indiana Battery, First Division, XXI Corps, Army of the Cumberland (Continued)

I formed my pieces forward into line, left oblique, leaving the infantry between me and the enemy, who was then advancing on our right. I moved in line as far as I possibly could, then broke into column of sections and finally into column of piece. When moving in this position the enemy burst upon us in such force as to render our holding (I mean the brigade) them back impossible. I then turned the head of my column to the left, moved across a corn-field to the crest of a hill about 400 yards distant. I then formed in battery and was told by Colonel Starling, of Major-General Crittenden's staff, to hold my fire till our own men got out of the timber. I immediately cautioned my lieutenants about holding fire till ordered, but a few minutes elapsed, however, till the enemy came up in splendid style in heavy lines to the right of my front. I ordered firing to commence with shell and canister.

I am confident that we killed and wounded hundreds of them as they came up. Other batteries were in the same line with mine and dealing perhaps equal destruction to the enemy, but just then, when I supposed that we were going to drive them back, we received a galling fire from the enemy who had got position in force on our right flank and rear; but a moment more and the enemy was charging us from the right. My horses were killed and disabled, and I could do nothing but leave the battery in his possession. [*O.R.*, XXX, Part I, pp. 677–678.]

From this position *Johnson's* division pushed to the western edge of this ridge, where he was able to command the Dry Valley Road.

If you walked to the position of the Union guns, return to the initial stopping point before you continue.

The patch of woods to your immediate right was smaller in 1863, but the woods to your left and rear are much as they were at the time of the battle. Poe Field is about 500 yards through the woods behind you. If you were to walk along the wood line to your left for about 125 yards and then into the woods for 10 yards, you would find a marker indicating the place *Major General John B. Hood* was wounded on September 20, 1863.

The northern part of Dyer's Field was marked by a fence that ran west from the Glenn-Kelly Road along the tree line to your right, crossed the stream, and continued to the high ground in front of you.

Hood's division—commanded by *Brigadier General E. McIver Law*—supported the leading brigades of *Johnson's* division during the Confederate breakthrough. It was deployed with *Law's* (*Sheffield's*) brigade forward, *Robertson's* brigade on the left, and *Benning's* brigade on the right, in the second line. After crossing the road, *Benning's* brigade turned right and attacked the flank of the Union troops defending Poe Field. *Law's* brigade continued in a northwest direction and eventually moved to a position to the right rear of *Johnson's* division. In the woods to your left this brigade made a partial right turn and began to move out of the woods and across the field. At the same time, *Robertson's* brigade moved up on the left of *Law's* brigade.

As *Law's* brigade moved out into the field, it was counterattacked by Harker's brigade of the First Division, XXI Corps, which had fallen back to that part of the ridge and lower ground just north of your location. Harker's brigade was deployed facing south with its right on the high ground and its left on the Glenn-Kelly Road. Here the division commander—Wood—picked up some stragglers from Buell's brigade, which also had been in Brotherton Field. The other parts of Buell's brigade had fallen back to join the four artillery batteries on the ridge.

Report of Brig. Gen. Thomas J. Wood, USA, Commanding First Division, XXI Corps, Army of the Cumberland (Continued)

Having turned our right and separated a portion of our forces from the main body, . . . [the enemy] was seeking the rear of our solid line of battle, to attack it in reverse, hoping thus to cut our communication with Chattanooga and capture and destroy the bulk of our army.

I had with me at the time but one brigade (Harker's) and a portion of Buell's. I immediately formed a line across the valley facing southward, determined, if possible, to check the advance of the enemy. He was in full and plain view in the open fields, and it was evident his force far outnumbered mine. But I felt that this was no time for comparing numbers. The enemy, at all hazards, must be checked. I was without the support of artillery and knew I had to depend alone on the musket.

I formed my line in a skirt of the woods reaching across the valley. In front of me was the open fields across which the enemy was advancing. It was a matter of great importance to get possession of the fence which bounded this field on the northern side. My line was some 150 or 200 yards from the fence on the north of it, while the enemy's lines were perhaps as much as 350 yards south of it. In person I ordered the One hundred and twenty-fifth Ohio, Colonel Opdycke commanding, to advance and seize the fence.

There was a momentary hesitation in the regiment to go forward. Its gallant colonel immediately rode in front of the center of his regiment, and taking off his hat, called on his men to advance. His regiment gallantly responded by a prompt advance, as men ever will under the inspiration of such leadership. The regiment quickly lined the fence, whence a sharp fire was opened on the enemy. Soon the Sixty-fourth Ohio . . . followed and formed along the fence on the left of the One hundred and twenty-fifth Ohio.

This bold and rapid offensive movement seemed to take the enemy by surprise and disconcert his movements, for his hitherto advancing lines halted. The other regiments, Sixty-fifth Ohio and Third Kentucky . . . of Harker's brigade, with the Fifty-eighth Indiana, of Colonel Buell's brigade . . . were formed on the right of the

One hundred and twenty-fifth Ohio, higher up the fence and on a hill dominating the field in which the enemy had halted. . . .

The movements of the enemy at this moment were so singular, and his blurred and greasy and dusty uniform so resembled our own when travel-stained, coupled with the fact that it was expected a part of McCook's command would come from that direction (the terrible disaster to his force on the right not then being known to us), that for a few minutes the impression prevailed and the cry ran along the line that the troops in front of us were our own. I ordered the firing to cease, the thought of firing on our comrades in arms being too horrible to contemplate. In a few moments, however, the delusion was dispelled, the enemy commencing to advance again in a way that left no doubt of his identity, for he advanced firing on us.

I do not mention this singular mistake on account of its possessing any particular importance *per se*, but rather to record it as an instance of the strange delusions that sometimes occur on the battlefield without any sufficient cause and without the possibility of a reasonable explanation. . . . The enemy was probably not more than . . . 350 yards distant, and was halted in a broad open field. But for the mistake we could have punished him most severely at the time he was halted. [*O.R.*, XXX, Part I, pp. 636–637.]

This counterattack against the right of *Law's* brigade threw it into confusion and caused it to retreat southeast towards the Dyer Road. Part of this confusion spread to the next brigade on the left—*Robertson's*—which temporarily halted.

The Third Confederate line in the breakthrough were two brigades—*Kershaw's* and *Humphreys'*—of *McLaws'* division, under the command of *Brigadier General Joseph B. Kershaw.* As the regiments of *Law's* brigade fell back before the Union counterattack, *Kershaw* entered the fight.

Report of Brig. Gen. Joseph B. Kershaw, CSA, Commanding McLaws' Division, Army of Northern Virginia

About 11 o'clock I was ordered forward with the command to report to *Major-General Hood.* Arriving, I found his troops engaged in front and a line of battle just going in. *General Hood* directed me to form line in his rear, with my center resting on the spot where I found him. . . . Forming line (*Humphreys* on my left) as rapidly as possible under fire . . . and in a thick wood, I moved . . . to the front. I had been directed to occupy a line of breastworks, but before reaching that point a staff officer of the lieutenant-general commanding was sent to direct me to a point farther in advance.

I crossed the La Fayette road near a house, and, crossing the open ground, entered the woods beyond and proceeded nearly to what I understood to be the Cove road [the Glenn-Kelly Road]. While passing through the last wood *Lieutenant-General Longstreet* directed me to look out for my right flank, and I had disposed of *Colonel Henagan's* Eighth South Carolina, my right regiment, in such a manner as to cover me in that direction. . . .

Having reached the point . . . the firing on my right became very heavy, and a portion of *General Hood's* division fell back along my line. I changed front almost perpendicularly to the right on *Colonel Nance's* Third South Carolina Regiment, my left center, which I had indicated as the directing battalion. This movement had just been accomplished when an officer of *Brigadier-General Law's* staff informed me of the unfortunate loss of *Major-General Hood*, and suggested that as senior brigadier I should assume the direction of the two brigades of that division on my right. *General Bushrod R. Johnson* was present, and called for a comparison of rank, which seemed to satisfy him. *Major Cunningham*, assistant inspector-general, *General Hood's* staff, who had been sent by the general to conduct me, made the opportune suggestion that the lieutenant-general commanding [*Longstreet*] be informed.

Relieved by this, I requested him to direct *General Humphreys* to move up and support me on my right, he having been thrown in my rear by my change of front. *General Johnson* had undertaken to advance a brigade on my left. The enemy occupied a skirt of wood on the farther side of the field around Dyer's house, his right extending into the woods beyond the field, his left crossing the Cove road. His colors were ostentatiously displayed along the lines.

The last of *Hood's* division engaged in my front had just retired when I ordered the advance, directing *Colonel Henagan* to extend to the right and engage the enemy in that direction until *Humphreys'* arrival, who was then in motion. The distance across the field was about 800 yards, with a fence intervening about one-fourth of the distance. As soon as we crossed the fence, I ordered bayonets fixed, and moved at a double quick, sending *Lieutenant-Colonel Gaillard*, Second South Carolina Regiment (my extreme left), to gain the enemy's right flank.

When within 100 yards of the enemy they broke, and I opened fire upon them along the whole line, but pursued them rapidly over the first line of hills to the foot of the second [Snodgrass Hill], when I halted under a heavy fire of artillery on the heights, sheltering the men as much as possible, and there awaited the coming of *Humphreys*, on my right. [*O.R.*, XXX, Part II, pp. 503–504.]

Report of Colonel Emerson Opdycke, USA, Commanding One hundred and twenty-fifth Ohio Infantry, Third Brigade, First Division, XXI Corps, Army of the Cumberland

The line stretched nearly across a long open field. One hundred yards to our rear was a ridge running parallel to the line, which ascended into quite a timbered hill 200 yards to my right. The enemy's line, which was 200 yards distant, reached beyond our flanks, and was advancing upon us. A severe encounter with small arms raged for a short time, when General Wood . . . ordered us to move forward. My regiment fixed bayonets and charged on the double-quick.

The enemy fled in confusion, and disappeared for a time. We pursued 400 yards and lay down behind a prostrate fence, which was upon another less tenable, but parallel ridge to the first one. This ridge also rose into a wooded hill 150 yards to our right. The other regiments of the brigade soon prolonged my line to the right and left.

Another line of the enemy, more formidable than the first, appeared in the distance, moving upon us. The terrible splendor of this advance is beyond the reach of my pen. The whole line seemed perfect and as if moved by a single mind. The musketry soon became severe and my losses heavy; the color-sergeant severely wounded, the standard shot in two the second time, and the colors riddled with balls. The regiment to my left gave way, and then that upon my right. . . . The enemy came on and themselves prolonged my line to the right, occupied the wooded hill there, and enfiladed my line with a destructive fire. . . . Numbers fell dead and more were seriously wounded, but the line was firmly maintained. Lieutenant Clark coolly remarked, "They can kill us, but whip us never."

Seeing no relief, I retired the regiment to the ridge in rear. In doing so, some troops passed obliquely through my right wing, which caused a little confusion there, but the ranks were closed immediately, and the crest occupied where ordered by General Wood. [*O.R.*, XXX, Part I, p. 708.]

From this position Harker's brigade and the remnants of Buell's brigade fell back north and took up position on an open finger of ground extending northeast from Snodgrass Hill. This placed them on the left flank of elements from Brannan's division and other regiments that had joined Brannan in establishing a defensive position on Snodgrass Hill. The critical delaying action by the Union regiments in this area bought the time necessary for Brannan to establish the final defense.

Return to your car for the drive to this position.

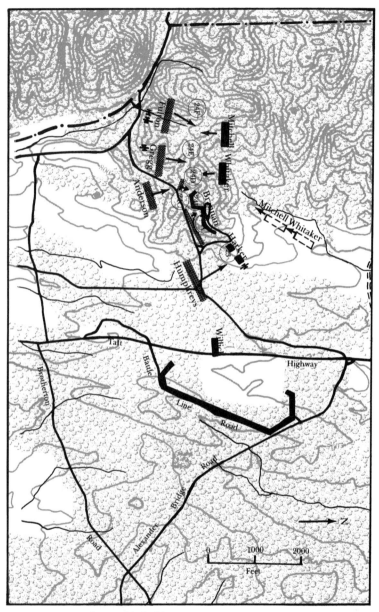

Stops 23 & 24
Situation Early–Mid Afternoon
September 20, 1863

THE FIGHT FOR SNODGRASS HILL

Afternoon September 20, 1863

Continue on the GLENN-KELLY ROAD for 0.4 mile. At the intersection, BEAR LEFT, drive 0.1 mile and BEAR RIGHT at the next fork on the SNODGRASS ROAD. Drive another 0.1. When you come out of the trees, and just before the road makes a hairpin turn to the left, park on the right side of the road. Dismount and walk down the line of monuments on your right to the monuments to the One hundred twenty-fifth and Sixty-fifth Ohio Regiments. Face right.

STOP 23, POSITION A – WOOD'S NEW LINE

You are now standing on an open finger of ground that runs northeast from Snodgrass Hill. The cabin on your right was the home of George Washington Snodgrass and his family. The high ground above the cabin, where the road continues, is Snodgrass Hill. About 1,100 yards (0.6 mile) south of you is Stop 23. The wood line to your front was farther to the south in 1863, and the area between the high ground and the woods to your left gave the appearance of a small open valley. Through the woods to your left, at a distance of 1,200 yards, was the center of the Union defensive position in the area of Kelly Field.

When the Union lines in Brotherton Field were broken and those in Poe Field outflanked, the defense was shifted to form almost two separate lines deployed at a right angle. The positions along Battle Line Road remained the same, except for the southern-most brigade – Turchin's – which made adjustments to face more southward on the northern edge of Poe Field. Elements of E. King's and Croxton's brigades, after being outflanked, moved north from Poe Field and went into position between Turchin's right and the La Fayette Road. Late in the afternoon Croxton's regiments rejoined their parent brigade on Snodgrass Hill and two of E. King's regiments were sent to General Brannan as re-enforcements. The ground between the La Fayette Road and the wood line east of you was covered by only one brigade – Willich's. This weak part of the Union reconstructed defense was never discovered by the Confederates.

A rear view of the Snodgrass house as seen from the finger of ground northeast of the house. (Archibald Gracie, *The Truth about Chickamauga* [Boston: Houghton Mifflin, 1911]).

The senior Union officer left on the field was Major General George H. Thomas, Commander of the XIV Corps. Thomas continued his defense around Kelly Field and also assumed control of the Union troops rallying and re-enforcing on Snodgrass Hill. After the afternoon of September 20, Thomas would always be known as "The Rock of Chickamauga."

Brigadier General John M. Brannan, who had been defending in the area of Poe Field with two brigades, retreated northwest with most of the regiments from his brigades. Upon reaching Snodgrass Hill and recognizing the importance of this ground, he began establishing a final defensive position.

The delaying action fought by Harker's brigade and part of Buell's brigade of Wood's division, in the northern edge of Dyer's Field, bought the time for Brannan to begin establishing a defense. After falling back from Dyer's Field, Harker's brigade went into position where you are now standing.

The attacks against this position were made by *Humphreys'* brigade and the right part of *Kershaw's* brigade, followed by two attacks of *Gracie's* brigade.

Report of Brig. Gen. Thomas J. Wood, USA, Commanding
First Division, XXI Corps, Army of the Cumberland
(Continued)

I . . . retired my command to a narrow and short ridge which shoots out nearly at right angles as a spur from the general ridge. . . . The short and narrow ridge extends athwart the valley in a nearly east-and-west course. The abruptness of the declivity on either side of it almost gives to this ridge the quality of a natural parapet. Troops holding it could load and fire behind it out of reach of the enemy's fire, and then advance to the crest of it to deliver a plunging fire on the advancing foe. In addition there was a moral effect in its command over the ground south of it which inspired the courage of the troops holding it. Here I determined to make an obstinate and stubborn stand. When General Brannan's right was turned (by the opening of the gap in our lines by the movement of my division to support General Reynolds), he had been compelled to fall back to the general ridge inclosing, on the west, the valley in which the great battle was fought. . . .

When I took position with Harker's brigade on the narrow ridge extending partially across the valley, General Brannan [had] formed his command on my right and higher up on the main ridge, thus giving to our united lines something of the shape of an irregular crescent, with the concavity toward the enemy. This disposition gave us a converging fire on the attacking column. Colonel Buell formed his command with General Brannan's. When my arrangements in this position were concluded it was probably 1 p.m. or a little after.

The enemy did not leave us long in the quiet possession of our new position. Soon a most obstinate and determined attack was made, which was handsomely repulsed. Similar attacks were continued at intervals throughout the entire afternoon. To describe each one in detail would . . . only add useless prolixity to my report. But I deem it proper to signalize one of these attacks specially.

It occurred about 4 o'clock, and lasted about 30 minutes. It was unquestionably the most terrific musketry duel I have ever witnessed. Harker's brigade was formed in two lines. The regiments were advanced to the crest of the ridge alternately, and delivered their fire by volley at the command, retiring a few paces . . . after firing to reload. The continued roar of the very fiercest musketry fire inspired a sentiment of grandeur in which the awful and the sublime were intermingled. [*O.R.*, XXX, Part I, pp. 637–638.]

Report of Col. Charles G. Harker, USA, Commanding
Third Brigade, First Division, XXI Corps, Army of the
Cumberland (Continued)

I retired, by battalions, to the crest of a hill, running nearly perpendicular to the general line of battle. General Brannan, having rallied a part of his command . . . together with fragments of other commands, formed on the hill at my right, while my brigade formed in two lines to the left of Brannan, fronting to the south and nearly perpendicular to Reynolds' division, then on my left. . . . Our line, now reduced and in the form of a crochet, must resist nearly the whole rebel force in our front, or itself be swept away, and the great Army of the Cumberland—the pride of the nation—be utterly routed. . . .

From about 1 p.m. until nightfall this line was repeatedly attacked, but remained unbroken. . . . It affords me great pleasure to refer to the grand volley firing of the regiments of my brigade. . . .

They were lying a little below the northern or eastern crest of the hill; the front line firing by volley would retire, when the rear would move forward and execute the same movement. Thus a continuous volley fire was kept up for some length of time. This system was resumed whenever the rebels made their appearance in force, and repulsed them on every occasion. It had never before been my fortune to witness so grand an example of effective musket firing. Twice we nearly exhausted our ammunition, but were furnished with new supplies. . . . I should mention that soon after taking our position on the hill . . . we were joined by about 40 men and a stand of colors of the Forty-fourth Indiana Volunteers, Lieutenant-Colonel Aldrich commanding. This little squad of men behaved most handsomely and Lieutenant-Colonel Aldrich deserves great praise for his conduct. [*O.R.*, XXX, Part I, p. 695.]

Harker was joined in this action also by the Eighty-seventh Indiana from Van Cleve's division, and the Thirty-seventh Indiana from Negley's division. These regiments had lost contact with their parent units and had moved to this position on their own.

One of Harker's regimental commanders provides a good description of the conditions of regiments as they went into position, the shifting of units laterally and the volume fire delivered to meet the Confederate attacks.

Report of Capt. Thomas Powell, USA, Commanding
Sixty-fifth Ohio Infantry, Third Brigade, First Division,
XXI Corps, Army of the Cumberland

While occupying the position on the hill [north of Dyer's Field], Major Brown was wounded, the command falling on me, the senior captain having been reported . . . wounded. The regiment fell back to the rear of the log house [Snodgrass cabin], where it rallied, and I was ordered by Colonel Harker, our brigade commander, to take position on the summit of the hill to the right of the log-house. Captain Tannehill took command of a number of men who had become separated from their companies, and took position at the left of the house.

The regiment, though having lost many of its best officers, and its ranks having been thinned by the loss of over one-third of its men, still held its position and did so for an hour and a half, when we were joined by Lieutenant-Colonel Bullitt with two companies of the Third Kentucky . . . and held the enemy in check till ordered by Colonel Harker to fall back to the rear of the log-house.

Here the regiment was formed, having been joined by Captain Tannehill and the men under his command. We were at this time supplied with cartridges to make up 40 rounds to the man. After a rest of about thirty minutes, I was ordered to take position on the left of the Sixty-fourth Ohio. The engagement then being renewed, we fired by volley, alternately, with the One hundred and twenty-fifth Ohio, until the enemy were repulsed, when I was ordered to take position on the right of the log house, still occupying position in the line on the left of the Sixty-fourth Ohio. This position was occupied till after dark. . . . [O.R., XXX, Part I, pp. 704–705.]

This short lateral move by Harker was to make room for the arrival of Colonel Hazen's Second Brigade of Palmer's division, which had been pulled out of its position in Kelly Field and sent to help hold Snodgrass Hill.

Report of Brig. Gen. William B. Hazen, USA, Commanding
Second Brigade, Second Division, XXI Corps, Army of the
Cumberland (Continued)

General Wood, General Brannan, and two divisions [brigades] of the Reserve Corps were formed in a line at right angles with and directly in rear of [my] position, . . . the left of this line [Harker] being about one-half mile from and opposite Reynolds' right.

At about 3 p.m. a fearful onslaught was made upon this line. The battle raged for one hour with apparently varying fortunes, when several general officers at our position expressed a sense of the necessity for a brigade to move over and strike the deciding blow. No one appeared to have any ammunition. I found, upon examination, that I still had 40 rounds per man, and immediately moved my men over at double-quick with a front of two regiments. Arriving near the scene of action, I caused a partial change of direction to the left, and was quickly pouring in volleys, my second line alternating with my first, the action lasting but a few minutes, the enemy retiring. There was no more fighting. . . . [*O.R.*, XXX, Part I, pp. 763–764.]

Narrative of Lieut. A. G. Bierce, USA, topographical
engineer, Second Brigade, Second Division, XXI Army Corps,
Army of the Cumberland

Had the Confederates made one more general attack we should have had to meet them with the bayonet alone. I don't know why they did not; probably they were short of ammunition. I know, though, that while the sun was taking its own time to set we lived through the agony of at least one death each, waiting for them to come on.

At last it grew too dark to fight. Then away to our left and rear some of *Bragg's* people set up "the rebel yell." It was taken up successively and passed round to our front, along our right and in behind us again, until it seemed almost to have got to the point whence it started. It was the ugliest sound that any mortal ever heard—even a mortal exhausted and unnerved by two days of hard fighting, without sleep, without rest, without food and without hope. There was, however, a space somewhere at the back of us across which that horrible yell did not prolong itself; and through that we finally retired in profound silence and dejection, unmolested. [*Works*, Vol. I, pp. 277–278.]

From this location you will next go to the high ground occupied by Brannan. Before departing, however, it is necessary to point out a Union force that would be an important re-enforcement to the defense of this area.

Face about and walk to position on the crest where you can look over the large field.

POSITION B—COMMITMENT OF THE UNION RESERVE

The La Fayette and Reed's Bridge Roads intersect one mile beyond the northeast corner of this field. Two and one-half miles farther north the La Fayette Road intersects with the Rossville Road. McAfee Church was one-half mile east of this intersection on Rossville Road.

Major General Gordon Granger's Reserve Corps was deployed around the church. Granger's mission was to protect the left flank of the Union army and the Rossville Gap through Missionary Ridge. Although called a corps, this force was really a two-brigade division commanded by Brigadier General James B. Steedman and a separate brigade commanded by Colonel Daniel McCook.

Report of Maj. Gen. Gordon Granger, USA, Commanding Reserve Corps, Army of the Cumberland

At 10:30 a.m. I heard heavy firing, which was momentarily increasing in volume and intensity on our right, in the direction of General Thomas' position. Soon afterward, being well convinced, judging from the sound of battle, that the enemy were pushing him hard, and fearing that he would not be able to resist their combined attack, I determined to go to his assistance at once. . . .

I started with General Whitaker's and Colonel Mitchell's brigades, under the immediate command of General Steedman, and left Colonel McCook's brigade at the McAfee Church in position to cover the Ringgold road. . . . We had not proceeded more than 2 miles when the enemy made his appearance in the woods on the left of our advancing column, about three-fourths of a mile from the road. They opened upon us quite briskly with their skirmishers and a section of artillery. I then made a short halt to feel them, and becoming convinced that they constituted only a party of observation, I again rapidly pushed forward my troops. . . .

At about 1 p.m. I reported to General Thomas. His forces were at that time stationed upon the brow of . . . a "horseshoe ridge." The enemy were pressing him hard in front and endeavoring to turn both of his flanks. To the right of this position was a ridge running east and west, and nearly at right angles therewith. Upon this the enemy were just forming. They also had possession of a gorge in the same, through which they were rapidly moving in large masses, with the design of falling upon the right flank and rear of the forces upon the Horseshoe Ridge. General Thomas had not the troops to oppose this movement of the enemy, and in fifteen minutes from the time when we appeared on the field, had it not been for our fortunate arrival, his forces would have been terribly cut up and captured.

As rapidly as possible I formed General Whitaker's and Colonel Mitchell's brigades, to hurl them against this threatening force of the enemy, which afterward proved to be *General Hindman's* division.

The gallant Steedman, seizing the colors of a regiment, led his men to the attack. [*O.R.*, XXX, Part I, pp. 854–855.]

We will rejoin Steedman, Whitaker and Mitchell later on top of the ridge. Return to your car. Continue driving up the paved road as it makes a sharp turn to the left and climbs to the top of Snodgrass Hill. Park where the road ends in a circular parking area. Dismount, walk to the wooden Park Service orientation sign, and continue to the Eighty-second Indiana monument on the high ground beyond.

STOP 24, POSITION A–BRANNAN ORGANIZES
THE DEFENSE

You are now on the eastern-most of a series of four knolls that form the east-west ridge called Snodgrass Hill or Ridge. The western portion of this ground has also been called Horseshoe Ridge. Confederate *Major General Thomas C. Hindman* describes the ground: "The enemy held the summit in strong force, his artillery, planted on the sundry sudden elevations, rising up like redoubts; his infantry between these, behind the crest, and further sheltered by breastworks of trees and rocks." [*O.R.*, XXX, Part II, p. 304.]

The semi-circular position outlined by the monuments around you and stretching out to the west to the next rise of ground was defended by nineteen regiments—or remnants of regiments—from seven different brigades of four divisions. Other than Brigadier General Thomas Wood, who was directing the defense around STOP 23, the only division commander here was Brigadier General John M. Brannan.

Connell's and Croxton's brigades of Brannan's division, which had retreated from Poe Field, stopped and were placed in position here by Brannan. They were joined by a brigade commanded by Colonel Timothy R. Stanley, several regiments of Brigadier General Samuel Beatty's brigade, a regiment from Colonel William Sirwell's brigade that had lost

Location of Brannon's headquarters on the afternoon of September 20, 1863. Ground shown in the western end of Snodgrass Hill. Attacks by Kershaw's Brigade came up the ground in the right of the picture. (Charles E. Belknap, *History of Michigan Organizations at Chickamauga, Chattanooga, and Missionary Ridge 1863* [Lansing, Mich.: R. Smith Printing Co., 1897]).

contact with its parent brigade, and two regiments from E. King's brigade, sent as re-enforcements from the south part of Kelly Field.

Report of Brig. Gen. John M. Brannan, USA, Commanding Third Division, XIV Corps, Army of the Cumberland (Continued)

Finding that the rebels were moving on my right . . . I swung back my right flank, and, moving about half a mile to the rear, took up a good position on a commanding ridge, General Negley (who had a portion of his command intact) having pledged himself to hold my right and rear.

Finding that this latter point was the key to the position so desired by the enemy, I made every preparation to defend it to the last, my command being somewhat increased by the arrival of portions of . . . [Van Cleve's] and Negley's divisions, and most opportunely re-enforced by Colonel Van Derveer's brigade which [had] . . . retired in good order, actually cutting its way through the rebels to rejoin my division. This gallant brigade was one of the few who maintained their organization perfect through the hard-fought passes of that portion of the field.

Nothing can exceed the desperate determination with which the rebels endeavored to gain possession of this point, hurling entire divisions on my small force in their fierce eagerness to obtain a position which would undoubtedly have given them the grand advantage of the day. My troops maintained their ground with obstinacy, evincing great gallantry and devotion in the most trying circumstances, until re-enforced about 3:30 p.m. by a portion of Granger's Reserve Corps, who took up the position that should have been occupied during the day by Negley's division.

General Negley, so far from holding my right as he had promised, retired, with extraordinary deliberation, to Rossville at an early period of the day, taking with him a portion of my division . . . and leaving me open to attack from the right as well as from the left and front (from which points the rebels attacked me simultaneously on four several occasions), and my rear so far exposed that my staff officers sent back for ammunition were successively cut off, and the ammunition, of such vital importance at that time, prevented from reaching me, thus necessitating the use of the bayonet as my only means of defense.

I remained in this position, heavily engaged, until sunset, re-enforced at intervals by the Ninth . . . Indiana . . ., sent me at my request by General Hazen, . . . and the Sixty-eighth and One hundred and first . . . Indiana . . . sent [from Kelly Field] by order of General Thomas, also the Twenty-first Ohio . . . all of whom remained in position and behaved with steadiness while their ammunition lasted. Colonel Stoughton, with a portion of a brigade [T. R. Stanley's], also rallied at this point and did good service.

Finding my ammunition almost entirely exhausted, some of the troops having none at all, and the remainder but one or two rounds, I ordered it to be reserved until the last final effort, and resort to be had to the bayonet as a means of defense. Several charges were made by the entire command during the last attack of the enemy, by which they were gallantly driven from the ridge, where they had obtained a momentary lodgment. My entire force during the day and afternoon on this ridge could not have been over 2,500 men, including the stragglers of various regiments and divisions, besides my own immediate command. . . .

The opportune arrival of Major-General Granger's command . . . saved the army from total rout. Being left my own resources by General Negley, whom I supposed to be on my right, I could not have held my position against another attack had not General Grang-

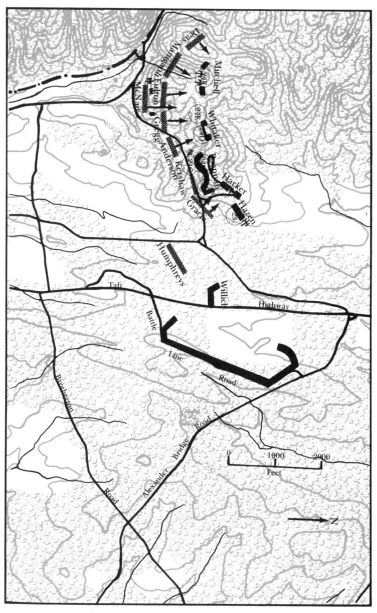

Stops 23 & 24
Situation Mid-Late Afternoon
September 20, 1863

er's troops got into position to prevent my being flanked on the right.
I am indebted to General Steedman for a small supply of ammunition
when I was depending solely on the bayonet for repulsing the next
assault. [*O.R.*, XXX, Part I, pp. 402–404.]

**Walk back through the parking lot and onto the next rise. Stop at
the monument to the Thirty-fifth Ohio.**

POSITION B – BRANNAN'S FIGHT

One of the last brigade-size units to arrive on this defensive position
was the Third Brigade of Brannan's division, which had moved from its
position near Kelly's cabin, where it had been resting after participating in
the counterattack against the Confederate forces in the northern part of
Kelly Field.

*Report of Col. Ferdinand Van Derveer, USA, Commanding
Third Brigade, Third Division, XIV Corps, Army of the
Cumberland (Continued)*

About 2 o'clock, hearing heavy firing on the right of the line, and
learning that the high ground in that direction was being held by
General Brannan with part of our division, I moved cautiously
through the woods, and at 2:30 p.m. reported my brigade to him for
duty. We were immediately placed in the front, relieving his troops,
then almost exhausted. The position was well selected and one
capable of being defended against a heavy force, the line being the
crest of a hill, for the possession of which the enemy made desperate
and renewed efforts.

From this time until dark we were hotly engaged. The ammunition failing, and no supply at hand, except a small quantity furnished
by Maj. Gen. Gordon Granger, our men gathered their cartridges
from the boxes of the dead, wounded, and prisoners, and finally fixed
bayonets, determined to hold the position.

Here again the Ninth Ohio made a gallant charge down the hill
into the midst of the enemy, scattering them like chaff, and then
returning to their position on the hill. For an hour and a half before
dark the attack was one of unexampled fury, line after line of fresh
troops being hurled against our position with a heroism and persistency which almost dignified their cause. At length night ended the

struggle, and the enemy, having suffered a terrible loss, retired from our immediate front. [*O.R.*, XXX, Part I, p. 430.]

In front of the Thirty-fifth Ohio's monument is a trail that goes down the hill. Follow this trail for 60 yards (passing the monument to the Fifty-eighth North Carolina) and find the small monuments to Kershaw's brigade and the Third South Carolina.

POSITION C – KERSHAW'S ASSAULT

If you were to walk south along this trail for another 75 yards, you would reach the Vittetoe Road. To cross this road and walk along the trail for another 300 yards would bring you to the ridge with the tall South Carolina Monument overlooking the north end of Dyer's Field and Stop 22.

Kershaw paused along this part of Dyer's Field after pushing back the Union delaying forces. *Humphreys'* brigade moved into position on his right. Around 1:30 p.m. both brigades moved forward to attack the high ground above you and the finger of open ground next to Snodgrass cabin.

Ground over which Gracie's and Kershaw's brigades assaulted the eastern end of Brannan's defensive position on Snodgrass Hill during the afternoon of September 20, 1863 (Henry V. Boynton, *Dedication of the Chickamauga and Chattanooga National Military Park* [Washington, D.C.: Government Printing Office, 1896]).

If you were to stand next to the Third South Carolina monument and look back up the hill, you would be in the left center of *Kershaw's* attacking formation. On your left would have been the Third South Carolina Battalion (also called *James'* battalion). Farther to the left, across the gully on the next finger, was the Second South Carolina.

To your right, on the finger of ground that leads to the parking area, were the Seventh South Carolina, Fifteenth Alabama, and Fifteenth South Carolina. Farther to the right and across the road were the Eighth South Carolina and *Humphreys'* brigade (four Mississippi regiments) who were attacking the finger of open ground.

Kershaw's report continues from the point where he pushed Harker's brigade back from Dyer's Field.

Report of Brig. Gen. Joseph B. Kershaw, CSA, Commanding McLaws' Division, Longstreet's Corps, Army of Northern Virginia (Continued)

I halted under a heavy fire of artillery on the heights, sheltering the men as much as possible, and there awaited the coming of *Humphreys*, on my right. My Seventh South Carolina, *Lieutenant-Colonel Bland*, my right center regiment, and Fifteenth South Carolina Regiment, *Lieutenant-Colonel Joseph F. Gist*, had obliqued to the right. *Colonel Henagan* [Eighth South Carolina] had pursued the enemy so far to the right that when *Humphreys* got up he occupied the interval between the Fifteenth and Eighth Regiments.

Colonel Oates, Fifteenth Alabama, *Law's* brigade, came up on the right of the Seventh [South Carolina], and occupied the line between that and the Fifteenth, and, with those regiments, advanced without orders. I had sent to the right to direct that I should be informed when *Humphreys* arrived. Hearing the firing renewed on my right, I advanced the left wing (Third South Carolina, *James'* battalion and Second South Carolina) and gained in some points the crest of the hill within a few yards of the enemy's lines.

After one of the most gallant struggles I have ever witnessed, especially on the part of the Third South Carolina and *James'* battalion, which occupied a position in front of the enemy's battery, I was compelled to fall back to a point about 250 yards back, where I determined to hold the enemy until re-enforcements arrived. The enemy soon advanced, but by a cool, deliberate fire were quickly repulsed. *General Humphreys* reported that he could make no farther advance on account of the heavy force of the enemy to his right. I directed him to make such disposition of his troops as would cover my right flank.

About 3 o'clock *Brigadier-General Anderson's* Mississippi brigade came to my support. I described to him the situation, and suggested an attack on the right flank of the position of the enemy. He acquiesced . . . and advanced his left preparatory to the movement, covering his front with skirmishers, who immediately became engaged, and drove in those of the enemy; but, raising a shout along their line, they advanced their line of battle at a charge, driving back *Anderson's* brigade in some confusion. With hearty cheers, the Second and Third South Carolina and *James'* battalion engaged with the utmost enthusiasm. *Anderson's* brigade promptly reformed and opened fire. His reserve regiment came up, and in ten minutes' time the enemy was driven pell-mell.

The Second South Carolina and *Anderson's* brigade dashed after him and drove him to the top of the hill, the Second South Carolina reaching the crest. The troops to his left having fallen back to their former position, *Lieutenant-Colonel Gaillard* says in his report "that he was obliged reluctantly to fall back." This was an attack on the right flank of the enemy, and the line was at an oblique angle to my line. . . .

About 4 o'clock *Gracie's* and *Kelly's* brigades came up and reported to me. I directed . . . the former to form on my rear and the latter to form on *Gracie's* left. *General Hindman* informed me that he was about to attack on *Anderson's* left, well on the right flank of the enemy, with two brigades of infantry with artillery. Soon after he opened heavily in that direction, but sent me word the attack was likely to fail unless a demonstration was made along the front. I determined on an attack, combining all our forces; *McNair's* brigade, which had come up, on my right, *Gracie's, Kelly's, Anderson's,* [and] my own Eighth, Fifteenth, and Second Regiments participating. The rest of my brigade, being in whole or in part out of ammunition, remained in reserve at their position.

This was one of the heaviest attacks of the war on a single point. The brigades went in magnificent order. *General Gracie,* under my own eye, led his brigade, now for the first time under fire, most gallantly and efficiently, and for more than an hour and a half the struggle continued with unabated fury. It terminated at sunset, the Second South Carolina being among the last to retire. [*O.R.*, XXX, Part II, pp. 504–505.]

Report of Brig. Gen. Archibald Gracie, Jr., CSA,
Commanding Brigade, Preston's Division, Buckner's Corps,
Army of Tennessee

Between 4 and 5 p.m. orders were received to support *Kershaw's* brigade. . . . Word was sent to *General Kershaw* that the brigade was ready, and he ordered it to advance. Passing through *Kershaw's* command, the brigade found itself suddenly in the presence of the enemy, strongly posted behind breastworks of logs and rails on the crest of an opposite hill. The fury of musketry, grape, and canister immediately commenced, but, undaunted, the brigade scaled the precipitous heights, driving the enemy before it, and took possession of the hill.

Holding these heights for nearly an hour, and ammunition becoming scarce, I informed *Brigadier-General Preston*, commanding division, that unless supported the brigade could not much longer hold out. . . . *Trigg's* and *Kelly's* brigades arriving, the command withdrew to replenish its empty cartridge boxes. . . .

The number of killed and wounded shows the desperate nature of the contest. Of about 1,870 carried into action, 90 were killed and 615 wounded. [*O.R.*, XXX, Part II, p. 421.]

Retrace your steps to the Thirty-fifth Ohio monument. Turn left and follow the top of the ridge line for 200 yards to the next piece of high ground. Walk to the monument to the Eighty-fourth Indiana.

POSITION D–GRANGER ENTERS THE FIGHT

This piece of rising ground and the next knoll 350 yards farther west were seized by the two brigades of Steedman's division. Brigadier General Walter C. Whitaker's First Brigade fought here while Colonel John G. Mitchell's Second Brigade defended the farther knoll. Both brigades came up the north side of the hill and gained the position just minutes before the emergence of the Confederate force, which was approaching from the south and southwest.

Report of Maj. Gen. Gordon Granger, USA, Commanding
Reserve Corps, Army of the Cumberland (Continued)

The gallant Steedman, seizing the colors of a regiment, led his men to the attack. With loud cheers they rushed upon the enemy, and, after a terrific conflict lasting but twenty minutes, drove them

from their ground, and occupied the ridge and gorge. The slaughter
. . . was frightful. General Whitaker, while rushing forward at the
head of his brigade, was knocked from his horse by a musket-ball,
and was for a short time rendered unfit for duty; while 2 of his staff
officers were killed, and 2 mortally wounded.

General Steedman's horse was killed, and he was severely
bruised, yet he was able to remain on duty during the day. This attack
was made by our troops, very few of whom had ever been in an
action before, against a division of old soldiers, who largely outnumbered them; yet with resolution and energy they drove the enemy
from his strong position, occupied it themselves, and afterward held
the ground they had gained with such terrible losses. The victory was
dearly won, but to this army it was a priceless one.

There was now a lull in the battle. It was of short duration,
however, for within thirty minutes after we had gained possession of
the ridge, we were impetuously attacked by two divisions of *Longstreet's* veterans.

Again the enemy was driven back, and from this time until dark
the battle between these two opposing forces raged furiously.

Our whole line was continually enveloped in smoke and fire.
The assaults of the enemy were now made with that energy which
was inspired by the bright prospect of a speedy victory, and by a
consciousness that it was only necessary to carry this position and
crush our forces to enable him to overthrow our army and drive it
across the Tennessee River. Their forces were massed and hurled
upon us for the purpose of terminating at once this great and bloody
battle. But the stout hearts of the handful of men who stood before
them as a wall of fire quailed not. They understood our perilous
position and held their ground, determined to perish rather than yield
it. Never had a commander such just cause for congratulation over
the action of his troops.

The ammunition which was brought in our train to this part of
the field was divided with Generals Brannan's and Wood's divisions
early in the afternoon, and we soon exhausted the remainder. All that
we could then procure was taken from the cartridge boxes of our own
and the enemy's dead and wounded. Even this supply was exhausted
before the battle was over, and while the enemy was still in our front,
hurling fresh troops against us. It was almost dark; the enemy had
been driven back, but we had not a round of ammunition left. All
now seemed to be lost if he should return to the contest.

Anticipating another attack, I ordered the command to be given to the men to stand firm, and to use the cold steel. After an ominous silence of a few minutes, the enemy came rushing upon us again. With fixed bayonets our troops gallantly charged them and drove them back in confusion. Twice more were these charges repeated and the enemy driven back before darkness brought an end to the battle. Night came, and the enemy fell back whipped and discomfited. [O.R., XXX, Part I, pp. 855–856.]

The initial attack against this western part of the Union line was made by two brigades of *Brigadier General Bushrod Johnson's* division. Throughout the afternoon these attackers were re-enforced by the remainder of *Johnson's* division, *Manigault's* and *Deas'* brigades of *Hindman's* division and *Trigg's* and *Kelly's* brigades of *Preston's* division.

These attacks were conducted in conjunction with the assaults made by the Confederate forces centered around *Kershaw's* brigade. Before it was over, eleven Confederate brigades had come into action against Snodgrass Hill and Horseshoe Ridge. The first attacks began shortly after 1:00 p.m. with five brigades. Throughout the afternoon fresh brigades were committed and exhausted units withdrawn to reform. The last attack was made just before dark when eight brigades were sent against the Union position.

Report of Brig. Gen. Walter C. Whitaker, USA, Commanding First Brigade, First Division, Reserve Corps, Army of the Cumberland

I was directed to drive the enemy from a ridge on which he had concentrated his forces in great numbers, supported by artillery, and was seriously threatening the destruction of our right by a flank movement, forming my command in two lines, the Ninety-sixth Illinois on the right, the One hundred and fifteenth Illinois in the center, the Twenty-second Michigan on the left of the first line; the Fortieth Ohio on the right, the Eighty-fourth Indiana in the center, and Eighty-ninth Ohio on the left of the second line.

Both lines advanced at a double quick pace against the enemy. The conflict was terrific. The enemy was driven near half a mile. Rallying, they drove my command a short distance, when they in turn were driven again with great loss. Both lines had been thrown into the conflict on the second charge, and the whole line kept up a deadly and well directed fire upon the enemy, who fought with great determination and vigor. . . .

The entire command bore themselves like veterans, under a most withering, murderous fire of musketry, grape, and canister for over three hours, firmly maintaining their ground until we were directed to retire, which was done in fair order, the enemy retiring also at the same time. . . . We fought, as I have been informed by prisoners, three divisions of the enemy, two of which were from *Longstreet's* corps. They fought like tigers, and with a zeal and energy worthy of a better cause. . . .

The available force of my brigade, . . . with the addition of the Twenty-second Michigan and Eighty-ninth Ohio Regiments, was 2877 rank and file; of the number there were killed, wounded and missing in the battle of the 20th . . . 1,225. [*O.R.*, XXX, Part I, pp. 862–863.]

Continue west on the ridge for another 100 yards to the small stone marker to the Third Tennessee Regiment of Johnson's division.

POSITION E – JOHNSON'S ASSAULT

You are now standing on ground repeatedly attacked by the right units of *Johnson's* division and the left regiments of *Anderson's* brigade.

Report of Brig. Gen. Bushrod R. Johnson, CSA, Commanding Provisional Division, Army of Tennessee attached to Longstreet's Corps, Army of Northern Virginia

The crest of the spur of Missionary Ridge north of Vidito's [Vittetoe's] extends east and west in its general direction, but curves to the south about the middle. . . . Toward the south the slope from the crest is gradual for some distance in several places, and especially so at the west end, and terminates toward the cove in an abrupt, serrated declivity, presenting to our approach from the south several secondary spurs or knobs with intervening short ravines. Along the crest of this spur the last desperate struggle of the Northern Army was made at the battle of Chickamauga.

Gregg's and *Johnson's* brigades, followed by *Dent's* and *Everett's* batteries, advanced in line toward the north, the left passing over the wagons, caissons, and pieces of artillery near Vidito's house and reaching to the Crawfish [Spring] road. There were a number of wounded Federals at Vidito's house. The ladies of the family who had taken shelter from danger on Saturday and Sunday beneath the floor now burst forth and greeted our soldiers with clapping of hands and shouts of joy, presenting an impressive scene. The brow of the secondary spurs north of Vidito's house was gained without resistance by *Gregg's* and *Johnson's* brigades and by *Anderson's*, which had come up on our right during our advance.

The line was then halted, the alignment corrected, and the two regiments of *Gregg's* brigade, which were formed on the left of my line in the morning, now returned to their brigade. Four of *Dent's* Napoleon guns and *Everett's* battery of three guns were placed in position on the spur occupied by *Johnson's* brigade, and two pieces of *Dent's* battery were placed upon the hill with *Gregg's* brigade [which was to the right of *Johnson's* brigade]. There was now no support on the left of *Johnson's* brigade, though *Deas'* brigade was every moment expected there.

A few minutes before 2 p.m., after the artillery had opened fire, the order was given to advance from this position with a view of gaining the main crest of the ridge in our front, which was some 1000 yards distant on our left, but much nearer on our right on account of its curvature to the south in the middle. The enemy opened fire on our left before it advanced 100 yards. Our movement was, however, continued for a time until my left found a position in which it was enabled to hold the enemy in check; but the Federals moved up on our flank along a secondary spur which united at the elevation at the west end of the main ridge with that upon which *Johnson's* brigade was fighting, and this movement was held in check some time by our troops firing obliquely to the left.

The advance of *Brigadier-General Anderson* on our extreme right was a gallant and impetuous charge. It encountered a heavy force of the enemy posted in a strong position, from which they poured a volume of fire that speedily repulsed the charge.

Gregg's brigade gained the crest of the ridge after a sharp contest, driving the foe down the northern slope of the ridge and delivering a damaging fire in the retreating masses; but the enemy returned to the attack, and there being now no support on our right, the line commenced falling back on that flank just after *Lieutenant-Colonel Tillman*, commanding the Forty-first Tennessee Regiment, was disabled by a wound.

The Third Tennessee Regiment, with about 40 men of the Fiftieth Tennessee and Seventh Texas Regiments, on the left of this brigade, claims to have held its advance position until *Johnson's* brigade fell back. . . . As my line fell back our artillery opened with canister, and was gallantly served under the fire of the enemy's infantry until the troops, rallying in line at the batteries, repulsed the charge of the foe.

I now gave orders to hold the hill, and await the re-enforcements from *Hindman's* division, momentarily expected. [*O.R.*, XXX, Part II, pp. 461–462.]

Report of Brig. Gen. Patton Anderson, CSA, Commanding Anderson's Brigade, Hindman's Division, Army of Tennessee

The attack was soon made by the whole line. It was stubbornly resisted from a very strong position just behind the crest of the hill. A portion of two of my regiments gained the crest of the hill and planted colors there, but the position was a hot one, and some breaking to the rear on the left caused the whole to give way for a time. The troops were rallied on the slope of the hill, lines re-formed, and all in readiness to resume the attack, when the enemy advanced his line immediately in my front down the hill with some impetuosity.

The line was instantly ordered forward to meet this charge and the command quickly responded to. The enemy was met by a volley and a charge which did much execution, his line broken, and his troops fled in some confusion; but as there was no corresponding forward movement by the brigades on my right and left, and as the hill near the crest was very difficult to ascend, he had time either to reform or to bring up a second line before we reached the top of the hill, and another repulse was the consequence. Troops never rallied more promptly and without confusion or clamor. [*O.R.*, XXX, Part II, p. 318.]

Continue to walk west for 200 yards to the cannons marking the position of Battery M, First Illinois Artillery.

POSITION F–HINDMAN TAKES CHARGE

You are now at the western end of the Union defensive line. South of your position, down the trail, is the spur where *Dent's* and *Everett's* batteries occupied the southern portion.

Report of Maj. Gen. Thomas C. Hindman, CSA,
Commanding Division, Army of Tennessee

While moving to the right and rear, I was met by . . . *Brig. Gen. Bushrod R. Johnson* . . . stating that he was hard pressed, and must have support forthwith. . . . I immediately placed *Anderson's* brigade under his orders. *Deas*, who was out of ammunition, obtained a partial supply from *Johnson's* wagons, and then marched west across the Crawfish Spring road and formed line of battle, facing west, at the top of the first ridge beyond. . . . *Manigault*, now coming up, was directed to form on *Deas'* right. . . . But . . . before *Manigault's* line had been established, brisk firing commenced to my right and rear, east of the Crawfish Spring road, and I received from *General Johnson* urgent requests for further support. *Deas* and *Manigault* at once moved in that direction and formed on his left. Previous to their arrival the firing had ceased.

General Johnson's line faced nearly north, about perpendicular to . . . our original line of battle. It was on the side of an extremely rough and steep projection of Missionary Ridge near Dyer's farm, and was extended eastwardly by the lines of *Anderson* and *Kershaw*. The height terminated in an open field near *Kershaw's* right. It was elsewhere densely wooded. The enemy held the summit in strong force, his artillery planted on sundry sudden elevations, rising up like redoubts; his infantry between these, behind the crest, and further sheltered by breastworks of trees and rocks.

At 3 p.m. a force of the enemy, probably that which I had recently confronted west of the Crawfish Spring road, appeared on my left. . . . I was apprehensive of an attack in rear, and sent to *General Longstreet* and *General Buckner* for reinforcements. At the same time, being the officer of the highest rank present and deeming concert of action necessary, I assumed command of *General Johnson's* troops and ordered an immediate and vigorous attack upon the enemy in our front, *Deas* and *Manigault* (with *Johnson's* command, all under the direction of that officer) to wheel to the right until faced east and then to advance, taking the enemy in flank, *Anderson* to move forward when the firing should begin. *General Kershaw* agreed to conform to the movements of the latter [*Anderson*]. I hoped to insure the capture or destruction of the enemy by driving him in confusion upon the Right Wing of our army. The movement began at 3:30. . . .

In a few minutes a terrific contest ensued, which continued at

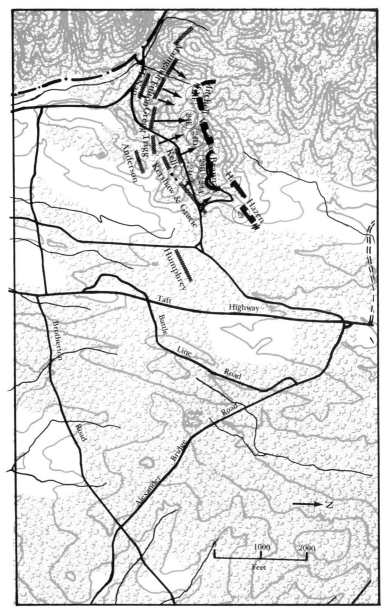

Stops 23 & 24
Situation Late Afternoon–Early Evening
September 20, 1863

close quarters without any intermission over four hours. Our troops attacked again and again with a courage worthy of their past achievements. The enemy fought with determined obstinacy and repeatedly repulsed us, but only to be again assailed. . . . On our extreme left the bayonet was used, and men also killed and wounded with clubbed muskets.

A little after 4 [o'clock] the enemy was re-enforced and advanced with loud shouts upon our right, but was repulsed by *Anderson* and *Kershaw*. At this time it became necessary to retire *Garrity's* battery, of *Anderson's* brigade, which had been doing effective service. . . . *Dent's* battery, of *Deas'* brigade, was engaged throughout the struggle. Notwithstanding the repulses of our infantry, the officers and men of this battery stood to their guns undaunted and continued firing, inflicting severe loss on the enemy and contributing largely to the success of my operations.

At 4:20 *Brigadier-General Preston*, of *Buckner's* corps, in answer to my application for help, brought me the timely and valuable re-enforcement of *Kelly's* brigade, and within an hour afterward the remaining brigades of his division—*Gracie's* and *Trigg's*. These brave troops as they arrived were conducted by officers of my staff to the right of my line, and promptly advanced, in conjunction with the rest, upon the enemy. From this time we gained ground; but, though now commanding nine brigades, with *Kershaw* co-operating, and all in action, I found the gain both slow and costly. I have never known Federal troops to fight so well. . . . I never saw Confederate soldiers fight better.

Between 7:30 and 8 p.m. the enemy was driven from his position, surrendering to the gallant *Preston* 600 or 700 prisoners. . . . This was the victorious ending of the battle. . . . [*O.R.*, XXX, Part II, pp. 304–305.]

Report of Brig. Gen. Bushrod R. Johnson, CSA,
Commanding Provisional Division, Army of Tennessee
attached to Longstreet's Corps, Army of Northern
Virginia (Continued)

Soon *Manigault's* brigade was seen advancing in line of battle through Vidito's [Vittetoe's] cornfield in the cove in our rear. As it came up on the left of my line *Brigadier-General Deas* reported in person, having with his brigade swept the ridge west of Crawfish [Dry Valley] road. Having sent a staff officer to place these two brigades on

The Viditoe House, showing the ground crossed by Johnson's and Hindman's divisions as they marched to attack the Union defenses on the western end of Snodgrass Hill (Henry V. Boynton, *Chickamauga National Military Park* [Washington, D.C.: Government Printing Office, 1902]).

my left, I rode toward the right and met *General Hindman*, who directed me to take command of the left wing and wheel to the right, making the right of my division the pivot. *McNair's* brigade, under *Colonel Coleman*, now came up and formed a line in rear of the left of my division. I also detailed 10 men from *Johnson's* brigade to assist in working the guns of *Dent's* battery.

Our line, from left to right, was formed of brigades in the following order, viz, *Deas'*, *Manigault's*, *Johnson's*, *Gregg's*, and *Anderson's*, with *McNair's* brigade in rear of *Johnson's*. *Deas'* brigade occupied the brow of the steep spur which forms the north side of the gorge through which Crawfish [Dry Valley] road passes Missionary Ridge. *Manigault's* stretched across the ravine and extended up the side of the adjacent spur to the right, on which *Johnson's* and *McNair's* brigades, with seven pieces of artillery, were posted. *Gregg's* brigade was formed on a spur of greater length, extending more toward the east, and separated in part from the main ridge by a hollow, with a piece of table land at its head to the west. *Anderson's* brigade was formed in two lines on the right, the front line extending up the slope of the spur on which *Gregg's* brigade was formed on the left and across the hollow on the right. The section of *Dent's* artillery with *Gregg's* brigade in the last attack were now moved to the hollow on the right, ready to be run up by hand on the main ridge as soon as it should be carried. *Kershaw's* brigade was somewhere on the right of, but not connected with, *Anderson's* brigade.

I proceeded in person to put the line in motion. Commencing with *Deas'* brigade, and giving careful instructions to preserve the dress and the connection to the right, I passed along the line until I saw it all moving gallantly forward. A most obstinate struggle now commenced for the possession of this spur of Missionary Ridge, the last stronghold of the enemy on the battlefield. . . . Our artillery opened on the brow of the ridge and the infantry became immediately engaged. The firing was very heavy on both sides, and showed that the enemy were in strong force in our front, supported by artillery posted near the junction of the two spurs on which *Deas'* and *Johnson's* brigades, respectively, moved. Our line pressed determinedly forward for some time, keeping up an incessant volley with small-arms.

But the enemy now evidently received re-enforcements of fresh troops, which advanced with a shout that was heard all along our lines, and we were driven back to our guns. . . . *Deas'* brigade and part of *Manigault's* next to it fell back to the foot of the hill. *Anderson's* fell back to its first position, and these three brigades, save two regiments of *Manigualt's* next to *Johnson's* brigade, did not again enter the fight.

In falling back on the spur on which *Johnson's* brigade and the two batteries fought, *McNair's* brigade, which formed a second line, mingled with the troops of the first line on the left of *Johnson's* and the right of the two regiments of *Manigault's* brigade, and continued to fight in that position during the rest of the day. [*O.R.*, XXX, Part II, pp. 462–463.]

The left of *Manigault's* brigade was centered astride the dirt road that you see going southwest from the Union battery. *Manigault's* left regiment extended across the draw west of this road to tie in with the right of *Deas'* brigade.

Report of Maj. John N. Slaughter, CSA, Commanding
Thirty-fourth Alabama Infantry, Manigault's Brigade,
Hindman's Division, Army of Tennessee

Moving forward across the abrupt spurs of this ridge, we ascended the steep and high hill on which the enemy were posted, formed in line, and lay down some hundred paces from the top of the hill. While lying in this position, *Deas'* brigade marched forward and formed 60 paces to our front, his right regiment overlapping the left of mine . . . and lay down. Previous to this I had thrown out *Lieutenant Colquitt's* company (E) as skirmishers to our front. The enemy's position was a strong one. . . . The ridge on which they were posted divided, and the apex was where three ridges met. The left of the Twenty-eighth Alabama rested on the one to my right, *Deas'* brigade extended over the one to my left, and the enemy occupied the one in my front, his battery being placed some 100 or 150 paces from the apex, being in a slight depression of the ridge which protected him from our fire. My regiment occupied an inclined plane between the first two ridges. The ground was such that the right and left of the regiment was exposed to a fire for 100 paces before the center. The moment the men appeared above the ridge they were exposed to a sweeping fire of the enemy's artillery and musketry.

We received orders at this juncture to move forward and govern ourselves by the movements of the Twenty-eighth Alabama, on our right, and *Deas'* brigade on our left. The regiment had moved forward with firmness some 50 or 60 paces up the hill when they were met by the right regiment of *Deas'* brigade falling back in disorder, they having come under a severe fire of canister and musketry, as did also the right companies of my regiment, which caused it to falter and fall back in confusion.

I attempted to rally them, and with the assistance of some of my officers a number were rallied, who moved forward with the colors, and kept their position with the Twenty-eighth Alabama . . . during the remainder of the battle. The rest became so confused with *Deas'* men and continued to fall back down the hill, that I could not rally them until they reached the top of the opposite hill. I ordered *Captain Carter* to the top of the hill, where, with assistance of other officers, he succeeded in rallying and forming them again. I was about returning to my position in line when I was ordered by the brigadier-general commanding to retire near my first position. . . .

Captain Huger, inspector-general, rendered me valuable assistance. . . . Riding fearlessly amid the shower of canister and Minie balls, waving his sword and calling upon the men to rally, and encouraging them by his heroic daring, he fell pierced through the heart and died almost instantly. [*O.R.,* XXX, Part II, pp. 352–353.]

EXCURSION

Walk 160 yards down the road to the southwest to see the ground as the Alabama regimental commanders saw it. Then turn left, and walk 100 yards up onto the high ground occupied by the Twenty-eighth Alabama where you will find a north-south trail and a small stone marker for the Tenth and Nineteenth South Carolina Regiments.

The Confederate artillery was 100 yards behind this line. Turn left (north) and follow the trail 125 yards over the ground where *Johnson's* brigade made several attacks. Stop at the location of Battery M, First Illinois Artillery.

Report of Col. John G. Mitchell, USA,
Commanding Second Brigade, First Division, Reserve
Corps, Army of the Cumberland

The order to charge was given, and in response the solid line rushed to the crest, drove the enemy from his position, and held it.

Three several times the enemy rushed upon us to hurl back our line, but in each instance he was met, and gallantly repulsed. In one of these charges, when the conflict had become hand-to-hand, the One hundred and twenty-first Ohio captured the flag of the Twenty-second Alabama Regiment, and bore it with them from the field.

For five hours the command remained in the position first gained, holding it against the repeated assaults of greatly superior numbers, and at sundown, after the last cartridge was fired, fell back to the ridge first in our rear. [*O.R.*, XXX, Part I, p. 867.]

Report of Capt. Harry T. Toulmin, CSA,
Commanding Twenty-second Alabama Infantry, Deas'
Brigade, Hindman's Division, Army of Tennessee

[The regiment], being ordered . . . to assault the enemy's line, it did so, but finding the enemy on a very high hill with a strongly posted battery, it was impossible to penetrate his line. The fire of grape and canister at this point was terrific, and although the command made bold and earnest efforts to rise the hill and storm the battery it was unsuccessful. Here, I regret to state, we lost our colors. *Private Braswell*, of Company A, who was then bearing them, fearlessly rushed to the front and in advance of the line, and was there literally riddled with balls, as was subsequently shown by the recovery of his body. The fire at this time was such as to throw the regiment into confusion, in which the loss of Private Braswell and colors was not discovered until too late to rescue them, for amid this confusion the regiment fell back, and was unable afterward to regain its lost position. Twice did it rally and attempt to recover its ground and lost colors, but the storm of grape and canister was so terrible and destructive that every effort proved unavailing. Having fallen back a third time in some disorder, the regiment retired to the foot of the hill and reformed there. This was done by the whole brigade. [O.R., XXX, Part II, pp. 336–337.]

Report of Brig. Gen. Bushrod R. Johnson, CSA, Commanding Provisional Division, Army of Tennessee, attached to Longstreet's Corps, Army of Northern Virginia (Continued)

All our troops had now suffered severely here and in other parts of the field. *Hindman's* division . . . had been especially weakened in the conflict before it came to our support. Neither *McNair's, Gregg's,* nor *Johnson's* brigades mustered over 500 guns. The part of *Manigault's* brigade adjacent to my division—about two regiments, under *Colonel Reid* . . . participated in the invincible spirit which fired our men, and continued to fight with us. I ordered that the hill should be held at all hazards, and determined that all should be lost before I would abandon it. I felt that this position on the extreme left was one of the utmost importance and might determine the fate of the day. . . .

The enemy were not whipped, and the conflict still raged with varying fortune. Repeatedly our men advanced, and were in turn forced to yield a portion of the ground they had gained. I directed our men to advance as far as possible, then hold their position and never retreat. We thus gradually approached the crest of the ridge. . . .

Over three hours passed in this conflict, in which officers and men toiled on and manifested more perseverance, determination, and endurance than I have ever before witnessed on any field. We had now slowly driven the enemy on the left up the gradual ascent about half a mile to the coveted crest of the ridge, where they made the last desperate resistance, and our lines gradually grew stronger and stronger. . . .

It was finally nearly sunset when a simultaneous advance swept along our whole lines, and with a shout we drove the enemy from the ridge. . . . [O.R., XXX, Part II, pp. 463-464.]

Depart from this location and retrace your steps back to the next knoll (Position D) and find the marker to the Eighty-ninth Ohio Regiment. Take care not to follow the service road that goes down the hill to your left.

POSITION G—DECISION TO WITHDRAW

Report of Maj. Gen. George H. Thomas, USA, Commanding
XIV Corps, Army of the Cumberland (Continued)

Every assault of the enemy . . . until nightfall was repulsed in the the most gallant style by the whole line. By this time the ammunition in the boxes of the men was reduced, on an average, to 2 or 3 rounds per man, and my ammunition trains having been unfortunately ordered to the rear by some unauthorized person, we should have been entirely without ammunition in a very short time had not a small supply come up with General Steedman's command. This, being distributed among the troops, gave them about 10 rounds per man.

General Garfield, chief of staff of General Rosecrans, reached this position about 4 p.m.. . . . [He] gave me the first reliable information that the right and center of our army had been driven, and of its condition at that time. I soon after received a dispatch from General Rosecrans, directing me to assume command of all the forces, and, with Crittenden and McCook, take a strong position and assume a threatening attitude at Rossville, sending the unorganized forces to Chattanooga for reorganization, stating that he would examine the ground at Chattanooga and then join me; also that he had sent out rations and ammunition to meet me at Rossville.

I determined to hold the position until nightfall, if possible, in the meantime sending Captains Barker and Kellogg to distribute the ammunition, Major Lawrence, my chief of artillery, having been previously sent to notify the different commanders that ammunition would be supplied them shortly. As soon as they reported the distribution of the ammunition, I directed Captain Willard to inform the division commanders to prepare to withdraw their commands as soon as they received orders. At 5:30 p.m. Captain Barker, commanding my escort, was sent to notify General Reynolds [in Kelly Field] to commence the movement, and I left the position behind General Wood's command [Stop 23] to meet General Reynolds and point out to him the position where I wished him to form line to cover the retirement of the other troops on the left.

In passing through an open woods . . . between my last and Reynold's position, I was cautioned by a couple of soldiers, who had been to hunt water, that there was a large force of the rebels in these woods, drawn up in line and advancing toward me. Just at this time I saw the head of Reynold's column approaching, and calling to the general himself, directed him to form line perpendicular to the State road, changing the head of his column to the left, with his right resting on that road, and to charge the enemy . . . in his immediate front. This movement was made with the utmost promptitude, and facing to the right while on the march, Turchin threw his brigade upon the rebel force, routing them and driving them in utter confusion entirely beyond Baird's left. In this splendid advance more than 200 prisoners were captured and sent to the rear.

Colonel Robinson, commanding the Second Brigade, Reynolds' division, followed closely upon Turchin, and I posted him on the road leading through the ridge to hold the ground while the troops on our right and left passed by. In a few moments General Willich, commanding a brigade of Johnson's division, reported to me that his brigade was in position on a commanding piece of ground to the right of the Ridge road. I directed him to report to General Reynolds, and assist in covering the retirement of the troops. Turchin's brigade, after driving the enemy a mile and a half, was reassembled, and took its position on the Ridge road with Robinson and Willich.

These dispositions being made, I sent orders to Generals Wood, Brannan, and Granger to withdraw from their positions. [*O.R.*, XXX, Part I, pp. 253–254.]

While the Union units were withdrawing, the Confederates increased their pressure and pushed onto the ridge. The result was some confusion at various places along the line. Several Union regiments were cut off and had many troops captured.

Continue east on the ridge for 200 yards to the next knoll.

POSITION H – THE BATTLE ENDS

Report of Col. Ferdinand Van Derveer, USA, Commanding Third Brigade, Third Division, XIV Corps, Army of the Cumberland (Continued)

During the latter part of the day the position directly on our right had been held by the division of Brigadier-General Steedman, but which early in the evening had been withdrawn without our knowledge, thus leaving our flank exposed. . . . Brigadier-General Brannan . . . ordered me to place the Thirty-fifth Ohio across that flank to prevent a surprise. This had scarcely been done when a rebel force appeared in the gloom directly in their front. A mounted officer rode to within a few paces of the Thirty-fifth Ohio and asked, "What regiment is that?" To this someone replied, "The Thirty-fifth Ohio." The officer turned suddenly and attempted to run away, but our regiment delivered a volley that brought horse and rider to the ground and put the force to flight. Prisoners said this officer was the rebel *General Gregg*.

At 7 p.m. an order came from Major-General Thomas that the forces under General Brannan should move quietly to Rossville. [*O.R.*, XXX, Part I, pp. 430–431.]

Return to the area where you parked your car.

POSITION I – THE AFTERMATH

Report of Maj. Gen. George H. Thomas, USA, Commanding XIV Corps, Army of the Cumberland (Continued)

I then proceeded to Rossville . . . and immediately prepared to place the troops in position at that point. One brigade of Negley's division was posted in the gap, on the Ringgold road, and two brigades on the top of the ridge to the right of the road, adjoining the brigade in the road; Reynolds' division on the right of Negley's and reaching to the Dry Valley road; Brannan's division in the rear of Reynolds' right, as a reserve; McCook's corps on the right of the Dry Valley road, and stretching toward the west, his right reaching nearly to Chattanooga Creek; Crittenden's entire corps was posted on the heights to the left of the Ringgold road, with Steedman's division of Granger's corps in reserve behind his left; Baird's division in reserve, and in supporting distance of the brigade in the gap. . . . Minty's brigade of cavalry was on the Ringgold road, about a mile and a half in advance of the gap. [*O.R.*, XXX, Part I, p. 254.]

C.A. Dana to Hon. E.M. Stanton, Secretary of War, September 20 — 4 p.m.

My report today is of deplorable importance. Chickamauga is as fatal a name in our history as Bull Run. The battle began late this morning. . . . Previous to 10 Rosecrans rode the whole length of lines. All seemed promising, except columns of dust within rebel lines moving north, and report from our right that enemy had been felling timber there during night. . . .

[*Longstreet's* Command] . . . suddenly burst over in enormous volume upon our center. . . . They came through with resistless impulse, composed of brigades formed in divisions. Before them our soldiers turned and fled. It was wholesale panic. Vain were all attempts to rally them. They retreated directly across two lines of considerable ridges running parallel to our line of battle, and then most of them made their way over Missionary Ridge. . . .

Our wounded are all left behind, some 6,000 in number. We have lost heavily in killed today. The total of our killed, wounded, and prisoners can hardly be less than 20,000, and may be much more. . . .

Rosecrans escaped by Rossville road. Enemy not yet arrived before Chattanooga. Preparations making to resist his entrance for a time.

8 p.m.

I am happy to report that my dispatch of 4 p.m. today proves to have given too dark a view of our disaster. Having been myself swept bodily off the battlefield by the panic-struck rabble into which the divisions of Davis and Sheridan were temporarily converted, my own impressions were naturally colored by the aspect of that part of the field.

It appears, however, that only those two divisions were actually routed, and that Thomas, with the remainder of the army, still holds his part of the field. Beside the two divisions of Davis and Sheridan, those of Negley and Van Cleve were thrown into confusion, but were soon rallied and hold their places. . . .

The latest report from Thomas is that he was driving back the advance of the rebels. . . .

September 21–1 p.m.

Deserters and captives both report that *Ewell's* corps is on its way [from Virginia] to join *Bragg*. One of the latter, taken this morning by Thomas, says the corps has arrived, though not in season to fight yesterday. Is now moving on the Tennessee River above this. *Long-street*, as we know, is here.

2 p.m.

Thomas seemed to have filled every soldier with his own unconquerable firmness, and Granger, his hat torn by bullets, raged like a lion wherever the combat was hottest with the electrical courage of a Ney.

Every division commander bore himself gloriously, and among brigade commanders, Turchin, Hazen, and Harker especially distinguished themselves. Turchin charged through the rebel lines with the bayonet, and becoming surrounded, forced his way back again. Harker, who had two horses shot under him on the 19th, forming his men in four lines, made them lie down till the enemy were close upon him when they suddenly rose and delivered their fire with such effect that the assaulting columns fell back in confusion. . . . When night fell this body of heroes stood on the same ground they had occupied in the morning, their spirit unbroken, but their numbers greatly diminished. . . . Thomas retired to Rossville after battle. Dispositions had been made to resist the enemy's approach on that line, but if *Ewell* be really there, Rosecrans will have to retreat beyond the Tennessee.

Thomas telegraphs this morning that the troops are in high spirits.

September 22–3 p.m.

The troops arrived here about midnight in wonderful spirits, considering their excessive fatigue and heavy losses. They have been working all day improvising rifle-pits. Line of defense is about 3 miles long. . . . It includes two redoubts . . . and is pretty strong. . . .

This army looks anxiously for re-enforcements.

September 23–11:30 a.m.

The net result of the campaign thus far is that we hold Chattanooga and the line of Tennessee River. It is true this result has been attended by a great battle with heavy losses, but it is certain that the enemy has suffered quite as severely as we have.

The first great object of the campaign, the possession of Chattanooga and the Tennessee line, still remains in our hands, and can be held by this army for from fifteen to twenty days against all efforts of the enemy, unless he should receive re-enforcements of overwhelming strength. But to render our hold here perfectly safe; no time should be lost in pushing 20,000 to 25,000 efficient troops to Bridgeport. If such re-enforcements can be got there in season . . . this place—indispensable alike to the defense of Tennessee and as the base of future operations in Georgia—will remain ours. [O.R., XXX, Part I, pp. 192–198.]

Vicksburg, Miss., via Memphis, September 22, 1863

Maj. Gen. H. W. Halleck
General-in-Chief:
Your dispatch . . . of the 15th instant directing re-enforcements to be sent to Major-General Rosecrans, is just received. I have ordered two divisions from here, one from each the Fifteenth and Seventeenth Corps. The one from the Seventeenth Army Corps is already on steamboats between Vicksburg and Helena. . . . Should more troops be required from here for Rosecrans, there is sufficient time for orders to reach before transportation can be had. An army corps commander will be sent in command of all troops from here.
U. S. Grant,
Major-General, Commanding
[O.R., XXX, Part I, p. 162.]

Washington, September 24, 1863

Colonel McCallum
Superintendent Military Railroad Transportation:
Colonel: The Secretary of War directs that you take charge of all matters of railroad transportation of the Eleventh and Twelfth Corps from Virginia to Tennessee, and that in everything connected with such transportation, loading and unloading the cars, etc., all officers of whatsoever grade will obey your instructions and give you all possible assistance. This will serve as your authority.
H. W. Halleck,
General-in-Chief
[O.R., XXIX, Part I, p. 153.]

Washington, D.C., October 16, 1863

Major-General Grant
Louisville, Ky:

General: You will receive herewith the orders of the President of the United States placing you in command of the Departments of the Ohio, Cumberland, and Tennessee. The organization of these departments will be changed as you may deem most practicable. You will immediately proceed to Chattanooga and relieve General Rosecrans. You can communicate with Generals Burnside and Sherman by telegraph. A summary of the orders sent to those officers will be sent to you immediately. It is left optional with you to supersede General Rosecrans by General G. H. Thomas or not. Any other changes will be made on your request by telegraph.

One of the first objects requiring your attention is the supply of your armies. Another is the security of the passes in the Georgia mountains to shut out the enemy from Tennessee and Kentucky. . . .

H. W. Halleck,
General-in-Chief

[*O.R.*, XXX, Part IV, p. 404.]

Report of General Braxton Bragg, CSA, Commanding Army of Tennessee (Continued)

Exhausted by two days' battle, with very limited supply of provisions, and almost destitute of water, some time in daylight was absolutely essential for our troops to supply these necessaries and replenish their ammunition before renewing the contest.

Availing myself of this necessary delay to inspect and readjust my lines, I moved as soon as daylight served on the 21st. On my arrival about sunrise near *Lieutenant-General Polk's* bivouac, I met the ever-vigilant *Brigadier-General Liddell*, commanding a division in our front line, who was awaiting the general to report that his picket this morning discovered the enemy had retreated during the night from his immediate front. Instructions were promptly given to push our whole line of skirmishers to the front, and I moved to the left and extended these orders. All the cavalry at hand . . . were ordered to the front. . . .

Our cavalry soon came upon the enemy's rear guard where the main road passes through Missionary Ridge. He had availed himself of the night to withdraw from our front, and his main body was already in position within his lines at Chattanooga.

Any immediate pursuit by our infantry and artillery would have been fruitless . . . with our weak and exhausted force. . . . Though we had defeated him and driven him from the field with heavy loss in men, arms, and artillery, it had only been done by heavy sacrifices, in repeated, persistent, and most gallant assaults upon superior numbers strongly posted and protected. [O.R., XXX, Part II, pp. 34–35.]

Headquarters, Near Chattanooga, September 26, 1863
Hon. J. A. Seddon,
Secretary of War:
Confederate States of America

Sir: May I take the liberty to advise you of our condition and our wants? On the 20th instant, after a very severe battle, we gained a complete and glorious victory – the most complete victory of the war, except, perhaps, the first Manassas. On the morning of the 21st *General Bragg* asked my opinion as to our best course. I suggested at once to strike at Burnside, and if he made his escape to march upon Rosecrans' communication in rear of Nashville. He seemed to adopt the suggestion, and gave the order to march at 4 o'clock in the afternoon. The Right Wing of the army marched some 8 or 10 miles, my command following the next day at daylight. I was halted at the crossing of the Chickamauga, and on the night of the 22d the army was ordered to march for Chattanooga, thus giving the enemy two days and a half to strengthen the fortifications here already prepared for him by ourselves. Here we have remained under instructions that the enemy shall not be assaulted. To express my convictions in a few words, our chief has done but one thing that he ought to have done since I joined his army. That was to order the attack upon the 20th. All other things that he has done he ought not to have done. I am convinced that nothing but the hand of God can save us or help us as long as we have our present commander.

Now to our wants. Can't you send us *General Lee?* The army in Virginia can operate defensively, while our operations here should be offensive – until we have recovered Tennessee, at all events. We need some such great mind as *General Lee's* (nothing more) to accomplish this. You will be surprised to learn that this army has neither organization nor mobility, and I have doubts if its commander can give it them. In an ordinary war I could serve without complaint under any one whom the Government might place in authority, but we have too much at stake in this to remain quiet under such distressing circumstances. Our most precious blood is now flowing in streams from the Atlantic to the Rocky Mountains, and may yet be exhausted before we have succeeded. Then goes honor, treasure, and independence. When I came here I hoped to find our commander willing and anxious to do all things that would aid us in our great cause, and ready to receive what aid he could get from his subordinates. It seems that I was greatly mistaken. It seems that he cannot adopt and adhere to any plan or course, whether of his own or of some one else. I desire to impress upon your mind that there is no exaggeration in these statements. On the contrary, I have failed to express my convictions to the fullest extent. All that I can add without making this letter exceedingly long is to pray you to help us, and speedily.

I remain, with the greatest respect, your obedient servant,

J. Longstreet,
Lieutenant-General
Confederate States Army

[*O.R.*, XXX, Part IV, pp. 705–706.]

Near Chattanooga, September 29, 1863

General S. Cooper
Adjutant and Inspector General:
Confederate States Army

Major-General Hindman and *Lieutenant-General Polk* have been suspended from their commands by my orders and sent to Atlanta, for not obeying orders on the 11th and 20th instant. This has been deemed necessary after grave consideration.

Braxton Bragg
General, Commanding
Army of Tennessee

[*O.R.*, XXX, Part II, p. 55.]

Bragg to General S. Cooper, Adjutant and
Inspector General, CSA, October 3, 1863

The anxiety of the Department is exhibited in dispatches for our advance against the enemy before he is re-enforced is fully shared. To attack him in front, strongly intrenched as he is, would be suicidal. To assail any other point requires us to cross the river.

For this movement supplies, which could only be had by railroad, were necessary, and our whole available means were promptly devoted to that end. The road being finished, our resources are now all devoted to the means of crossing the river, and we hope soon to be ready. In the meantime all our available cavalry is operating on the enemy's communications, and I hope soon to hear of his supplies being cut off.

The Department will, I trust, appreciate the embarrassments of an army with inadequate means of transportation; largely and hastily re-enforced without the slightest addition to these means, and just at the time of a very large loss in battle, especially of artillery horses, which makes a drain upon other resources. [*O.R.*, XXX, Part IV, p. 726.]

Near Chattanooga, Tenn., October 13, 1863

General Braxton Bragg,
Commanding near Chattanooga, Tenn:

General: I have received your application of the 11th instant, for the removal of *Lieut. Gen. D. H. Hill* from a command in the Army of Tennessee. Regretting that the expectations which induced the assignment of that gallant officer to this army have not been realized, you are authorized to relieve *General D. H. Hill* from further duty with your command.

Very respectfully, and truly, yours,

Jefferson Davis

[*O.R.*, XXX, Part II, pp. 148–149.]

General Orders, War Dept., Adjutant-General's Office
No. 322   Washington, September 28, 1863

I. The President of the United States directs that the Twentieth and Twenty-first Army Corps be consolidated and called the Fourth Army Corps, and that Maj. Gen. Gordon Granger be the commander of this consolidated corps.

II. It is also directed that a court of inquiry be convened, the detail to be hereafter made, to inquire and report upon the conduct of Major-Generals McCook and Crittenden, in the battles of the 19th and 20th instant. These officers are relieved from duty in the Department of the Cumberland, and will repair to Indianapolis, Ind., reporting their arrival, by letter, to the Adjutant-General of the Army.

By order of the Secretary of War:

E. D. Townsend,
Assistant Adjutant-General

[*O.R.*, XXX, Part III, p. 911.]

APPENDIX I.
MEDICAL PRACTICES AND
THE HANDLING OF WOUNDED IN
THE CIVIL WAR:
THEORY AND APPLICATION

Colonel Ralph M. Mitchell

For four bloody years of the Civil War men and boys left home to fight for causes they barely understood. All possibilities considered, the odds were two to one against their safe return. They could be struck down by disease or enemy bullets and could die from either. At best, they could escape both and return home bearing the lifetime scars.

Disease had always been the greatest killer in war. Field sanitation and hygiene were ignored, and few diseases had known cures. Treatment consisted of long rest periods followed by slow recovery or death. Compared to the Mexican War, where ten Americans had died of disease for each one killed in battle,[1] casualty rates for the Civil War showed great improvement. Three Confederate soldiers died of disease for each one killed in battle. The ratio for the Union Army was a more respectable two to one.[2] Disease remained the greatest crippler of armies, but its force as a killer was slowly being reduced. Immunization and other medical techniques such as isolation were controlling epidemics and reducing morbidity.

Handling massive numbers of wounded soldiers was entirely another matter. Prior to the Civil War, the system had been haphazard. Frederick the Great had used Prussian executioners as surgeons. He and Napoleon I both left wounded to die on the battlefield without medical care or, at best, removed them to nearby structures and abandoned them.[3] Americans had never had to deal with large numbers of wounded and were not prepared for such undertakings at the beginning of the war.[4] Prewar medical organizations and administration were entirely inadequate and unsuitable for large armies. It is a credit to American resourcefulness that Civil War surgeons were able not only to improvise and adapt to a countless variety of situations, but to provide modern medicine with many important innovations as well.

Critics of Civil War medical practices tend to isolate them from all other aspects of the war and evaluate them against twentieth century standards. This results in a distorted picture of successes and failures. Only when viewed in proper historical perspective and evaluated as components of vastly different logistics systems can the handling of wounded by Confederate and Union Medical Departments be judged properly.

Efforts by the Confederacy to support its army were hampered by shortages of capital, labor, food, supplies and transportation. These shortages kept its logistics systems in the embryonic stages of development throughout the war. The Union, on the other hand, was able to support its army for exactly the opposite reasons. An abundance of capital, labor and raw materials combined with an excellent transportation network and a strong industrial base to insure the success of Union logistics and, in a war of attrition, to guarantee victory.

THE CONFEDERATE MEDICAL SYSTEM

The handling of wounded was clearly influenced by the Surgeons General of the respective armies. Nine days after the Battle of First Bull Run (Manassas), on 30 July 1861, the leadership of the Confederate Medical Department fell upon the capable shoulders of Samuel Preston Moore, who held the post for the duration of the war.[5] Despite "liberal appropriations" from Congress, Moore found his department pressed for money, trained men, supplies and transportation. These shortcomings demanded that Medical Department surgeons be skilled in improvisation and adaptation. Such skills, early learned and often practiced, would carry them through periods when they would be left to fend for themselves.[6] Moore was the right man for the job. He wasted no time in bringing order out of chaos and putting together a medical service which, if logistically supported, would have been comparable to that of the North.

Of the six thousand Confederate surgeons who entered the service, only twenty-six had any previous military experience. Twenty-four of those had resigned from the United States Army to serve the Confederacy. Most were assigned organizing and administrative duties, leaving only a handful of experienced medical officers to care for the wounded in the field.[7] Skilled surgeons were hard to find. All Southern medical schools except the Medical College of Virginia had been forced to close during the war, yet somehow the Confederacy managed to overcome shortages of medical personnel and provide care to the wounded.[8]

Procurement of medical supplies required imagination. Pharmaceutical laboratories had been established but were still unable to meet the demand for medicines. Native plants and trees, it was discovered, offered satisfactory substitutes for many scarce drugs. Battle victories also gave Confederate forces the medical spoils of war when military necessity did not require their destruction.[9]

In theory, the systems for handling Confederate wounded from battlefield to General Hospital were the same as those used by the Union Army. In application, there was a clear distinction, especially after the first year. During and after a battle, stretcher bearers detailed from each regiment delivered wounded to regimental aid stations where emergency treatment could be administered. From there the wounded were taken by stretcher or ambulance to the brigade field hospital where they received more definitive care, were operated on if necessary and evacuated to a general hospital if recovery could not be accomplished in the field. Men with slight scratches arrived at field hospitals in the protective arms of a host of friends, many of whom they had never met. Adept as they were in finding the field hospitals, such "friends" always seemed to have trouble finding the front lines again.[10]

Wounded soldiers fortunate enough to be recovered from the battlefield had several obstacles to overcome before starting on the road to recovery. One of them was a ride in a Confederate ambulance. Each regiment was authorized two four-wheeled and two two-wheeled ambulances. Few ever saw that number. Ambulance shortages noted at First Manassas persisted throughout the war. The best Confederate ambulances were those captured from Union forces. The most that can be said of the Confederate ambulance service during the war is that it barely survived.[11] Without strong centralized control, field hospitals fared no better and achieved the same results. Only the general hospital system enjoyed success.

In 1861 the Confederacy devoted little time to consideration of the general hospital problem. In 1862, after the spring and summer campaigns against the city, Richmond became one vast hospital. Mortality was high, and something had to be done about it. Large hospitals, capable of efficient administration and much better care, had to be constructed. Toward the end of that year a system of general hospitals was being organized. By the early months of 1864 there seemed to be little need for further hospital expansion. To ease the logistics burden, small hospitals were closed in favor of larger ones. There was one notable exception. The Robertson Hospital, managed by Sally L. Tompkins and always containing less than one hundred patients, was permitted to remain open because of its overwhelming success in returning men to duty. Since those in charge of military hospitals had to be military personnel, President Davis gave Miss Tompkins a commission as Captain of Cavalry. She was the only woman to earn a regular commission in the Confederate Army.[12] In a time of crisis few dared argue with success.

Operating in the shadow of an overburdened logistics system, the Confederate Medical Department did well to survive. But the department was not conspicuous for its survival. It was conspicuous for its achievements. Against overwhelming odds, Samuel Preston Moore developed a system to handle sick and wounded and made that system work. It had many defects, but the job got done. No one who understood the poverty of Confederate logistics could have asked for more.

THE UNION MEDICAL SYSTEM

At the outbreak of war the Union Medical Department under Surgeon General Thomas Lawson had an organization with performance capabilities far below those of Imperial Rome, when a physician was assigned to practically every legion and warship. Bandages and instruments were available, and some hospitals had plumbing, kitchens and pharmacies.[13] In the time of Lawson, the Medical Department was designed to care for fifteen thousand men scattered throughout the country. There were scarcely more than one hundred doctors, a handful of clinical thermometers, a gross or two of surgical kits, few hospitals and ambulances and none worthy of the designation.

Lawson died in May of 1861 and was replaced by Surgeon General Clement A. Finley, a man of equal incompetence. Under both men inefficiency, inaction and confusion characterized Medical Department activities. Until these "old guard" surgeons were removed, younger, more capable men would be frustrated by bureaucratic inertia.[14] United States Sanitary Commission Director Frederick Law Olmsted best summed up the major problem of Medical Department administration in 1861. In a scorching critique of Surgeon General Finley he wrote,

> It is criminal weakness to entrust such important responsibilities as those resting on the surgeon-general to a self-satisfied, supercilious, bigoted, block-head, merely because he is the oldest of the old mess-room doctors of the frontier-guard of the country. He knows nothing, and does nothing, and is capable of knowing nothing and doing nothing but quibble about matters of form and precedent, and sign his name to papers which require that ceremony to be performed

before they can be admitted to eternal rest in the pigeonholes of the bureau.[15]

With that vote of confidence, Finley led his department to war. Numbering more than twice their Confederate counterparts and armed with varying degrees of medical knowledge, Union surgeons took to the field in 1861. Soon came the stark realities that neither surgeons nor line officers understood the actual duties of medical officers. As late as April 1862, during the Battle of Shiloh, the Army of the Ohio was moved to the battlefield with such haste that it was forced to leave all tents, bedding, ambulances and medical supplies behind. Naturally, the wounded suffered terribly.[16] Later that month William A. Hammond, a brilliant regular army surgeon, replaced Finley as Surgeon General. From that time forward the Medical Department achieved spectacular successes. Among his many accomplishments, the farsighted Hammond recommended the establishment of an ambulance corps, a corps of medical assistants, an army medical school and the first permanent general hospital in Washington. He was succeeded by Joseph K. Barnes in August of 1864. Barnes, a man of equal intelligence and competence, executed most of Hammond's programs to the benefit of the Medical Department and the Union Army.[17]

Soon to emerge as two of the most innovative surgeons in the Union Army were Charles Tripler, Medical Director of the Army of the Potomac, and Jonathan Letterman, who replaced Tripler on 4 July 1862. Tripler recommended changes in the organization of the medical department to give it autonomy and greater efficiency. Letterman was the pathfinder for the Union Army. By September of 1862, he had revamped the medical supply system, devised a workable system of field hospitals, and organized an efficient ambulance corps.[18] Hammond approved, but getting organized took time. Medical departments of western armies took another year to adopt the Letterman system. Not until the Battles of Chickamauga and Chattanooga did the Army of the Tennessee have a battle-proven medical department capable of supporting it under extremely adverse conditions.[19]

Centralization was the major theme of medical departments during 1864. Regimental and brigade field hospitals were replaced by more efficient division and corps field hospitals. The ambulance corps followed similar lines.[20] Purveying depots sprang up in the East and West and were liberally outfitted. Thirty depots and countless sub-depots were in operation by the end of the war. If success can be measured by the ability to transport medical items of ancillary value, it is noteworthy that by the end of the war field hospitals had received almost fifty thousand tons of ice through the supply system.[21]

Still there were many problems. Surgeons often refused treatment to men outside their regiments, causing an inequitable distribution of work during battles. Seeking greater efficiency, Tripler in 1862 was the first to combine regimental hospitals into brigade hospitals. That same year Letterman organized brigade hospitals into division hospitals. By 1863 corps hospitals were introduced to make the best possible use of medical personnel and equipment in large battles.[22] Division hospitals, however, remained the mainstay of the Union medical effort for the remainder of the war. In the process of upgrading hospital care, surgeons also designed mobile hospitals. Near the end of the war, a train bearing hospital personnel and equipment was introduced in the Army of the Potomac as an advance movable depot hospital. Lee's surrender at Appomattox shortened its field use to only eighteen days.[23]

Second only to an efficient hospital system was an efficient ambulance system. Vehicles designed for the express purpose of carrying sick and wounded soldiers were unknown in the United States Army prior to 1858. But in the years immediately before the war one model of a four-wheeled ambulance and two models of a two-wheeled ambulance had been approved for experimentation. The four-wheeler was the only one tested, and it achieved satisfactory results. For reasons yet unknown, the untested two-wheeled ambulances were adopted and recommended by a board of officers as the best for transporting badly wounded men. Experience would show that these were utterly unfit for any such purpose.[24]

The system needed improvement even more than the ambulances. Tripler saw the need for a separate and distinct ambulance corps of volunteers organized into companies with officers and non-commissioned officers to lead them. Letterman concurred. Deciding that an efficiently run ambulance corps could not be under quartermaster control nor under the direct control of surgeons whose battlefield requirements precluded their attention to such details, Letterman obtained Major General G. B. McClellan's permission to test the new organization in the Army of the Potomac.[25] Antietam and Fredericksburg were the first testing grounds. Both battles proved the system's viability. Wounded soldiers were recovered from the battlefield faster than ever before without confusion or disorder.

Other departments soon followed the Army of the Potomac. In March of 1863 the Department of the Tennessee, at the insistence of its medical director, E. P. Vollum, and with the hearty endorsement of its commander, Major General Ulysses S. Grant, adopted a similar system. Still, it was not until 11 March 1864 that an Act of Congress gave the Medical Department authority over the ambulance corps. That act, based on Letterman's system, made the ambulance system uniform throughout the Union Army.[26]

General hospitals presented a unique problem. In 1861 the largest military hospital, located at Fort Leavenworth, Kansas, had forty-one beds. Like those of the Confederacy, all early Union general hospitals were extemporized, utilizing former schools, warehouses, factories, hotels, large private residences, churches and town halls. The first general hospital was opened in May of 1861 in Washington, D.C. Other hospitals quickly opened in other major eastern and western cities.[27]

Two major questions had to be considered in the construction of general hospitals. Would the layout permit efficient administration, and would it provide proper ventilation? Lessons were learned by trial and error, and surgeons and architects concluded that the pavilion system seemed the most logical and least objectionable. The accomplishments attributed to hospital design were amazing. In four years the Union Army had developed a general hospital system which provided the basis for today's general hospitals. By 1865 there were two hundred and five hospitals capable of handling 136,894 patients.[28] The achievement was remarkable.

Unlike the South, which had nothing at the national level, there were several national organizations for soldiers' relief in the North. First sanctioned on 13 June 1861, the United States Sanitary Commission was designed to investigate and advise on matters of "sanitary and hygienic interest." Operating largely in the eastern theater, this precursor of the American Red Cross brought about instead a purging and cleansing of the Medical Department. It inspected all medical activities, exposing negligence and incompetence whenever discovered. Its workers went to the field to nurse and nourish and distribute medical supplies, food and clothing. Relief lodges were set up in large cities to feed and shelter soldiers in transit and disabled soldiers. The Western Sanitary Commission complemented its work. Organized on 5 September 1861, it performed similar services for western armies.[29]

Another organization welcomed in most camps was the United States Christian Commission. Members of the commission donated vast stores of food to the armies but were remembered most for performing personal services for the wounded that regular hospital attendants could not or would not do.[30]

To a large extent the Union Medical Department reflected the logistics system of which it was a part. Success spawned success. But the Medical Department went beyond that. As the Union logistics system began to operate smoothly, surgeons dared to be innovative. With sufficient resources at their command, they boldly changed ambulance and hospital systems. But, procedures had to be perfected, lessons had to be learned on the battlefield, and, as always, the wounded paid the price.

THE HANDLING OF WOUNDED: BATTLEFIELD EXPERIENCES

There were many ways men on both sides could be wounded in the Civil War. Muskets and pistols accounted for ninety-three percent of all wounds, artillery accounted for only six percent, and bayonets and sabers accounted for less than one percent.[31] Having been wounded in some manner, soldiers on both sides found themselves still much at risk. The ebb and flow of clashing forces might place the wounded alternately on Union or Confederate held ground and subject them to fire from both sides. Those able to move ran, walked or crawled to the rear in search of aid stations. The incapacitated remained where they fell, awaiting medical assistance and hoping not to be wounded again or killed by screaming artillery shells and whizzing bullets. Surviving these dangers, they still faced the possibility of being trampled or run over by friendly or enemy soldiers or by horses and wagons passing back and forth in waves of panic or controlled frenzy. If they were still alive after that, they could only hope that help would come quickly. If it did not, they might bleed to death, starve, die of thirst or succumb to the elements.

No adequate system of battlefield first aid was developed. Hemorrhage was a major problem for the wounded soldier, and his suffering prior to receiving medical attention was usually intense. Both sides suffered in the battle for Fort Donelson in February of 1862. The battlefield was cold, wet and muddy. There, Union and Confederate wounded had to be removed with picks and axes from the mud into which they had frozen fast. Some of the Union wounded who tried to stop Confederate stragglers from stripping them and taking their valuables were pinned to the earth with bayonets and their items then taken. Those who did not die from the bayonet wounds lay frozen in the mud for a day, stripped and alive, but unable to move. A Union officer left for dead remained alive only because his bleeding wounds had frozen. For twenty-four hours he lay with his head frozen to the ground while opposing forces fought for, and twice passed over, the ground where he fell. Miraculously, he survived the ordeal.[32]

During the Second Battle of Bull Run in August of 1862, the ordeal of one soldier defied belief. Wounded in the shin, the 2nd Wisconsin's Sheldon E. Judson arrested the bleeding with his handkerchief. He was placed in an ambulance and taken to some woods on the battlefield where others needing medical attention had been collected. There he was propped against a tree and promptly attacked by a swarm of hornets. After a painful night he and his group were abandoned, taken prisoners by Confederate pickets, abandoned again and shelled by Union artillery. Following several futile attempts to get help from passing Confederate troops and ambulances, Judson and the others were finally collected by some sympathetic "rebs" and deposited alongside several hundred other wounded Union soldiers. There they remained for six days without treatment and with but one cracker per day to sustain them. Judson spent two of those days and one night lying without protection in a pool of water. A truce finally ended his immediate suffering, and he was taken to a general hospital in Washington where he recovered. Another soldier of the same regiment decided that help would never come and crawled nine miles to the nearest Union field hospital to have his shattered leg amputated. One embarrassed soldier, bleeding profusely from a wound in the buttocks, was ordered to the rear by a member of the medical corps. Cursing loudly, the soldier announced that he would not leave the field until he received "a more honorable wound."[33] Whatever the outcome, one thing was certain—he belonged to the army which lost the field, and the wounded of that army could expect to suffer more.

Less than a month later at Antietam the situation was reversed. Victorious Union forces collected their wounded as fast as they fell, but retreating Confederate forces left behind over two thousand of theirs. Good weather and rapid collection and care of Confederate wounded saved them from a fate similar to that suffered by Union soldiers at Second Bull Run.[34]

Despite improved methods of casualty collection, men suffered and died waiting for help. Fire was always a great threat to wounded soldiers. At Chancellorsville and Chickamauga in 1863 and the Wilderness in 1864, many wounded on both sides were burned to death as the dense thickets in which they fell caught fire.[35]

But such tragedies were the exception; after 1862 wounded soldiers, particularly those from the Union, could be reasonably sure that their comrades would make every effort to recover them from the battlefield. Ambulance systems had been established and recovery techniques practiced. Still, recovery under fire was a dangerous undertaking. During the siege of Petersburg in September of 1864, one Union corps lost ten killed, six wounded and nineteen captured trying to recover its wounded. In the process two ambulances took direct hits from enemy artillery.[36]

EVACUATION TO FIELD HOSPITALS

Litter bearers from each regiment collected all who could not walk and delivered them to an aid station located just beyond enemy musket range. Those who could not be evacuated under fire were evacuated under the cover of darkness or as soon after the battle as possible. An assistant surgeon at the aid station examined the wounds, applied dressings and ligatures where needed and sent the men by ambulance to the nearest field hospital. These hospitals were initially located out of the range of enemy artillery (about 1½ to 2 miles from the front lines), but were often subjected to its fire when battle lines shifted. If ambulances were not available, litter bearers would have to carry wounded soldiers to the hospitals.[37]

At the First Battle of Bull Run not one wounded Union soldier made the twenty-seven mile trip back to Washington in an ambulance. Later in the first year of the war, those forced to ride in makeshift ambulances could justifiably complain of being "jolted to death." Most ambulances were little more than springless wagons, pulled over rough roads by debilitated animals. After the Second Battle of Bull Run one hundred and fifty ambulances were dispatched to enemy-held territory to recover the wounded. Only one reached its destination. With Tripler's and Letterman's corrections, however, the Union ambulance system was finally functioning effectively by September of 1862. Lack of a responsive ambulance system under the Confederate Medical Department, however, combined with a shortage of animals and vehicles to produce crisis management. This inability to establish an ambulance system plagued the Confederacy for the duration of the war.[38]

Antietam marked the turning point in the evacuation of wounded to field hospitals. There, on the bloodiest day in American history, members of the newly formed ambulance corps manned three hundred ambulances under a new system. Evacuation was quick and orderly, and by the day after the battle the field was completely cleared of wounded. Ten thousand Union and four thousand Confederate soldiers were brought in to field hospitals for treatment.[39]

As news of Letterman's success flowed west, his ambulance system was adopted everywhere as the best form of evacuation. As early as 29 December 1862 a variation of his system was tried with good results at Murfreesboro. Confederate soldiers were so amazed at the efficiency with which wounded from both sides were recovered that they preferred to watch rather than fire upon the ambulance corps as it went about the battlefield.[40] Both sides understood the significance of rapid and unbridled handling of the wounded. After Chancellorsville, splendid cooperation between Lee and Hooker and the medical directors of both sides resulted not only in a transfer of the captured wounded, but in a transfer made efficient by the free flow of surgeons, ambulances and supplies within each other's lines.[41]

Gettysburg marked the high point of Letterman's ambulance system. The battle lasted three days and ended on July 3, 1863. By early morning, July 4th, one thousand ambulances had evacuated 14,193 Union and 6,000 Confederate wounded.[42] That feat represented the ultimate combination of abundant equipment and an efficient system.

FIELD HOSPITALS

Union and Confederate wounded arriving at field hospitals had mixed emotions. With the tents or building pressed into service in sight, there was a feeling of relief that the jolting had stopped and medical care was at hand. That feeling was marred by a concomitant fear of the unknown. Horrible stories of brutal treatment by surgeons passed quickly from soldier to soldier and were known to all. Each expected the worst.

Wounds introduced a special form of bacterial contamination. Bullets fired at slow speeds did not create sufficient air friction to be self-purifying. Upon entering the body they contained germs from the hands of the men who fired them and pushed into the wound bits of filthy clothing they happened to strike. If the wound did not become infected from the bullet or clothing, it soon would become so as surgeons' dirty hands and instruments and unsterile cleansing and bandaging procedures introduced deadly microbes. Those germs produced toxemia, septicemia, pyemia, tetanus and hospital gangrene among the more direct effects, and produced numerous indirect diseases as well. Recovery from the wound was often secondary to fighting infections.[43]

Paradoxically, the South, with a dearth of medical supplies, was better able to prevent the formation and spread of infection than the North. Wounds were cleansed with *boiled rags* instead of contaminated sponges. Unsterile lint in bandages was replaced by *sterile cotton* baked in ovens. *Boiled horse hair* replaced silk in ligatures and sutures. These improvisations presented unsuspecting Confederate surgeons with the basic principles of asepsis.[44] Having no time to analyze what they had seen, they relinquished the laurels of discovery and went about the grim business of broken bodies.

Surgeons worked days without food or sleep to clear field hospitals of wounded. What little time they had away from the operating tables was spent examining and dressing wounds. Three of every four operations were amputations. Chloroform or a mixture of chloroform and ether was generally available, but there were occasions when amputations were performed without anesthesia. Brave was the man who submitted to unanesthetized surgery, but braver still were those detailed to hold him still.[45]

To the passer-by a field hospital in operation was a horrible sight. Groans and moans could be heard everywhere. Surgeons with bloody hands and clothing worked quickly on patients as a steady flow of fresh blood seemed to drip from the operating tables. Completing the macabre scene was the ever-present pile of amputated arms and legs which caused even hardened veterans to grow queasy and hurry on.[46] But, given the primitive state of the art, surgeons did well to save as many lives as they did.

Away from the operating table, those cases deemed hopeless were made as comfortable as possible, while surgeons turned their attentions to those whose injuries were afforded a chance of recovery. All wounds were treated first with simple water dressings. As they began to suppurate, a mild soothing ointment called simple cerate (two parts fresh lard and one part white wax) was applied. Maggots frequently infested the wounds, causing patients much anxiety. They served a useful purpose in cleaning the wound, but few could tolerate their annoying presence. If a patient survived the infection, he had a chance to recover. If not, he wasted away quickly.

Field hospitals were grim indeed, but not entirely without humor. One captain from Kentucky was shot in the mouth while leading a charge at the Battle of Nashville. The bullet knocked out some front teeth, struck his tongue and apparently disappeared. Examining surgeons could find no trace of it. The next day nature extracted the bullet which, it turned out, the captain had swallowed.[47] It was a case of "biting the bullet" taken to its literal extreme.

At field hospitals, surgeons always tried to improve techniques. After Chickamauga they noticed how quickly their wounded recovered in open air tents and mild weather. Lessons such as that were duly recorded and disseminated so other surgeons could learn.[48] But tents were not always so highly regarded. Before sanitary inspections became routine, hospital tents contained ten men so close together that there was hardly walking room between them. The floor was often muddy and foul with excrement and the patients' clothing was filthy with vomit and rank with perspiration. Flies and body lice were in constant attendance. Male nurses would not or could not do much to help. Female nurses would not stand for such filth. They made their presence felt and appreciated.[49]

Lack of organization and centralization plagued Confederate field hospitals throughout the war. Surgeons simply had to adapt and improvise as needed to ensure adequate care for the wounded. In contrast, division field hospitals for the Union were so well organized by early 1864 that they could operate practically independent of the units to which they were assigned. Typical of the service the wounded could expect to receive for the remainder of the war was that furnished by Sherman's combined Armies of the Cumberland, Tennessee and Ohio during the campaign through Georgia. A large mobile field hospital containing one hundred tents and all appurtenances followed the armies, keeping near the rail lines at all times. It received most of the wounded and provided them with the necessary care until they were well enough to be sent back to Chattanooga. A permanent detail of commissary officers provided food comparable to that served in general hospitals. In the campaign as far as Atlanta, the hospital was moved eight times without incident.[50] Its successful functioning over a four month period clearly demonstrated the ability of the Medical Department to support sustained combat operations.

TRANSPORTING WOUNDED FROM FIELD TO GENERAL HOSPITALS

After treating their wounded at field hospitals, surgeons on both sides made arrangements for the disposition of each case. The lightly wounded would remain at the field hospital or convalesce in an area nearby until they were able to rejoin their units. Those requiring further treatment and those no longer fit for field service were evacuated to general hospitals. Despite system improvements toward the end of the war, the trip was usually a painful ordeal. Typical of what a wounded soldier might expect was the plight of surgeon John G. Perry of the 20th Massachusetts Regiment, who accompanied the rear guard during Hooker's withdrawal from Chancellorsville. Along the way Perry's horse kicked him and broke his leg in several places. The rear guard left him where he lay, but a surgeon friend found him and placed him in an ambulance headed north. For several days he received an excruciatingly painful jolting. Making the trip more unbearable was the fact that his ambulance mate who had died early on the trip rolled on top of him each time they went over a bump. Upon reaching the railroad depot, Perry was placed in a freight car half filled with corn and sent to Alexandria, Virginia. There, car and passenger were switched to a railroad siding and abandoned. Having finally been discovered in the car, Perry was taken to a general hospital where he was told his leg had developed gangrene and would have to be taken off. To save his leg he "escaped" from that hospital and secured passage on a steamboat to Washington where he prevailed on a surgeon at a general hospital there to help him get home. Through the United States Sanitary Commission he secured passage on a hospital train bound for his home in New York. Upon arriving there he was unable to locate a doctor who could set the broken leg, so with the help of his brother-in-law, he set the leg himself with good and permanent results.[51]

From the beginning of the war the South had little to offer in the way of transportation to general hospitals. Steamers were pressed into service on the Mississippi River until the fall of Vicksburg, but railroads accepted the burden of evacuating most of the Confederacy's wounded. Ambulances and springless wagons transported the wounded from field hospitals to railroad depots or steamer landings. Then the men would be taken to large cities and transferred by ambulance or wagon to general hospitals.[52]

Typical of the difficulties experienced in transporting wounded to general hospitals were the problems encountered by Confederate medical officers attempting to evacuate the Chickamauga casualties. Railroads were from ten to twenty-five miles from the battlefield. Roads were bumpy, and ambulances were in short supply. Most of the fifteen thousand wounded required evacuation. It took the ambulances more than a week to deliver them to the railroad depots where some had to wait another week to obtain further transportation. The only good rail lines near Chickamauga led to Atlanta; so, regardless of ultimate destination, more than ten thousand wounded soldiers were received into general hospitals in that city which, at the time, had a hospital capacity of only eighteen hundred.[53]

In contrast, the Union Medical Department had developed a system of sequential transfer by 1862. Before or during large engagements, patients were removed from general hospitals near the battlefield and sent to others further north. Thus freed, the evacuated hospitals could accept large numbers of patients without taxing their facilities. By 1863 passenger cars were being converted into hospital cars. This was the first of many innovations. As the war progressed, most trains were equipped with kitchens, dispensaries, stoves, sanitary facilities, quarters for nurses and doctors and offices for the latter. Some trains were used as general hospitals and had capacities of up to two hundred patients. By the end of the war, hospital trains had transported 225,000 sick and wounded patients to general hospitals.[54]

On occasions when railroads were inaccessible, the wounded were bound to suffer more. After Gettysburg Confederate wounded had to be taken all the way to Virginia by wagon. On the way they were attacked by

Union raiding parties which captured wounded officers and destroyed wagons. Brigadier General John D. Imboden's cavalry brigade escorted one ambulance column seventeen miles long. During the trip Imboden listened to the shrieks of the wounded as they were bounced and jostled over rutty roads. Many pleaded to be shot or left beside the road to die peacefully. At one point where the ride was particularly rough, Imboden wrote: "During this one night I realized more of the horrors of war than I had in all the two preceding years."[55]

Originally under control of the Quartermaster Department, Union hospital steamers carried the wounded up coastal waterways and western rivers. Evacuation by water transports was hampered by the uncertainty of their use. Early in the war some steamers were filled with wounded soldiers and sent off without a surgeon on board. One steamboat Captain from Ohio refused to take on board any wounded but those from his state. Vessels fitted for medical evacuation would be taken without notice by Quartermaster officers and returned later, filthy and stripped of everything necessary for patient comfort. Medical officers complained, but little action was taken by anyone before 1865. Through an Act of Congress in February of that year, the Medical Department assumed complete control over all hospital steamers assigned to it. It was no wonder that wounded soldiers hated steamers. Most were overcrowded and uncomfortable. The trip took at least several days, during the course of which patients had to be treated and even operated upon, and bandages had to be changed. For the wounded, each day was just an extension of their agony. One hospital volunteer told of having to put her fingers in her ears to avoid the shrieks of the men as doctors examined them and changed their dressings. When the steamers finally reached their destinations, there was still the painful wagon ride to the hospital awaiting each man.[56] Going to the general hospital was an ordeal few ever forgot. Only those who died enroute were relieved of their suffering.

Were it not for Letterman's evacuation system, countless more wounded soldiers would have died before reaching general hospitals. There were many success stories. After Fredericksburg, one group of fifteen hundred wounded Union soldiers made the trip to Washington in seventeen hours without the loss of a single man. At Gettysburg the evacuation system was put to its most severe test. In the two weeks following the battle, 15,425 wounded were moved to general hospitals.[57] The North had proven beyond a doubt that it could handle mass casualties. Time and distance directly influenced mortality rates. Reducing both increased survivability.

TREATMENT AT GENERAL HOSPITALS

Soldiers who survived the trip and found themselves in general hospitals were still not sanguine about their chances for recovery. Facing overcrowded and unsanitary conditions, it is no wonder that they developed the attitude that being placed in a general hospital meant certain death. When offered the opportunity, most preferred to risk a long and painful journey in order to recuperate at home.[58] Infections similar to those found in field hospitals were also present in general hospitals. Patients already weakened by months of hard campaigning succumbed quickly as deadly germs attacked their emaciated bodies. Little could be done except to let the infection run its course and hope the patient was strong enough to survive. Surgeons, seeking to check the spread of infection, were unaware that with their contaminated hands and instruments they were spreading it themselves.[59]

Women were employed as hospital matrons, nurses and cooks. Their zeal and industry were a blessing to doctors and patients alike. The major problem with women was that there were not enough of them in the general hospitals where, throughout the war, the ratio of male to female nurses remained five to one.[60]

Of the 150 general hospitals constructed by the Confederacy, Chimborazo was the largest. With 150 pavilions (40–60 beds each), 100 Sibley tents (8–10 beds each) and a staff of 120 medical personnel, the hospital had accommodation for eight thousand patients. It was totally self-sustaining and even managed to lend the Confederate Government three hundred thousand dollars during the war.[61]

While Chimborazo thrived, smaller general hospitals often went weeks without quartermaster or commissary support. Such occurrences were expected. The failing fortunes of the Confederacy had an adverse effect on the general hospital system, in the end reducing efficiency to the point of failure.[62] In four years a hospital system had been instituted, developed and destroyed. Severely limited by logistics problems, medical officers did well to keep general hospitals in operation until the end of the war.

Early Union general hospitals were much the same as those in the Confederacy. All were extemporized. Surgeon General Hammond was no less enthusiastic than his counterpart in the South in pressing for the construction of pavilion hospitals. In all, 201 were built during the war. Their capacities ranged from one hundred to thirty-five hundred. The largest was Satterlee Hospital in Philadelphia. As a rule, a one thousand bed hospital would contain between 120 and 200 staff members.[63]

After being admitted to General Hospitals, patients went through a thorough inprocessing. They were weighed and measured and had their complete medical description recorded. Also recorded were their units, states and, for obvious reasons, names of next of kin.[64] Surgeons constantly had to guard against the spread of infection. Their tasks were made all the more difficult by their limited knowledge of asepsis and antisepsis. Bromine and iodine, first considered cleaning solutions, were unknowingly used as disinfectants in latrines and on floors, hospital furniture and bedpans, but apparently not on medical instruments. By 1863 bromine was being used to cure hospital gangrene.[65] This antiseptic measure was not recognized as such since only the cure for, and not the cause of, the infection was known.

Long stays were the rule in Confederate and Union general hospitals; to be discharged in less than six weeks for anything but minor surgery was practically unheard of, and some patients remained for more than a year. It was difficult for soldiers in general hospitals to understand that surgeons were trying to give all patients the best care possible. One officer recounted how each day for weeks his wounds were probed without anesthetic to a depth of six inches. Another patient complained about the poor way his wounds were dressed, and recorded bouts with erysipelas and gangrene to support his contention. Similar stories came from all general hospitals. Soldiers felt alone and afraid in large impersonal wards far from their comrades and often just as far from their homes. After visiting several of those establishments, Letterman was convinced that, "life in a General Hospital tends to destroy the good qualities of a soldier."[66] Good morale was an important part of recovery. The will to live frequently determined whether a soldier would survive the long ordeal of hospitalization, so it was important to keep him as happy as possible.

Patients convalesced at hospitals or were discharged if boards of medical officers found them unfit for further service. If a board deemed them fit for further service, they returned to the battlefield, usually with their former regiments.[57] When it was decided that a man should return to the battlefield, he could be sent there directly or by way of a convalescent camp. If he had the misfortune of being sent to a convalescent camp to complete his recovery, he could expect to trade a bed in a warm ward for bare ground in an unheated tent. Morale would be low and mortality high. Life in a general hospital was difficult, but in a convalescent camp it was pure misery.[67]

From field to general hospitals, the Union Army had a transportation system far superior to that used by the Confederate Army. As the assets of the latter diminished, those of the former grew. The same held true for general hospitals. The Confederacy went far toward meeting the needs of its wounded, but in the end its general hospitals could not function without logistical support. As they collapsed one by one, those in the North flourished under the aegis of a sound logistical system. In 1863 Union general hospitals had a capacity of 58,715 beds. By the end of the war that number had been increased to 136,894. After 1863 the hospitals were never filled to capacity. Still, in four years over one million patients had been cared for in a hospital system limited in size only by the scope of the conflict.[68]

Critics of Civil War medical practices often evaluate them against twentieth century standards. There is also a tendency to isolate a study of medical activities from all other aspects of the war. This results in a distorted picture of successes and failures. Confederate and Union Medical Departments operated as part of overall logistics efforts in their respective armies. The mutuality of that arrangement allowed the departments not only to reflect the fortunes of their logistics systems, but to be contributing factors in those fortunes as well. Seen in proper historical perspective, the activities of both medical departments clearly indicate how successful each was in caring for its wounded.

From a military standpoint, Civil War medical contributions had far-reaching effects. Along with major equipment improvements and innovations there was established an efficient medical organization controlled by a competent surgeon general. Equally important was the establishment of supply, field hospital and ambulance systems. The results achieved from such efficient systems astonished European medical experts and led to improved methods in caring for the sick and wounded in armies throughout the world.[69] Letterman's field hospital system dictated the basic structure of United States Army medical care through World War II. His ambulance system remained in effect until the introduction of helicopters in the Korean War rendered it obsolete.[70]

In any large organization there is always room for improvement. During the Civil War Confederate and Union Medical Departments seemed to substantiate that observation with alarming regularity. Surgeons did their best to solve the myriad problems which confronted them daily, but in the process mistakes were made and patients suffered the consequences. As members of medical departments reflecting the fortunes of sharply contrasting logistics systems, surgeons relied on their skills in improvisation, adaptation, and innovation to give their wounded the best available care. In the Union Medical Department those skills meant constant improvement; in the Confederate Medical Department they meant survival.

APPLICATION

*Narrative of Thomas G. J. Doughman, Co. G, 89th Ohio
Volunteer Infantry, First Brigade, First Division, Reserve Corps,
Army of the Cumberland*

In the morning (Sept. 20) we were taken out of our brigade (the 89th was attached to Whitaker's brigade, Steedman's division at this time) and carried sugar and coffee along, issued to us as we marched. We were being ordered to Rosencrantz's extreme right, where Longstreet's fresh troops that came up from the eastern army was pressing Rosencrantz right wing.

As we was marching over some cleared land on the edge of a field near some woodland, we could see some troops off to our left. Seeing horses off to our left worrying Colonel –?– (looks like Nathes) raised his glasses to his eyes and said, "Lay down, boys!" We had hardly gotten down when we saw smoke rise where we saw the horses. Rebs had artillery–rifle battery–in position to shell us. (Nathan B. Forrest) The first shell dropped some distance in front of us, the second coming nearer. The Colonel gave command, "Forward double quick–right oblique into woods!" to avoid shell fire. They did fire, and came near getting us. We went into the woods double-quick.

It was not long before we came to the foot of Snodgrass Ridge. On striking the ridge, here came an Illinois regiment down the hill Pel Mel with the rebs right behind. Our Colonel, seeing the situation, ordered the 89th to "Fix bayonets, charge!" We formed a line of battle, and with a cheer no Johnny could equal, we started. Seeing us and hearing us coming, the rebs give "about face" up the hill. The Rebel line broke back up the ridge, the Illinois troops did about face and were right behind them, and us close behind them.

In reaching the top of the ridge, our Colonel halted us giving command, "Lie down boys". As soon as the rebs saw we were not coming further, they about faced and charged the Illinois troops, and back the Illinois troops came, passing over our regiment, their Colonel passing within 5 feet of where I lay. That put us in front.

We opened fire on them, and proceeded to fight them laying down, since we was not so much exposed as when standing. Our Colonel had already instructed us to shoot the collor barers. "Get the collors down!" We succeeded in checking them. While doing that, the firing ceased on our part of the line, from their side. Comrade, W. S. Thacker and myself of our company got up from the ranks and advanced perhaps 3 or 4 paces in front of the company and looked down over the crest of the ridge to see what the enemy was about.

We seen they was forming fresh troops to attack us again. Thacker went back to the ranks and laid down with the company. I, however, laid down just where I was, in exposed position.

They soon came marching up four abreast. They got in close range and wheeled into line of battle, their collors bright as then they were unfurled for the first time. They were just opposite me. Thinking that now was my chance to get a collor barer, I got up on my feet right by a small sapling, resting my gun on the sapling and went to firing at the collor barer, supposing that my regiment would raise, but they did not—still remained firing while lying down.

The first ball coming my way cut off my canteen string and my canteen was thrown to the ground. Another ball pierced my haversack. I had fired several times and had my gun at ready when I was struck by one of those explosive musket balls—within half inch of the joint of left hip.—For technical description see medical record—passing through lower bowel and exploded in right hip.

I turned half around, facing my company, and fell on my hands and knees. Held on to my gun tightly and crawled back through my regiment which was still laying down behind me, to the rear. One of the boys asked, "Jeff, you wounded?"

"Yes, the S. O. B.'s, go after them!"

One says, "Where?"

I said, "In the foot", as it numbed my left limb at the time. Had the sensation of foot asleep. I crawled to the rear of the regiment and all I thought of was doing some big shooting again. But I got sick—nausea and faintness—and the balls were coming thick and fast, and I began to fear being hit again. An old stump just in front of me offered protection for the time being and I crawled to its shelter. But seeing a ball knock a chunk out of my log, I concluded I had better remain where I was.

Soon Seargeant J. H. Hall (sic.) of my company came to me asking, "Jeff, can you walk?"

I answered, "I don't know. I'll try." He helped me to my feet and not until then did I discover where I was wounded. I then saw the blood coming down my left pants leg and could feel the ball just under the skin under my right hip.

I threw my gun down, took off my belt and cartridge box and discarded them, having nothing left but haversack and blanket. I put my arm around the Seargeant's neck and he helped me back down side of ridge out of the range of Reb guns.

There met Michael Paul of my company who had gone to the rear. Seargeant Hall gave him my blanket and haversack and he helped me a little farther, where we met a soldier that said he belonged to an Indiana Regiment and had exhausted his ammunition.

Knowing Paul had plenty, as we entered fight with 100 rounds to the man, I told him to give me my things and then handed them to the other soldier and said to Paul, "Go back." I let go of Paul and leaned on the other man. I told Paul to go back and stay with the boys, not run off in this style, that he was needed at the front. But he would not go, insisted on accompanying us.

At the foot of the ridge where the Colonel of the Illinois Regiment was trying to get his men in line to go back and support the 89th, we passed just in front of the Colonel's horse. Seeing two men with me, and Paul not assisting me, he drew his sword over Paul's head and commanded him to get into the ranks right there, that one man with me was enough.

Did not go but little farther until we came to an old house—cottage. We went in and he fixed a bed for me on the floor. One wounded man was already in there. Soon after, another wounded man was brought in and put on the floor with me. He was shot through the groin.

As night came on and one man who was not wounded stayed there. This was the afternoon of Sunday 20th and Rosencranz's (sic.) army fell back on Chattanooga that night and there was numerous confused stragglers. The Indiana man went out and shut the door and it was not long until dark came.

I knew nothing more until next morning (Sept. 21) about sun up. About daylight Monday—the door opened and in stepped two Reb soldiers with guns and took the soldier who spent the night with us, prisoner. I said—jig was up, I considered myself a prisoner now. During Monday morning, Nathen Cooper, (sic.) and his wife and two small children, and his mother—whose home was this house—he being a confederate soldier was allowed to visit his home.—Corresponded with him for 15 years. A widow lady with two boys also occupied this house.

I asked them if they knew where there was a doctor. They said there was one close by, and I requested they send the boys for him. When the M. D. came in, I saw he was one of our captured surgeons.

I was told that he was belonged to the 105th Ohio Volunteer Infantry. I told him I'd like the ball in my hip removed—and after the examination he said he could do nothing, as the Rebs had taken all his instruments.

I told him to cut away with what he had and do the best he could. After cutting in he removed a number of fragments of ball and remarked, "I guess you were shot with a button." After probing further he removed a one ounce lead ball—round except a flattening on one side. The outside covering of the main ball is steel about the thickness of a knife blade. This part exploded. I know this to be true and still possess the ball.

There being a number of Reb stragglers prowling around robbing the dead, one came in. And I having removed my shoes and put them close beside me—he wearing a worn out pair of boots, wanted to know how I'd like to trade my shoes for his boots. I remarked that I wouldn't trade, that I intended wearing them. He said, "You'll never wear them again," and I didn't for he picked them up and walked out without removing his delapidated boots.

Soon after, another big Confederate came in with gun in hand. He swore a terrific oath and wanted to know where I was wounded. I told him. He raised his gun saying, "I guess I'll knock your brains out!" and was putting his threat into execution when Old Lady Cooper catched his arm, arrested the blow and turned him around. She remarked that he shouldn't abuse these men since they were wounded and prisoners. He left swearing.

Not a mouthful of food in the house, with the small children crying for food. I told Mrs. Cooper there were several pieces of hard tack and coffee in my haversack.

They all went away that night but those two boys stayed. The wounded man on the bed with me wanted water in the night. I called to the boys, got them to get some water. I got him quiet, but soon he wanted water again, but I could not get him any more. I got him quieter, but before daylight he died and I laid in bed with him until about 11 o'clock before they took his body out. They was all very kind to me.

The third or fifth day the Rebs came with their government wagon and hauld me about 3 mile where they were getting our wounded together. There was about 500 there wounded. My, my, to see the different wounds. It is still fresh in my mind yet. They then took our names and command in order to ship us South to prison.

They had to haul us about 12 miles to put us on a train to ship south, so they proceeded to commence hauling. When they got all those they thot would be able to again go into our Service, they sent a Rebble doctor around to examin the rest of us, and when he examined me he shook his head and said I was too near dead. Consoling, was it not?

When they got through with that part, they proposed an exchange with Rosencrantz. So Rose sent his mule train through after us, but they would not allow our drivers to come closer than the Pickett Post.

They came to me about noon on wednesday. I told them to let me down and see if I could bear my weight on my feet. I could not tell when my feet touched the ground. Went down like a rag.

Raining, got soaking wet, got to Chattanooga, 14 miles, at daylight thursday morning. They had no hospital and put us in an old store room. Had no one to wait on us.

While in Reble hands we got ½ pint of gruel per day. Got ½ pint of gruel on wednesday morning and nothing more until thursday eve, then they brought us some hard tack and bacon. They gave each man a handful of hard tack and about 2 pounds of bacon. Ate it raw. you should have seen us eat.

On the 6th day of October they carried me up to the Crutchfield house and put me in the 3rd ward, 3rd storry. I had not had my wounds dressed since the ball was taken out on the 21st day of September. John Peters and Charles Holley were my first nurses after Geo Teter. (sic.) I laid on my back over two months until the bed sores with gangrene in them got so bad they turned me over on my face, and I laid that way for three months. I could not move a particle, only my hand while in that position. My feet extended over the end of the bunk—no socks—and that cold Newyears I got my feet frozen by the time my Father got there to bring me home. But he had to wait until I rallied some, as my wound had healed up on the outside of the wound in my right hip and had to be cut open again.

Then they transfered me to Nashville, Tennessee. Took me out of the hospital car and put me in an ambulance, thinking I was an officer, and hauled me up to the officers hospital on the hill. Then back down town to the hospital where they took me out of the car. (sic.) I have a scar on one of my knees yet that was caused by me being bumped around over the rough streets.

While laying on my face, I laid on a ring which caused severe bed sores, coming near cutting my abdomen. I was put under chloraform at Nashville and they scraped the bone then burned it out, in order to nail gangrene.

—another soldier busy nearby, ripped out an oath saying, "You're young to get a discharge," he said, "ha ha!" gut up, took his knapsack. In hospital near depot.

Next day father tried to secure furlough with the results the same as at Chattanooga. They claiming I was subject to discharge. He returned to me and I refused discharge after —?— at difficult times for two weeks. They finally granted me a furlough of 30 days with the understanding that I was to report at Nashville after the expiration of that time. Father believing that I would not live until we arrived home, remarked that a dead man would have to report. I had refused a discharge a number of times.

Father had been so annoyed by graybacks (lice) himself, that when we were ready to board the boat, he purchased a new suit of clothes to rid himself of his uninvited guests. The boat that we boarded had transported soldiers and was well infested. The soldiers leaving many of their lice behind, with the result that father was the unwilling host of numerous new guests.

As we were on the boat a week going from Nashville to Cincinnati, he would go to bed sleeping in the bunk above mine, and about the time he was nearly to sleep, the graybacks would begin their serenade, driving him from his bunk—strike a light and hunt for graybacks. He would repeat this several times during the night. It amused me since I had become so accustomed to my guests that I was no longer much annoyed.

We landed at the Cincinnati warf and they carried me to the Penn R. R. depot. From there to Milford, Ohio. And from Milford to Goshen, Ohio, by hack. Nine miles by hack driven by Louis Wellner. Landing at Goshen about 6 P.M. My home in '62.

Father bringing me home all the way from Chattanooga lying on my face on the same mattress that I had laid so long, and had used in the hospital in Chattanooga and Nashville. Arrived home about the middle of February 1864.

Having refused a discharge a number of times, on the 20th day of February, 1864, at Nashville, Tennessee, they filled out my discharge and sent it to me by mail. It arrived just a few days before my furlough expired.

I was able to walk on crutches about June of '64, and used them for some time. My first venture out on crutches was to the —?—

church, (initials, but illegible) which was close by. Col. Tetor (or Tebor) was supt of Sunday School, not noticing me when I entered. He discovered my presence. He came to me and wanted me to go up front. I asked the Colonel to excuse me since I had been to the front once too often now.

I still have my old disabilities to contend with, but feel thankful that I am as well as I am.

Thomas J. Doughman
Co. G 89th O. V. I.
Goshen
Clermont County, Ohio

(Letter in possession of Thomas J.
Doughman, Maitland, Florida)

NOTES

1. George W. Adams, *Doctors in Blue: The Medical History of the Union Army in the Civil War* (New York: Henry Schuman, Inc., 1952), p. 3.

2. H. H. Cunningham, *Doctors in Gray: The Confederate Medical Service* (Baton Rouge: Louisiana State University Press, 1958), p. 5. See also Otto Eisenschiml, "Medicine in the War," *Civil War Times Illustrated*, Vol. 1, No. 2 (May, 1962), 5.

3. George W. Smith, *Medicines for the Union Army: The United States Army Laboratories During the Civil War* (Madison, Wisconsin: American Institute of the History of Pharmacy, 1962), p. 1.

4. It is estimated that 617,528 men died in the Civil War. Of that total 359,528 were Union soldiers and 258,000 were Confederate. Of those, 110,070 and 94,000, respectively, died from wounds. Assuming the above figures are correct, Thomas L. Livermore's figures indicate that of 385,245 Union soldiers wounded, 110,070 died and 275,175 survived. Similarly, of 329,000 Confederate soldiers wounded, 94,000 died and 235,000 survived. Some deaths occurred before medical attention could be given, but others did not occur until the wounded had been cared for by medical personnel. From this it is reasonable to assume that Union medical officers cared for over 300,000 wounded and Confederate medical officers cared for over 250,000 wounded. See Stewart Brooks, *Civil War Medicine* (Springfield, Illinois: Charles C. Thomas, 1966), p. 125; Thomas L. Livermore, *Numbers and Losses in the Civil War in America: 1861-65* (Bloomington: Indiana University Press, 1957), pp. 63–64; Charles B. Johnson, *Muskets and Medicine or Army Life in the Sixties* (Philadelphia: F. A. Davis Company, 1917), p. 250.

5. Horace H. Cunningham, *Field Medical Services at the Battles of Manassas*, University of Georgia Monographs, No. 16 (Athens, Georgia: University of Georgia Press, 1968), p. 23. See also Brooks, *Civil War Medicine*, pp. 20–21; Carrington Williams, "Samuel Preston Moore, Surgeon General of the Confederate States Army," *Virginia Monthly*, LXXXVIII (October, 1961), 623.

6. Frank E. Vandiver, *Their Tattered Flags* (New York: Harper's Magazine Press, 1970), pp. 114–115.

7. Cunningham, *Doctors in Gray*, p. 20. See also Henrietta Runyon Winfrey, "Virginia Military Hospitals" (Richmond: Medical College of Virginia, n.d.). (Mimeographed), 5–6; Williams, "Samuel Preston Moore," p. 623.

8. John Q. Anderson, *A Texas Surgeon in the C.S.A.*, Confederate Centennial Studies, No. 6 (Tuscaloosa, Alabama: Confederate Publishing Company, Inc., 1957), p. 9; See also Cunningham, *Field Medical Services*, p. 24; Bell Irvin Wiley, *They Who Fought Here* (New York: The MacMillian Company, 1959), p. 276. Williams, "Samuel Preston Moore," pp. 624–625; Bell Irvin Wiley, *The Life of Johnny Reb, The Common Soldier of the Confederacy* (New York: The Bobbs-Merrill Company, 1943), p. 268.

9. Williams, "Samuel Preston Moore," p. 625. See also Eisenschiml, "Medicine in the War," p. 29; *War of the Rebellion: A Compilation of the Official Records of the Union and*

Confederate Armies, Series 1, Volume 12.1 (Washington: Government Printing Office, 1880–1901, pp. 719–720 (Hereafter cited as *O.R.*).

10. Cunningham, *Field Medical Services*, pp. 75–76, 79.

11. Wiley, *They Who Fought Here*, p. 230. See also Cunningham, *Field Medical Services*, p. 72; Brooks, *Civil War Medicine*, pp. 36–37.

12. H. H. Cunningham, "Confederate General Hospitals: Establishment and Organization," *The Journal of Southern History*, Vol. 20, No. 3 (August, 1954), 376–383.

13. Brooks, *Civil War Medicine*, p. 12.

14. A. Howard Meneely, *The War Department, 1861: A Study in Mobilization and Administration* (New York: Columbia University Press, 1928), pp. 227–229.

15. Meneely, *War Department*, p. 228.

16. *Medical and Surgical History of the War of the Rebellion*. (1861–65). Part 1, Vol. 1, (Washington: Government Printing Office, 1875–1883), pp. App. 31, App. 38 (Hereafter cited as M.S.).

17. Brooks, *Civil War Medicine*, pp. 18–20.

18. *O. R.*, Series 1, Volume 11.1, pp. 192–198, 211. See also *M.S.*, Part 1, Volume 1, p. App. 70.

19. *M. S.*, Part 1, Volume 1, pp. App. 269–274, App. 330–331.

20. *M. S.*, Part 1, Volume 1, pp. App. 156, App. 199.

21. *M. S.*, Part 3, Volume 1, pp. App. 964–966. See also *M. S.*, Part 1, Volume 1, pp. App. 46, App. 182..

22. *M. S.*, Part 1, Volume 1, p. App. 48. See also Cunningham, *Field Medical Services*, p. 45; Adams, *Doctors in Blue*, pp. 63–65.

23. Jonathan Letterman, *Medical Recollections of the Army of the Potomac* (New York: D. Appleton and Company, 1866), pp. 58–61, 78. See also *M. S.*, Part 1, Volume 1, pp. App. 167, App. 204, App. 259–261, App. 301, App. 314.

24. *M. S.*, Part 3, Volume 2, p. 944. See also *M. S.*, Part 1, Volume 1, p. App. 49.

25. *O. R.*, Series 1, Volume 5, p. 102. See also Letterman, *Medical Recollections*, pp. 23–30; *M. S.*, Part 1, Volume 1, p. App. 96; Brooks, *Civil War Medicine*, p. 36; Thomas T. Ellis, *Leaves From the Diary of an Army Surgeon; or, Incidents of Field Camp and Hospital Life* (New York: John Bradburn, 1863), pp. 183–184; *O.R.*, Series 1, Volume 11.1, pp. 217–219.

26. *M.S.*, Part 3, Volume 2, pp. 935–943. See also *Letterman, Medical Recollections*, pp. 31, 73–75, 161–178; J. R. Weist, *The Medical Department in the War* (Cincinnati, Ohio: H. C. Sherick and Co., 1886), p. 15.

27. *M. S.*, Part 3, Volume 1, p. 896–899. See also Brooks, *Civil War Medicine*, p. 41.

28. *M. S.*, Part 3, Volume 1, pp. 927–930, 943–951, 960. *M. S.*, Part 3, Volume 2, p. 902; Brooks, *Civil War Medicine*, p. 43.

29. Brooks, *Civil War Medicine*, p. 18. See also Howard D. Kramer, "Effect of the Civil War on the Public Health Movement," *Mississippi Valley Historical Review*, Vol. 35, No. 3 (December, 1948), 455; Linus P. Brockett, *The Philanthropic Results of the War in America* (New York: Sheldon and Company, 1864), pp. 46–47, 70–73; William Y. Thompson, "The U.S. Sanitary Commission," *Civil War History*, Vol. 2, No. 2 (June, 1956), 53.

30. James O. Henry, "The United States Christian Commission in the Civil War," *Civil War History*, Vol. 6, No. 4 (December, 1960), 382–383.

31. Brooks, *Civil War Medicine*, pp. 6–7. See also John Allan Wyeth, *With Sabre and Scalpel: The Autobiography of a Soldier and Surgeon* (New York: Harper and Brothers, 1914), p. 213; *M. S.*, Part 1, Volume 1, pp. App. 340–341.

32. Marjorie Barstow Greenbie, "Lincoln's Daughters of Mercy," *The Reader's Digest*, XLIII (August, 1943), 90. See also A. H. Hoge, *The Boys in Blue; or Heroes of the "Rank and File"* (New York: E. B. Treat and Company, 1867), p. 41; James O. Churchill, "Wounded at Fort Donelson," *Civil War Times Illustrated*, Vol. 8, No. 4 (July, 1969), 19–23.

33. Cunningham, *Field Medical Services*, pp. 51–52, 58.

34. Ellis, *Leaves*, pp. 280–281. See also Letterman, *Medical Recollections*, p. 46.

35. *M. S.*, Part 1, Volume 1, pp. App. 140, App. 151. See also Adams, *Doctors in Blue*, pp. 90–91; Wyeth, *Sabre and Scalpel*, p. 255; William F. Drum, "Work of the Fifth Corps Ambulance Train, Spring and Summer of 1864," *Glimpses of the Nation's Struggle: Third Series*, ed. Edward D. Neill (New York: D. D. Merrill Company, 1893), p. 81.

36. *M. S.*, Part 1, Volume 1, p. App. 173.

37. Adams, *Doctors in Blue*, pp. 66–67. See also Drum, "Fifth Corps Ambulance Train," p. 80; Johnson, *Muskets and Medicine*, p. 99; *M. S.*, Part 1, Volume 1, p. App. 184.

38. Cunningham, *Doctors in Gray*, pp. 118, 125–126. See also Wiley, *Life of Johnny Reb*, pp. 263–265; Williams, "Samuel Preston Moore," p. 625; Adams, *Doctors in Blue*, pp. 74–75; Ellis, *Leaves*, pp. 209–213; *M. S.*, Part 1, Volume 1, pp. App. 111, App. 125–126.

39. *O. R.*, Series 1, Volume 19.1, p. 110. See also Adams, *Doctors in Blue*, pp. 76–79; Ellis, *Leaves*, pp. 280–281; *M. S.*, Part 1, Volume 1, p. App. 98.

40. *O. R.*, Series 1, Volume 20.1, pp. 220–221.

41. *M. S.*, Part 1, Volume 1, pp. App. 138–140. See also Adams, *Doctors in Blue*, pp. 90–91; Letterman, *Medical Recollections*, pp. 129, 138–142.

42. Francis Trevelyan Miller (ed.), *The Photographic History of the Civil War*, Vol. VII, *Prisons and Hospitals* (New York: A. S. Barnes and Company, Inc., 1957), p. 232; See also Letterman, *Medical Recollections*, p. 158; Adams, *Doctors in Blue*, p. 91; *M. S.*, Part 1, Volume 1, p. App. 142.

43. Paul E. Steiner, *Disease in the Civil War, Natural Biological Warfare in 1861–1865* (Springfield, Illinois: Charles C. Thomas, 1968), pp. 11–12. See also Miller, *Photographic History*, p. 236.

44. Winfrey, "Virginia Military Hospitals," p. 5. See also Miller, *Photographic History*, p. 246; *O. R.*, Series 1, Volume 11.1, p. 199.

45. F. E. Daniel, *Recollections of a Rebel Surgeon or in the Doctor's Sappy Days* (Austin, Texas: Von Boeckmann, Schultz and Company, 1899), pp. 68–69. See also Miller, *Photographic History*, p. 264; Brooks, *Civil War Medicine*, p. 97; Wiley, *Life of Johnny Reb*, p. 265; Wiley, *They Who Fought Here*, p. 232.

46. Eisenschiml, "Medicine in the War," p. 30. See also Anderson, *Texas Surgeon in the C.S.A.*, p. 97.

47. Johnson, *Muskets and Medicine*, pp. 99, 104–105. See also Stephen C. Ayres, "The Battle of Nashville, With Personal Recollections of a Field Hospital," *Sketches of War History, 1861–1865, Volume 5*, eds. W. H. Chamberlin and others (Cincinnati: The Robert Clark Company, 1903), p. 295.

48. Miller, *Photographic History*, p. 266.

49. Nina Brown Baker, "Cyclone in Calico," *The Reader's Digest*, LXI (December, 1952), 144.

50. *M. S.*, Part 1, Volume 1, pp. App. 150, App. 299.

51. Martha D. Perry, *Letters from a Surgeon of the Civil War* (Boston: Little, Brown and Company, 1906), pp. 48–55. For another account of the journey from battlefield to complete recovery see A. B. Isham, "The Story of a Gunshot Wound," *Sketches of War*

History 1861–1865, Volume 4, ed. W. H. Chamberlin (Cincinnati: The Robert Clark Company, 1896), pp. 429–443.

52. Cunningham, *Doctors in Gray*, p. 118. See also Wiley, *Life of Johnny Reb*, pp. 263–265.
53. Cunningham, *Doctors in Gray*, pp. 124–125. See also Livermore, *Numbers and Losses*, p. 106.
54. *O. R.*, Series 1, Volume 12.3, p. 766. See also *M. S.*, Part 3, Volume 2, pp. 962, 964, 968; Brooks, *Civil War Medicine*, p. 37.
55. William H. Ridinger, "Hospitalization of the Armies at Gettysburg Battle, 1863" (Unpublished Graduation Thesis, Gettysburg College, 1942), p. 44. See also Cunningham, *Doctors in Gray*, p. 121.
56. *M. S.*, Part 3, Volume 2, pp. 984–986. See also Brooks, *Civil War Medicine*, pp. 13, 37; John H. Brinton, *Personal Memoirs of John H. Brinton, Major and Surgeon U.S.V. 1861–1865* (New York: The Neale Publishing Company, 1914), p. 178; Weist, *Medical Department in the War*, p. 17; *M. S.*, Part 1, Volume 1, pp. App. 29, App. 38, App. 43; *O. R.*, Series 1, Volume 7, pp. 241–243; *O. R.*, Series 1, Volume 10.1, p. 298; Katharine Prescott Wormeley, *The Cruel Side of War with the Army of the Potomac* (Boston: Roberts Brothers, 1898), p. 26; Ellis, *Leaves*, p. 79.
57. *M. S.*, Part 1, Volume 1, p. App. 143. See also *M. S.*, Part 3, Volume 2, p. 957; Weist, *Medical Department in the War*, pp. 15–16.
58. Cunningham, "Confederate General Hospitals," pp. 383–385. See also Cunningham, *Doctors in Gray*, pp. 48–49; Anderson, *Texas Surgeon in the C.S.A.*, p. 10.
59. Anderson, *Texas Surgeon in the C.S.A.*, p. 10.
60. Cunningham, *Doctors in Gray*, p. 73. See also Winfrey, "Virginia Military Hospitals," p. 4; Brooks, *Civil War Medicine*, p. 51.
61. John R. Gildersleeve, "History of Chimborazo Hospital, Richmond, Va., and Its Medical Officers During 1861–1865," *Confederate Historical Society Journal*, Vol. 3, No. 1 (March, 1965), 17–21. See also Brooks, *Civil War Medicine*, pp. 46–47; Williams, "Samuel Preston Moore," pp. 625–626.
62. Cunningham, *Doctors in Gray*, p. 69.
63. Brooks, *Civil War Medicine*, p. 43.
64. General DeChanal, "Good Order and Cleanliness," *Civil War Times Illustrated*, Vol. 6, No. 6, (October, 1976), 42–43.
65. Eisenschiml, "Medicine in the War," p. 28. See also Brinton, *Personal Memoirs*, p. 227.
66. Gordon W. Jones, "Wartime Surgery," *Civil War Times Illustrated*, Vol. 2, No. 2 (May, 1963), 30. See also Elbridge J. Coop, *Reminiscences of the War of the Rebellion, 1861–1865* (Nashua, New Hampshire: The Telegraph Publishing Company, 1911), pp. 473–474; James Madison Stone, *Personal Recollections of the Civil War* (Boston: James Madison Stone, 1918), pp. 181–185; Letterman, *Medical Recollections*, p. 143.
67. Brooks, *Civil War Medicine*, pp. 60–62; See also DeChanal, "Good Order and Cleanliness," pp. 43–44; *O. R.*, Series 1, Volume 5, pp. 94–95; Hoge, *Boys in Blue*, pp. 87–91.
68. Brooks, *Civil War Medicine*, p. 43. See also *M. S.*, Part 3, Volume 1, p. 964; Smith, *Medicines for the Union Army*, p. 1.
69. Brooks, *Civil War Medicine*, pp. 122–124. See also Weist, *Medical Department in the War*, p. 12.
70. Wiley, *They Who Fought Here*, p. 226. See also James A. Huston, *The Sinews of War: Army Logistics 1775–1953*, Army Historical Series. Washington: U.S. Government Printing Office, 1966, p. 241.

APPENDIX II
ORDER OF BATTLE

Organization of the Army of the Cumberland, Maj. Gen. William S. Rosecrans, U.S. Army, commanding, September 19 and 20, 1863.

FOURTEENTH ARMY CORPS (Maj. Gen. George H. Thomas)

First Division (Brig. Gen. Absalom Baird)

First Brigade (Col. Benjamin F. Scribner)
38th Indiana
2d Ohio
33d Ohio
94th Ohio
10th Wisconsin

Second Brigade (Brig. Gen. John C. Starkweather)
24th Illinois
79th Pennsylvania
1st Wisconsin
21st Wisconsin

Third Brigade (Brig. Gen. John H. King)
15th United States, 1st Battalion
16th United States, 1st Battalion
18th United States, 1st Battalion
18th United States, 2d Battalion
19th United States, 1st Battalion

Artillery
1st Michigan Light, Battery A
(1st Brigade)
Indiana Light, 4th Battery (2d Brigade)
5th United States, Battery H
(3d Brigade)

Second Division (Maj. Gen. James S. Negley)

First Brigade (Brig. Gen. John Beatty)
104th Illinois
42d Indiana
88th Indiana
15th Kentucky

Second Brigade (Col. Timothy R. Stanley)
(Col. William L. Stoughton)
19th Illinois
11th Michigan
18th Ohio

Third Brigade (Col. William Sirwell)
37th Indiana
21st Ohio
74th Ohio
78th Pennsylvania

Artillery
Illinois Light, Bridges' Battery
(1st Brigade)
1st Ohio Light, Battery M (3d Brigade)
1st Ohio Light, Battery G (3d Brigade)

Third Division (Brig. Gen. John M. Brannan)

First Brigade (Col. John M. Connell)
82d Indiana
17th Ohio
31st Ohio
38th Ohio (not engaged)

Second Brigade (Col. John T. Croxton)
(Col. William H. Hays)
10th Indiana
74th Indiana
4th Kentucky
10th Kentucky
14th Ohio

Third Brigade (Col. Ferdinand
Van Derveer)
87th Indiana
2d Minnesota
9th Ohio
35th Ohio

Artillery
1st Michigan Light, Battery D
(1st Brigade)
1st Ohio Light, Battery C (2d Brigade)
4th United States, Battery I
(3d Brigade)

Fourth Division (Maj. Gen. Joseph J. Reynolds)

First Brigade (Col. John T. Wilder)
(Detached from its division and serving as
mounted infantry)
92d Illinois
98th Illinois
123d Illinois
17th Indiana
72d Indiana

Second Brigade (Col. Edward A. King)
(Col. Milton S. Robinson)
68th Indiana
75th Indiana
101st Indiana
105th Ohio

Third Brigade (Brig. Gen. John B. Turchin)
  18th Kentucky
  11th Ohio
  36th Ohio
  92d Ohio

Artillery
  Indiana Light, 18th Battery (1st Brigade)
  Indiana Light, 19th Battery (2d Brigade)
  Indiana Light, 21st Battery (3rd Brigade)

TWENTIETH ARMY CORPS (Maj. Gen. Alexander McD. McCook)

First Division (Brig. Gen. Jefferson C. Davis)

First Brigade (Col. P. Sidney Post) (not engaged)
  59th Illinois
  74th Illinois
  75th Illinois
  22d Indiana
  Wisconsin Light Artillery, 5th Battery

Second Brigade (Brig. Gen. William P. Carlin)
  21st Illinois
  38th Illinois
  81st Indiana
  101st Ohio
  Minnesota Light Artillery, 2d Battery

Third Brigade (Col. Hans C. Heg) (Col. John A. Martin)
  25th Illinois
  35th Illinois
  8th Kansas
  15th Wisconsin
  Wisconsin Light Artillery, 8th Battery

Second Division (Brig. Gen. Richard W. Johnson)

First Brigade (Brig. Gen. August Willich)
  89th Illinois
  32d Indiana
  39th Indiana
  15th Ohio
  49th Ohio
  1st Ohio Light Artillery, Battery A

Second Brigade (Col. Joseph B. Dodge)
  79th Illinois
  29th Indiana
  30th Indiana
  77th Pennsylvania
  Ohio Light Artillery, 20th Battery

Third Brigade (Col. Philemon P. Baldwin)
(Col. William W. Berry)
6th Indiana
5th Kentucky
1st Ohio
93d Ohio
Indiana Light Artillery, 5th Battery

Third Division (Maj. Gen. Philip H. Sheridan)

First Brigade (Brig. Gen. William H. Lytle)
(Col. Silas Miller)
36th Illinois
88th Illinois
21st Michigan
24th Wisconsin
Indiana Light Artillery, 11th Battery

Second Brigade (Col. Bernard Laiboldt)
44th Illinois
73d Illinois
2d Missouri
15th Missouri
1st Missouri Light Artillery, Battery G

Third Brigade (Col. Luther P. Bradley)
(Col. Nathan H. Walworth)
22d Illinois
27th Illinois
42d Illinois
51st Illinois
1st Illinois Light Artillery, Battery C

TWENTY-FIRST ARMY CORPS (Maj. Gen. Thomas L. Crittenden)

First Division (Brig. Gen. Thomas J. Wood)

First Brigade (Col. George P. Buell)
100th Illinois
58th Indiana
13th Michigan
26th Ohio

Second Brigade (Brig. Gen. George D. Wagner) (Not engaged)
15th Indiana
40th Indiana
57th Indiana
97th Ohio

Third Brigade (Col. Charles G. Harker)
3d Kentucky
64th Ohio
65th Ohio
125th Ohio

Artillery
Indiana Light, 8th Battery (1st Brigade)
Ohio Light, 6th Battery (3d Brigade)

Second Division (Maj. Gen. John M. Palmer)

First Brigade (Brig. Gen. Charles Cruft)
31st Indiana
1st Kentucky
2d Kentucky
90th Ohio

Second Brigade (Brig. Gen. William B. Hazen)
9th Indiana
6th Kentucky
41st Ohio
124th Ohio

Third Brigade (Col. William Grose)
84th Illinois
36th Indiana
23d Kentucky
6th Ohio
24th Ohio

Artillery (Capt. William E. Standart)
1st Ohio Light, Battery B (1st Brigade)
1st Ohio Light, Battery F (2d Brigade)
4th United States, Battery H
(3d Brigade)
4th United States, Battery M
(3d Brigade)

Third Division (Brig. Gen. Horatio P. Van Cleve)

First Brigade (Brig. Gen. Samuel Beatty)
79th Indiana
9th Kentucky
17th Kentucky
19th Ohio

Second Brigade (Col. George F. Dick)
44th Indiana
86th Indiana
13th Ohio
59th Ohio

Third Brigade (Col. Sidney M. Barnes)
35th Indiana
8th Kentucky
21st Kentucky
51st Ohio
99th Ohio

Artillery
Indiana Light, 7th Battery
Pennsylvania Light, 26th Battery
Wisconsin Light, 3d Battery

RESERVE CORPS (Maj. Gen. Gordon Granger)

First Division (Brig. Gen. James B. Steedman)

First Brigade (Brig. Gen. Walter C. Whitaker)
96th Illinois
115th Illinois
84th Indiana
22d Michigan
40th Ohio
89th Ohio
Ohio Light Artillery, 18th Battery

Second Brigade (Col. John G. Mitchell)
78th Illinois
98th Ohio
113th Ohio
121st Ohio
1st Illinois Light Artillery, Battery M

Second Division

Second Brigade (Col. Daniel McCook)
85th Illinois
86th Illinois
125th Illinois
52d Ohio
69th Ohio
2d Illinois Light Artillery, Battery I

CAVALRY CORPS (Brig. Gen. Robert B. Mitchell)

First Division (Col. Edward M. McCook)

First Brigade (Col. Archibald P. Campbell)
2d Michigan
9th Pennsylvania
1st Tennessee

Second Brigade (Col. Daniel M. Ray)
2d Indiana
4th Indiana
2d Tennessee
1st Wisconsin
1st Ohio Light Artillery, Battery D (section)

Third Brigade (Col. Louis D. Watkins)
4th Kentucky
5th Kentucky
6th Kentucky

Second Division (Brig. Gen. George Crook)

First Brigade (Col. Robert H. G. Minty)
3d Indiana (battalion)
4th Michigan
7th Pennsylvania
4th United States

Second Brigade (Col. Eli Long)
2d Kentucky
1st Ohio
3d Ohio
4th Ohio

Artillery
Chicago (Illinois) Board of Trade Battery

Organization of the Army of Tennessee, General Braxton Bragg, C.S., commanding,
September 19–20, 1863

RIGHT WING (Lieut. Gen. Leonidas Polk)

Cheatham's Division (Maj. Gen. Benjamin F. Cheatham)

Jackson's Brigade (Brig. Gen. John K. Jackson)
  1st Georgia (Confederate), 2d Battalion
  5th Georgia
  2d Georgia Battalion Sharpshooters
  5th Mississippi
  8th Mississippi

Smith's Brigade (Brig. Gen. Preston Smith)
  (Col. Alfred J. Vaughan, Jr.)
  11th Tennessee
  12th Tennessee
  47th Tennessee
  13th Tennessee
  154th Tennessee
  29th Tennessee
  Dawson's Battalion Sharpshooters

Maney's Brigade (Brig. Gen. George Maney)
  1st Tennessee
  27th Tennessee
  4th Tennessee (Provisional Army)
  6th Tennessee
  9th Tennessee
  24th Tennessee Battalion Sharpshooters

Wright's Brigade (Brig. Gen. Marcus J. Wright)
  8th Tennessee
  16th Tennessee
  28th Tennessee
  38th Tennessee
  Murray's (Tennessee) Battalion
  51st Tennessee
  52d Tennessee

Strahl's Brigade (Brig. Gen. Otho F. Strahl)
  4th Tennessee
  5th Tennessee
  19th Tennessee
  24th Tennessee
  31st Tennessee
  33d Tennessee

Artillery (Maj. Melancthon Smith)
  Carnes' (Tennessee) Battery
  Scogin's (Georgia) Battery
  Scott's (Tennessee) Battery
  Smith's (Mississippi) Battery
  Stanford's (Mississippi) Battery

HILL'S CORPS (Lieut. Gen. Daniel H. Hill)

Cleburne's Division (Maj. Gen. Patrick R. Cleburne)

Wood's Brigade (Brig. Gen. S. A. M. Wood)
16th Alabama
33d Alabama
45th Alabama
18th Alabama Battalion
32d Mississippi
45th Mississippi
15th Mississippi Battalion
Sharpshooters

Polk's Brigade (Brig. Gen. Lucius E. Polk)
1st Arkansas
3d Confederate
5th Confederate
2d Tennessee
35th Tennessee
48th Tennessee

Deshler's Brigade (Brig. Gen. James Deshler)
(Col. Roger Q. Mills)
9th Arkansas
24th Arkansas
6th Texas Infantry
10th Texas Infantry
15th Texas Cavalry (Dismounted)
17th Texas Cavalry (Dismounted)
18th Texas Cavalry
24th Texas Cavalry
25th Texas Cavalry

Artillery (Maj. T. R. Hotchkiss)
(Capt. Henry C. Semple)
Calvert's (Arkansas) Battery
Douglas' (Texas) Battery
Semple's (Alabama) Battery

Breckinridge's Division (Maj. Gen. John C. Breckinridge)

Helm's Brigade (Brig. Gen. Benjamin H. Helm)
(Col. Joseph H. Lewis)
41st Alabama
2d Kentucky
4th Kentucky
6th Kentucky
9th Kentucky

Adams' Brigade (Brig. Gen. Daniel W. Adams)
(Col. Randall L. Gibson)
32d Alabama
13th Louisiana
20th Louisiana
16th Louisiana
25th Louisiana
19th Louisiana
14th Louisiana Battalion

Stovall's Brigade (Brig. Gen. Marcellus A.
Stovall)
   1st Florida
   3d Florida
   4th Florida
   47th Georgia
   60th North Carolina

Artillery (Maj. Rice E. Graves)
   Cobb's (Kentucky) Battery
   Graves' (Kentucky) Battery
   Mebane's (Tennessee) Battery
   Slocomb's (Louisiana) Battery

RESERVE CORPS (Maj. Gen. William H. T. Walker)

Walker's Division (Brig. Gen. States R. Gist)

Gist's Brigade (Brig. Gen. States R. Gist)
   (Col. Peyton H. Colquitt)
   (Lieut. Col. Leroy Napier)
  46th Georgia
  8th Georgia Battalion
  16th South Carolina (not engaged)
  24th South Carolina

Ector's Brigade (Brig. Gen. Matthew D. Ector)
  Stone's (Alabama) Battalion
    Sharpshooters
  Pound's (Mississippi) Battalion
    Sharpshooters
  29th North Carolina
  9th Texas
  10th Texas Cavalry (Dismounted)
  14th Texas Cavalry (Dismounted)
  32d Texas Cavalry (Dismounted)

Wilson's Brigade (Col. Claudius C.
Wilson)
   25th Georgia
   29th Georgia
   30th Georgia
   1st Georgia Battalion Sharpshooters
   4th Louisiana Battalion

Artillery
   Howell's (Georgia) Battery (formerly
   Martin's)

Liddell's Division (Brig. Gen. St. John R. Liddell)

Liddell's Brigade (Col. Daniel C. Govan)
2d Arkansas
15th Arkansas
5th Arkansas
13th Arkansas
6th Arkansas
7th Arkansas
8th Arkansas
1st Louisiana (Regulars)

Walthall's Brigade (Brig. Gen. Edward C. Walthall)
24th Mississippi
27th Mississippi
29th Mississippi
30th Mississippi
34th Mississippi

Artillery (Capt. Charles Swett)
Fowler's (Alabama) Battery
Warren Light Artillery (Mississippi Battery)

LEFT WING (Lieut. Gen. James Longstreet)

Hindman's Division (Maj. Gen. Thomas C. Hindman)
(Brig. Gen. Patton Anderson)

Anderson's Brigade (Brig. Gen. Patton Anderson)
(Col. J. H. Sharp)
7th Mississippi
9th Mississippi
10th Mississippi
41st Mississippi
44th Mississippi
9th Mississippi Battalion Sharpshooters
Garrity's (Alabama) Battery

Deas' Brigade (Brig. Gen. Zach. C. Deas)
19th Alabama
22d Alabama
25th Alabama
39th Alabama
50th Alabama
17th Alabama Battalion Sharpshooters
Dent's (Alabama) Battery (formerly Robertson's)

Manigault's Brigade (Brig. Gen. Arthur M. Manigault)
24th Alabama
28th Alabama
34th Alabama
10th South Carolina
19th South Carolina
Waters' (Alabama) Battery

BUCKNER'S CORPS (Maj. Gen. Simon B. Buckner)

Stewart's Division (Maj. Gen. Alexander P. Stewart)

Johnson's Brigade (Brig. Gen. Bushrod R. Johnson)
(Col. John S. Fulton)
17th Tennessee
23d Tennessee
25th Tennessee
44th Tennessee

Bate's Brigade (Brig. Gen. William B. Bate)
58th Alabama
37th Georgia
4th Georgia Battalion Sharpshooters
15th Tennessee
37th Tennessee
20th Tennessee:

Brown's Brigade (Brig. Gen. John C. Brown)
(Col. Edmund C. Cook)
18th Tennessee
26th Tennessee
32d Tennessee
45th Tennessee
23d Tennessee Battalion

Clayton's Brigade (Brig. Gen. Henry D. Clayton)
18th Alabama
36th Alabama
38th Alabama

Artillery (Maj. J. Wesley Eldridge)
1st Arkansas Battery
T. H. Dawson's (Georgia) Battery
Eufaula Artillery (Alabama Battery)
Company E, 9th Georgia Artillery
Battalion (Billington W. York's Battery)

Preston's Division (Brig. Gen. William Preston)

Gracie's Brigade (Brig. Gen. Archibald Gracie, Jr.)
43d Alabama
Hilliard's (Alabama) Legion
63d Tennessee

Trigg's Brigade (Col. Robert C. Trigg)
1st Florida Cavalry (Dismounted)
6th Florida
7th Florida
54th Virginia

Third Brigade (Col. John H. Kelly)
65th Georgia
5th Kentucky
58th North Carolina
63d Virginia

Artillery Battalion (Maj. A. Leyden)
Jeffress' (Virginia) Battery
Peeples' (Georgia) Battery
Wolihin's (Georgia) Battery

Reserve Corps Artillery (Maj.
Samuel C. Williams)
Baxter's (Tennessee) Battery
Darden's (Mississippi) Battery
Kolb's (Alabama) Battery
McCants' (Florida) Battery

Johnson's Division (Brig. Gen. Bushrod R. Johnson)

Gregg's Brigade (Brig. Gen. John Gregg)
(Col. Cyrus A. Sugg)
3d Tennessee
10th Tennessee
30th Tennessee
41st Tennessee
50th Tennessee
1st Tennessee Battalion
7th Texas
Bledsoe's (Missouri) Battery

McNair's Brigade (Brig. Gen. Evander
McNair)
(Col. David Coleman)
1st Arkansas Mounted Rifles
(Dismounted)
2d Arkansas Mounted Rifles
(Dismounted)
25th Arkansas
4th and 31st Arkansas and 4th
Arkansas Battalion (consolidated)
39th North Carolina
Culpeper's (South Carolina) Battery

LONGSTREET'S CORPS (Maj. Gen. John B. Hood)

McLaws' Division (Brig. Gen. Joseph B. Kershaw)
(Maj. Gen. Lafayette McLaws)

Kershaw's Brigade (Brig. Gen. Joseph B.
Kershaw)
2d South Carolina
3d South Carolina
7th South Carolina
8th South Carolina
15th South Carolina
3d South Carolina Battalion

Humphreys' Brigade (Brig. Gen.
Benjamin G. Humphreys)
13th Mississippi
17th Mississippi
18th Mississippi
21st Mississippi

Hood's Division (Maj. Gen. John B. Hood)
(Brig. Gen. E. McIver Law)

Robertson's Brigade (Brig. Gen. Jerome
B. Robertson)
(Col. Van H. Manning)
3d Arkansas
1st Texas
4th Texas
5th Texas

Law's Brigade (Brig. Gen. E. McIver
Law)
(Col. James L. Sheffield)
4th Alabama
15th Alabama
44th Alabama
47th Alabama
48th Alabama

Benning's Brigade (Brig. Gen. Henry L.
Benning)
  2d Georgia
  15th Georgia
  17th Georgia
  20th Georgia

RESERVE ARTILLERY (Maj. Felix H. Robertson)

Barret's (Missouri) Battery
Le Gardeur's (Louisiana) Battery
Havis' (Georgia) Battery

Lumsden's (Alabama) Battery
Massenburg's (Georgia) Battery

CAVALRY (Maj. Gen. Joseph Wheeler)

Wharton's Division (Brig. Gen. John A. Wharton)

First Brigade (Col. C. C. Crews)
  Malone's (Alabama) Regiment
  2d Georgia
  3d Georgia
  4th Georgia

Second Brigade (Col. Thomas Harrison)
  3d Confederate
  3d Kentucky
  4th Tennessee
  8th Texas
  11th Texas
  White's (Tennessee) Battery

Martin's Division (Brig. Gen. William T. Martin)

First Brigade (Col. John T. Morgan)
  1st Alabama
  3d Alabama
  51st Alabama
  8th Confederate

Second Brigade (Col. A. A. Russell)
  4th Alabama (Russell's Regiment)
  1st Confederate
  J. H. Wiggins' (Arkansas) Battery)

FORREST'S CORPS (Brig. Gen. Nathan B. Forrest)

Armstrong's Division (Brig. Gen. Frank C. Armstrong)

Armstrong's Brigade (Col. James T.
Wheeler)
  3d Arkansas
  2d Kentucky
  6th Tennessee
  18th Tennessee Battalion

Forrest's Brigade (Col. George G. Dibrell)
  4th Tennessee
  8th Tennessee
  9th Tennessee
  10th Tennessee
  11th Tennessee
  Shaw's Battalion, O. P. Hamilton's
    Battalion, and R. D. Allison's
    Squadron (consolidated)
  Huggins' (Tennessee) Battery (formerly
    Freeman's)
  Morton's (Tennessee) Battery

Pegram's Division (Brig. Gen. John Pegram)
Davidson's Brigade (Brig. Gen. H. B.
Davidson)
  1st Georgia
  6th Georgia
  6th North Carolina
  Rucker's (1st Tennessee) Legion
  Huwald's (Tennessee) Battery
                Scott's Brigade (Col. John S. Scott)
                  10th Confederate
                  Detachment of John H. Morgan's
                    command
                  1st Louisiana
                  2d Tennessee
                  5th Tennessee
                  N. T. N. Robinson's (Louisiana) Battery
                    (one section)

INDEX